INDIAN CONSTITUTION
Under Communal Attack

INDIAN CONSTITUTION
Under Communal Attack

Ram Khobragade

GYAN PUBLISHING HOUSE
New Delhi–110 002

INDIAN CONSTITUTION: Under Communal Attack
(Law, Constitution)

Rs. 540

ISBN: 81-212-0780-0

Published in 2002 in India by
Gyan Publishing House
5, Ansari Road, Darya ganj,
New Delhi–110 002
E-mail: gyanbook@vsnl.com

Lasertypesetting at: Varsha Graphics, Delhi
Printed at: Mehra Offset Printers, New Delhi

Dedicated to

All those thousands and thousand of
BAMCEF Activists, Artists and my
Colleagues who sacrificed
Comforts of their life, wealth and
Precious time of their career
To build-up,strengthen and consolidate

FULE–AMBEDKARITE MOVEMENT ALL OVER INDIA

With their Blood, Sweat and Tears
On the call of Kanshi Ramji, then President of
BAMCEF, D-S4 and now Bahujan Samaj Party,
But today they matter nowhere
In the same very Movement !

And to

My beloved wife Vasantmala
Who also could never enjoy the
Family life in real sense for many years
From the day first we got married
Because of my total involvement in the same very Movement
And who, while remaining away from me from Delhi for years
At my native place, caring my old parents but
Never complained for lack of facilities and
Co-operated with me fully without a word of Murmur !

Contents

विश्वनाथ प्रताप सिंह

1–तीन मूर्ति मार्ग,
नई दिल्ली–110001
दूरभाष: 3792202

क्रमांक......................

दिनांक 01-12-2001

Foreword

Khobragade has very rightly titled this book as—*Indian Constitution Under Communal Attack.* I observe, he has very carefully carved out various incidents, occasions and statements to prove as to how the communalism of RSS-VHP brand has made in-roads in each and every sphere of State activity and adversely affected national integration and brotherhood among the people. His another observation that secular democratic forces are interested only in short-term gains and never aspire for long-term planning to counter saffronisation move by strengthening an all-India non-political base to sustain the failure of political move, is also an important point for introspection of all those who really desire to protect and maintain secular democratic nature of the polity.

Our Constitution has proved during the past 50 years that it has never been an hurdle in the socio-economic development of the country. Therefore, what we need today is not the review of the Constitution but to protect it from the ongoing attacks, which appear dead-set not only to change the colour and concept but the content of the Constitution also. In this context, Adv. Khobragade's this timely venture is definitely worth appreciating and also an eye-opener for all those who really desire to maintain the sanctity of the Constitution and secular polity.

I fully agree with the views of Dr. Rajendra Prasad, first President of our Republic and Chairman of the Constituent Assembly that "... After all, a Constitution like a machine, is a lifeless thing. It acquires life because of the men who control it and operate it, and India needs nothing more than a set of honest men who will have the interest of the country before them ..."

I wish many more such ventures by the author.

(Vishwanath Pratap Singh)
Former Prime Minister of India

विश्वनाथ प्रताप सिंह

Foreword

Khobragade has very aptly titled this book as—*Indian Constitution Under New Attacks*. I observe, he has very carefully carved out various incidents, measures and statements to prove as to how the communalism of RSS–VHP brand had made in-roads in each and every sphere of State activity and adversely affected national integration and livelihood among the people. His another observation that secular democratic forces are interested only in short-term gains and never aspire for long-term planning to counter-communalism move by strengthening an all-India non-political base to assist in the failure of political move, is also an important point for introspection of all those who really desire to protect and maintain secular democratic nature of the polity.

Our Constitution has proved during the past 52 years that it has never been any hurdle in the socio-economic development of the country. Therefore, what we need today is not amendments in the Constitution, but to protect it from the various attacks, which appear dedicated not only to change the letter and concept but the content of the Constitution also. In this context, Adv. Khobragade's this timely venture is definitely worth appreciating and also an eye-opener for all those who really desire to maintain the sanctity of the Constitution and secular polity.

I fully agree with the views of Dr. Rajendra Prasad, first President of our Republic and Chairman of the Constituent Assembly that "... After all, a Constitution like a machine, is a lifeless thing. It acquires life because of the men who control it and operate it, and India needs today nothing more than a set of honest men who will have the interest of the country before them."

I wish many more such ventures by the author.

(Vishwanath Pratap Singh)
Former Prime Minister of India

Preface

I had no plan to write a book and that, too, on the Indian Constitution. When I was National Secretary of BAMCEF and very closely associated with D-S_4 and BSP right from the day. First of those formations at New Delhi and looking after all publications, including *The Oppressed Indian* (English Monthly Magazine) and *Bahujan Sangathak* (Hindi Weekly), I wrote a number of editorials and articles to build-up, strengthen and consolidate Phule-Ambedkarite Movement and Phule-Ambedkarite journalism under the leadership of Kanshi Ramji.

Indian Constitution initially came under severe attack by the Communists and Socialists to which Dr. Ambedkar replied perfectly during his life time only. It was again under discussion when the Swarn Singh Committee was appointed by Indira Congress and when its report was debated. Eminent jurist and spokesman of capitalist society N.A. Palkhiwala, wrote three articles in the *Times of India,* supporting American style of Executive. Vasant Sathe favoured vigoroubly the American Presidential form of Executive.

Supersession of senior judges of the Supreme Court to favour the appointment of A.N. Ray to reverse Allahabad High Court judgement in Raj Narayan Vs. Indira Gandhi case, withdrawal of Judicial Review Power through 42nd Constitution Amendment Act of 1976 and imposition of emergency by Indira Gandhi intensified the debate on constitutional changes. The RSS and its off-shoot organisations including BJP were never happy with the present Constitution. They got this golden opportunity to demand for review of the Constitution.

When an opportunity came to their way BJP did not spare any time in appointing the Constitution Review Commission under Justice M.N. Venkatachalaih. In fact there appeared during that very period a number of articles and comments in print media for and against the review. I also wrote two articles on the issue, published in *Nav Bharat of Nagpur,* the largest circulated Hindi daily in Central India. However, I was not happy. I could not do justice to the subject in those two short articles. And that very feeling kept on haunting me. Finally, I decided to venture in this project in December 2000. Unfortunately, I got severe double heart-attack on January 2, 2001, while earlier day, I wished many of my friends and colleagues 'Happy New Year'. Luckily I survived. I was hospitalised for 13 days at Chandrapur and Nagpur. My venture was automatically stood postponed for four months. Finally, I could finish it in September 2001.

For writing this book, I had to take references from various books, periodicals, news papers and research papers for which I take this opportunity to thank all learned editors, writers and researchers. I am very grateful to one of my fast and most intimate friends - P.K.R. Tilak of Hyderabad, who supplied me the books of references without delay at a very short notice and without caring for the cost. Even otherwise also he helped me a lot on different accasions. I also thank my all colleagues in All India IFC Employees Association, in New Delhi who always extended their hands of help and co-operation. My thanks are due to my cousin Abhishek and Rupesh Ringane of MAS Computers, Ballarpur and its proprietor Anand Sathe who did the job of DTP timely and efficiently and Ms. Jayanti Thomas, English teacher of Montfort Hr. Secondary School, Ballarpur who teaches English to my son Akshay and Pranay and who helped me in final proof-reading.

The cover design is an art by Prakash Patil of Faridabad, my cousin, who has done lot of arts work for the Movement of BAMCEF, D-S_4 and BSP right from 1978 when he was doing M.F.A. in B.H.U., Varanasi and whose major contribution in the Movement was *Ambedkar Mela on Wheels* (100 oil-paintings on canvass) which Kanshi Ramji carried with him from place to place for educating and organising the people.

I cannot forget to thank and express my gratitude to Dr. R.M. Pal of Indian Social Institute, New Delhi and prominent Human Rights Activist, who has always been a source of encouragement and inspiration for me in this venture and many other ways. I shall be failing in my duty if I forget to mention the co-operation extended by my friend Advocate R. Santhan Krishanan of Supreme Court, G.S. Tripathi of IFCI and many other friends at various places. I also thank Shri B.P. Garg of Gyan Publishing House, New Delhi without whose active and timely support this venture could not have seen the light of day.

New Delhi
November 26, 2001 **Ram Khobragade**

1
The Dooms–Day

It was the 6th December, 1992

The 37th Mahaparinirvana Day of Babasaheb Dr. B.R. Ambedkar, the architect of Indian Constitution and the Messiah of the millions of oppressed and exploited communities, to whom he generated the spirit of their socio-political status in the land of disparities-the land to which they could not call their mother-land and where at the centuries old discriminatory socio-religious system of Hinduism had made them live the life of less than animals. Babasaheb Dr. Ambedkar, who himself had undergone the treachery and tyranny of Hindu religion's *Varnashram-caste system* and suffered a lot of humiliation - mentally and physically, made those miserable human beings - nay - the miserable human-animals, speak and live the honourable life in this land of disparities.

Dr. Ambedkar attacked Hinduism vehemently and exposed the fallacy and various vicious myths of Hindu religion and *Varnashram social system.* He said, " To me, this *Chaturvarnya* with its old labels is utterly repellent and my whole being rebels against it.... There can not be a more degrading system of social organisation than *Chaturvarnya*. It is the system which deadens, paralyses and cripples the people from helpful activity.... I feel I should not consent to live in a society which cherishes wrong ideals or a society which having right ideals will not consent to bring its social life in conformity with those ideals. If I am disgusted with Hindus and Hinduism, it is because I am convinced that they cherish wrong ideals and live a wrong social life. My quarrel with Hindus and Hinduism is not over the imperfections of their social conduct. It is over their ideals".[1] Criticising bitterly Mahatma Gandhi on his defence of Hinduism, caste system and *Varnashram social system,* Dr. Ambedkar said, "Individually it is a folly and a crime. One class and one class alone to be entitled to education and learning ! One class and one class alone to be entitled to arms ! One class and one class alone to trade ! One class and one class alone to serve !.... Ninety percent of the Hindus—*Brahmins*, *Vaishyas* and *Shudras* - could not bear arms under the Hindu social system. How can a country be defended if its army can not be increased in the hour of its peril.... the *Puranas* and other *Shashtras* were a treasure house of sharp practices which the shrewd Hindus employed to befool, beguile and swindle the common mass of poor, illiterate and superstitious people"[2] He ruthlessly attacked not only *Varnashram social system* and Brahminism; but rocked the whole of the Hindu society to its foundation by his furious onslaught on the outdated customs, traditions, orthodox ideas, beliefs in fate and salvation after death and authority of the Hindu scriptures. He was critical of the claim of Hindus that they were a nation and belonged to the rich heritage of ancient culture and civilisation. He questioned the very concept of Hindus as to how they could constitute a nation in the political and sociological sense as to when the people of this land are shamelessly divided into thousands of castes, "Is there any society in the world which has unapproachables, unshadowables and unseenables ? Is there any society which has got a population of criminal tribes ? Is there a society in which there exists today the primitive people who live in Jungles, who do not know even to clothe themselves ? How many do they count in numbers ? I wish they numbered a paltry few. The tragedy is that they have to be counted in millions, millions of untouchables, millions of criminal tribes, millions of primitive tribes !! One wonders whether the Hindu civilisation,is a civilization or infamy" ?[3]

Dr. Ambedkar was the bitter critic of Hindu Religion. He was well-aware that it was that very religion and the various *Vedic* and Hindu religious scriptures which were the root-cause of all the ills of the oppressed and exploited people and their socio-economic sufferings. He, therefore, initiated endless war against those instruments of oppression and exploitation of the untouchables—*Shudras* and *Ati-shudras*, till the last breath of his life. But that does not mean that he was irreligious or anti-religious. On the contrary he was the most religious man. His religious concepts were entirely different from that of Hinduism and most reasonable, logical and scientific in outlook and contents. He was in agreement with Burke when the latter said, "True religion is the foundation of society, the basis on which all true civil Governments rest and have their sanction". According to him, "A religious act may not be correct act but must at least be a responsible act. To permit of this responsibility, religion must mainly be a matter of principle only. It cannot be a matter of rules".[4] He, therefore, questioned Marx and Angel's concept of religion, "Religion is not an opium as it is held by some. What good things I have in me or whatever have been the benefits of my education to society, I owe them to the religious feelings in me. I want religion but I do not want hypocrisy in the name of religion.... Some people think that religion is not essential to society. I do not hold this view. I consider the foundations of religion to be essential to life and practices of society.... Man could not live by bread alone.... Man was also a cultural being who could hardly live without religion"[5]

"Dr. Ambedkar's concept of religion had a close link with social morality, people's empirical welfare. It was not abstract or illusory. It was essentially a system of right relation and was entirely on social ethics i.e. liberty, equality and fraternity. It is for man's own good that he must follow these principles"[6] It was in that context only that he laid more emphasis on principles, "Religion must mainly be a matter of principles only. It cannot be a matter of rules. The moment it degenerates into rules it ceases to be religion, as it kills responsibility which is the essence of a truly religious act"[7]

Therefore, in the opinion of Dr. Ambedkar, "A people and their religion must be judged by social standard based on social ethics. No other standard would have any meaning if religion is held to be necessary good for the well-being of the people"[8] And when religion fails to inculcate these principles and teaches the disciples to discriminate and differentiate between man and man, Dr. Ambedkar attacks such religion very bitterly and of course with logic. "The religion which discriminates between two followers is partial and the religion which treats crores of its adherents worse than dogs and criminals and inflicts upon them insufferable disabilities is no religion at all. Religion is not the appellation for such an unjust order. Religion and slavery are incompatible".[9] A true religion, for Dr. Ambedkar, is that which consists of the following four characterstics :

(i) Religion, in the sense of morality, must therefore, remain the governing principle in every society.

(ii) Religion, if it is to function, must be in accord with reason which is merely another name for science.
(iii) Its moral code must recognise the fundamental tenets of liberty, equality and fraternity.
(iv) Religion must not sanctify or ennoble poverty".[10]

Dr. Ambedkar, right from the day he realised that the real and main cause for degradation of the untouchables—*Shudras* and *Ati-Shudras*, was the teaching and the so called scriptures of Hinduism, he initiated his bitterest attack on both the teachings and scriptures and exposed their hollowness and made them naked.

In fact, Dr. Ambedkar had a doubt in his mind that the word Hindu was native. He observed, "The first and foremost thing that must be recognised is that Hindu society is a myth. The name is itself a foreign name. It was given by the Mohammedans to the native for the purpose of distinguishing themselves. It does not occur in any *Sanskrit* work prior to the Mohammedan invasion.... Hindu society as such does not exist. It is only a collection of castes.... There is no Hindu conciousness of kind. In every Hindu the conciousness that exists is the conciousness of his caste. That is the reason why the Hindus cannot be social to form a society or a nation.... The literature of the Hindu is full of caste geneologies in which an attempt is made to give a noble origin to one caste and an ignoble origin to other castes"[11]

Dr. Ambedkar not only criticised very bitterly Hinduism but he also attacked *Brahminism*, the basis of Hinduism, "By *Brahminism* I do not mean the power, privileges and interests of the *Brahmins* as a community. That is not the sense in which I am using the word. By *Brahminism* I mean negation of the spirit of liberty, equality and fraternity. In that sense it is rampent in all classes and is not confined to *Brahmins* alone though they have been its originators. The effects of *Brahminism* were not confined to social rights such as inter-dining and inter-marrying. It also denied them civic rights. So omniscient is *Brahminism* that it even affects the field of economic opportunities"[12] And, therefore while addressing *The Mahar* Conference on 30–31 May 1936 at Dadar, Bombay, which was arranged on the advice of Doctor Saheb to declare his intention to discard the Hindu Religion, he said, "I tell you, religion is for man and not man for religion. If you want to organise, consolidate and be successful in this world, change this religion. The religion that does not recognise you as human beings or give you water to drink or allow you to enter the temples is not worthy to be called a religion. The religion that forbids you to receive education and comes in the way of your material advancement is not worthy of the appellation 'religion'. The religion that does not teach its followers to show humanity in dealing with its co-religionists is nothing but a display of force. The religion that asks its adherents to suffer the touch of animals but not the touch of human beings is not religion but a mockery. That religion which precludes some classes from education, forbids them to accumulate wealth and bear arms, is not religion but a mockery. The religion that compels the ignorant to be ignorant and the poor to be poor, is not religion but a visitation !"[13] It is in this context that Mahatma Gandhi alerted and warned his *Sanatan co-religionists* that, "Dr. Ambedkar is a challenge to Hinduism"[14]

It was not Dr. Ambedkar alone who raised critical remarks against Hinduism and *Varnashram* caste system. The great freedom fighter and Arya Samaj leader Lala Hardayal also criticised Hinduism and caste system, "Caste is the curse of India. Caste, in all its forms, has made us a nation of slaves. It is not Islam, it is not England, that has destroyed India. No, our enemy is within us. Priestcraft and caste have slain us. India can never establish and maintain a free state so long as caste rules in our society. You may deliver speeches, pass resolutions, sign Commonwealth Bills ad *infinitum,* but caste Hindus cannot work together or establish a free state or create a victorious army".[15] "Others who criticised caste and untouchability include," the saints like Ramanand, Kabir, Nanak, Ravidas, Chokhamela, Dayanand, Vivekanand, Ramtirath, Tagore, Gandhi; the reformes like Raja Ram Mohun Roy, Ranade, Lala Lajpat Rai, Tilak, Aurobindo, J.P. Narayan, Vinoba Bhave and the politicians like Patel, Rajendra Prasad, Radhakrishnan, V.V. Giri, Nehru, Shastri and a host of others condemned caste and untouchability. They also denounced the stereo types in Hindu social system. However no conservative Hindu cared about the criticism voiced by these persons. They criticised only the visible effects of a system, not its root otherwise these great men would have been opposed by the conservative Hindus. They did not wish to ask for the abolition of *varna-dharma* in order to destroy caste and untouchbility since they know that their criticism of *shashtras* and *Varna-Dharma* was sure to invite opposition to them. Rather most of them upheld *Varna-Vyavastha* as a remedy to social evils prevalent in India".[16]

Dr. Ambedkar was considered the only one social reformer, educationist, philosopher, politician and statesman of the highest stature, who did not care for the opposition of the conservative Hindus and attacked Hinduism and *Varnashram* caste system with all intellectual vigour and vitality at his command and demolished the dome of fallacy, treachery and conspiracy the conservative Hindus had planned, devised and designed to build the Hindu social order depriving the majority of population of this land from asserting their legal, moral and legitimate right to better life in this land of disparities and discrimination. He was a big challenge to the Hinduism and Hindu social order of the country. Nobody, except Dr. Ambedkar could expose the fallacy and treachery of the so-called Hindu scriptures and their teachings. This is the reason why conservative and orthodox Hindus even today hate him, though apparently, on face, they try to show that they respect him. *The RSS, Vishwa Hindu Parishad, Bajrang Dal* and even BJP as on date in the heart of their hearts bitterly hate Dr. Ambedkar, who made their religion thoroughly naked for centuries to come.

It is in this context we have to view the unfortunate day - the 6th December 1992, the Dooms Day, when the six hundread years old *Babri Masjid* was demolished by fanatic caste Hindus on the instigation and inspiration of *RSS* and its affiliate organisations like *Vishwa Hindu Parishad, Bajrang Dal* and even *Shiv Sainiks*. Those Hindus wanted to give a message to the country-men that the legally elected Parliament, Executive and Judiciary of the country are all helpless before Hinduism of this country and they do not accept or rather they do not have faith in those organs of the State, which have been created by the Constitution of the country. And the most alarming message to the million of people of this land was that these *RSS* sponsored organisations do not have faith in the present Constitution that was drafted by Dr. B. R. Ambedkar, an untouchable, *Ati-shudra* to whom they had treated less than an animal. He had publically burnt the *Manusmriti* and demolished the Hindu social order. In other sense

Dr. Ambedkar was the architect of the morden social order of this country and this very thing these *Manuvadis*, the protagonists of *Manuvadi* social system could not digest and consequently on his 37th *Mahaparirvan Day* they showed to the entire world that hence forth India would be governed not by the Constitution of Dr. Ambedkar but by the social order created by *Manu Maharaj* and other religious scriptures created by various *rishis* and saints - the supporters of *Varnashram caste system.*

The leaders of Bhartiya Janata Party had given an assurance to the Supreme Court of India and even to the Parliament of India that the structure of the *Babri Masjid* would not be touched by the *Karsevaks*. The Uttar Pradesh Government headed by BJP Chief Minister Kalyan Singh had filed an affidavit to that effect in the Supreme Court that the structure of the *Babri Masjid* would be protected at all costs. Despite all assurances and affidavit by the Sanghi leaders, the *Doom of Faith of Indian Secularism* was destroyed at one stroke by the communalists and caused irreparable damage to the concept of secularism, enshrined in our Constitution, which was upheld and cherished by our countrymen for the last fifty years and the founding fathers of Indian Constitution had conceived after a long and heated deliberations in the Constituent Assembly. It was the beginning of bad old days - those days which are known in the History of India as the Blackest Days of Indian History.

References

1. Annihilation of Caste : Dr. B.R. Ambedkar p. 124-125.
2. Ranade, Gandhi and Jinnah : Dr. B.R. Ambedkar.
3. Ranade, Gandhi and Jinnah : Dr. B. R. Ambedkar p. 20.
4. Annihilation of Caste : Dr. B.R. Ambedkar p. 71
5. Dr. Ambedkar : Life & Mission: Dhananjay Ker p. 304 and 258.
6. The Buddha and Karl Marx : Dr. D.R. Jatava p. 182-186.
7. Annihilation of Caste : Dr. B.R. Ambedkar p. 87.
8. Annihilation of Caste : Dr. B.R. Ambedkar p. 124.
9. Dr. Ambedkar : Life and Mission : D. Keer p. 92.
10. Buddha and the Future of His Religion (Artice) : Dr. B.R. Ambedkar.
11. Annihilation of Caste : Dr. B.R. Ambedkar.
12. Dr Ambedkar : Life and Mission : Dhananjay Keer p. 302.
13. Dr Ambedkar : Life and Mission : Dhananjay Keer p. 273.
14. The Critics of Dr. Ambedkar : Dr. D.R. Jatava p. 5.
15. Dr. Ambedkar : Life and Mission : D. Keer p. 271.
16. The Critics of Dr. Ambedkar : Dr. D. R. Jatava p. 3.

2
Constitution: Philosophy, Procedure and Performance

While addressing the special function in the Central Hall of the Parliament on 27th January 2000, on the eve of Golden Jubilee of Indian Republic as well as on completing 50 successful working years of the Constitution, President K.R. Narayanan alerted and warned the countrymen, - "Today when there is much talk about revising the constitution or even writing a new constitution, we have to consider whether it is the constitution that has failed us or it is we who have failed the constitution".

What is the reason that the warning to our countrymen by the President on this occassion was necessitated ? Bhartiya Janata Party and the protagonists of Presidential form of government, in place of Parliamentary form of government, had initiated a debate long back, during the period of Smt. Indira Gandhi's Prime Ministership. Mr. Vasant Sathe, then Information and Broadcasting Minister in Indira Gandhi's government and eminent jurist Nani Palkiwala of Tata Group, spokesman for the capitalist system, advocated the theory of presidential form of government. Simultaneously a section of RSS intellectuals also, who are always busy and committed to establish and search out various probable equations, theories, suggestions and schemes for BJP, the political child of the mother *RSS*, supported the view, enunciated by the protagonists of the presidential system; but for different reasons. The RSS could not digest the present Constitution of India, for various reasons, one among them being that they want to establish *Hindu Rashtra* in this country and our constitution propounded the secular state.

Bhartiya Janata Party for the first time in 1996, in their Manifesto declared their intention to review/revise the constitution if they would return to power. In 1998 election also, their commitment to review the constitution was in tact. Unfortunately in 1996 and 1998 their long-cherished dream could not materialise for the reasons that the Vajpayee government had to resign firstly within 13 days and secondly within 13 months. But their commitment to *Hindu Rashtra* did not change. In 1999 they again declared in their Joint Manifesto of National Democratic Alliance for review of the Constitution. And, finally 11 members Constitution Review Commission was announced by the Union government on Sunday 13th February 2000, headed by former Supreme Court Chief Justice M.N. Venkatchalaiah. The terms of reference for the commission include the provisions to examine the working of the Constitution in its five decades after Independence and make suggestions how it could be applied to the changing needs of an efficient, smooth, effective system of governance, social economy and democracy. It would recommend changes that would be required in the constitution without interfering with its basic structure and features.

The interpretation of the terms of reference would be done by the Commission itself and it would talk to political parties for report which would be placed before the Parliament.

Ever since the NDA government headed by Vajpayee declared their intention to set up a panel for review of the Constitutiton, there was lot of *HALAGULA* in the political circles for and against the move of Vajpayee government. Except NDA partners all other political parties condemned the move of the government to review the Constitutiton. Apart from political parties, the eminent personalities of the country including those from legal arena also condemned the move of NDA government. There were instant reactions from those who wanted to oppose the move.

Rebuttal/Reactions

Smt. Sonia Gandhi, president of Indira Congress and Leader of Opposition in the Lok Sabha, addressing a rally on the birth anniversary of Dr. B.R. Ambedkar on the 14th April 2000 in New Delhi's Dr. Ambedkar stadium launched a blistering attack on the BJP led National Democratic Alliance's decision to review the Constitution, saying it was a conspiracy against democracy. It was aimed at establishing a "communal and fascist autocracy". She assured the gathering that the Congress (I) would fight such moves tooth and nail and would protect the Constitutiton at any cost. Mrs Gandhi also accused the NDA of "twisting" India's culture and history to give it a communal colour by trying to change the curriculum in educational institutions. The Constitution "review" now being undertaken was an insult to the country's founding fathers and a move to destroy their dreams and ideas.[1]

Another national political party - Bahujan Samaj Party also declared to oppose the move of NDA government to review the Constitution. BSP president Kanshi Ram said on January 30, 2000 that his party would oppose "tooth and nail" any attempt by BJP-led government to review the Constitution and change its basic features. The idea of reviewing the Constitutiton was floated by the "minority" BJP led government as the political advancement of backwards and scheduled castes was preventing single party rule. The BSP, he said, had no objection to amending the constitution, if it was necessary but would oppose in parliament and on the streets "every move to undermine its socio-economic spirit and to do everything to save its basic features including a responsible parliamentary form of government. .... welcoming "the warning sounded by the president about the government's move to review the constitution", the BSP chief said its basic framework included important provisions for safeguarding the interests of the downtrodden section of society which was sought to be reviewed".[2]

Bahujan Samaj Party also organised country-wide agitational programme against the review of the Constitution by NDA government and which finally culminated in a big rally at New Delhi on 6th December 2000.

Mr. Sharad Pawar, National President of Nationalist Congress Party (NCP), former Chief Minister of Maharashtra and Defence Minister of the country when the structure of Babri Masjid was being demolished and destroyed, opined at a press conference at Mumbai on February 2, 2000 that there was nothing wrong in moving amendments to the Constitutiton, but "the NCP and other like-minded parties will not tolerate changes in the basic structure of the Constitution".[3]

Samajwadi Party, Rashtriya Janata Dal, CPI and CPI (M) and RPI (all groups) also condemned the move initiated by BJP led NDA government to review the Constitution. The move also did not find favour with the eminent intellectuals. A sort of conspiracy was visible to most of them. The Polit bureau of the Communist Party of India (Marxist) observed that "an executive decision will have no legitimacy, as only parliament is competent to undertake such a review". The CPI (M) made a distinction between specific amendments by parliament and a roving review, which it was unwarranted. The CPI demanded that the move be put off and parliament be taken into confidence. The party's central secretariat alleged that the objective of the BJP-led government clearly was to tamper with the Constitution and creat an atmosphere of doubt about its republican character 3(a).

Mr. Lalit Bhasin, Honorary General Secretary of Bar Association of India and a senior Supreme Court Lawyer said that, " The proposed move to set up a Constitution Review Committee for a complete review of the constitutiton is a retrogade step, initiated for political consideration and petty short term gains. The constitution has stood the test of time and if properly enforced it can ensure social justice, economic improvement and general well-being and welfare of the people of this country. Any attempt to tamper with constitution would be suicidal .... There do not seem to be major anomalies in the constitution although there may be certain areas which have been called as "zones of silence, vagueness and uncertainties" .... Here again it would be preferable to retain these "zones of silence ...." because the constitution has left it to the wisdom of the political leadership, the healthy convention and to evolve a code of conduct which would be in the proper governance of the country in conformity with the basic principle of the rule of Law".[4]

Justice J.S. Verma, former Chief Justice of India and presently Chairman of the National Human Rights Commission, in his speech delivered at a recent seminar in New Delhi on the topic—*The Constitution : A Case of Rethinking,* observed that, "The Preamble to the constitution contains the objective of the document, including the constitutional promise made therein. The machinery provisions later are enacted to indicate the manner in which the constitutional promise is meant to be realised. In my view, there is nothing to rethink or review in the preamble to the constitution which is laudable and the exercise is, therefore, required to be confined to the later machinery provisions. In the performance of this exercise, attention has to be focused on the later specific provisions to determine whether the failure to achieve the objective to the extent expected in fifty years of work is on account of any deficiency or defect in any provision so enacted or it is in the manner of its working. Unless any defect is found in the provision itself, the occasion to recast the provision would not arise and the need would be only to improve its operationalisation".[5]

Justice Verma further mentioned that, "The operation of any provision of the constitution through the instrument devised for that purpose is essentially by some human agency. It is the improvement of the human agency in that situation which is warranted. We have to then think of the process by which the improvement can be made. There may, however, be some area in which the provision is found deficient or there is a gap which needs to be filled by enacting some specific provision to fill the vacuum because unfortunately it has not yet been filled by the development and acceptance of a proper convention for that purpose. May be, in practice for sometime, possibly at the beginning, foundation has been laid of a healthy convention to fill the gap or to regulate the operation of that provision and later it was not uniformly respected".[6]

And, further, Justice Verma said, "As I saw it, except for a few areas, there is a case essentially for improving the performance. That would require working of every provision by the best quality of human agency available in the country". He lamented on this pity situation which has emerged in the political scenario and thus he observed very sadly that, "This, unfortunately has not happened always in the recent past. How to cure that defect appears to me the most important aspect of the problem. Good government assured by improvement of machinery to work the constitutional provision in order to translate the constitutional provisions into reality is there all task before us. The debate needs to be focussed on this aspect more than any thing else .... The situation brings to mind the thought—"A bad workman quarrels with the tools". I for one do not think that we need new tools. All we need is sharpening of the tools and making the best use of them, if need be with only some modifications".[8]

His Lordship, finally, observed that, "My own view is that

the basic structure of the constitution is sound requiring no rethinking. The only change required may be in some parts of the machinery which provides for implementing the constitutional programme because of the deficiencies revealed in its working and the margin available in the existing system for its subversion by the unscrupulous, which tendency is increasing. There are only some areas in which experience has shown that there is need for some change to strengthen the constitutional fabric and to provide some effective measures to achieve the constitutional goal. Such areas are only a few where some amendments may be necessary or fresh provisions need to be enacted, but that too is only to realise the constitutional promise initially made".[9]

His Lordship very emphatically said, "It is my firm belief that the aberations found in the working of the constitution are more because of the failure of or deficiency in those who have worked certain provisions at different times. This is the reason why the same provision as originally enacted has not been found wanting for quite some time initially even though its working later on has given rise to a debate for its alteration".[10]

Justice V. R. Krishna Iyer, who has also been co-opted as Chairman on the Fundamental Rights Committee by the Constitutional Review Commission and is known in legal fraternity as the most progressive judge, whose epoch-making judgements have changed to a great extent the socio-economic concept in context to the service matters, though agreed to work on the committee under persuasion, even friendly pressure from Soli Sorabji and Justice Venkatcheliah, he had initially opposed the 'review' ploy.

In an article, published in Hindu (Delhi Ed.) dated April 12, 2000 Justice Iyer could not help expressing his real intent and views about the probable machinations the BJP led NDA government might have in their mind in the setting up of Constitution Review Commission. He wrote, "Now we know blackguardly blockheads and blockheadly blackguards do gain access to power. Reviewing the constitutiton is sensible only if the National Charter has failed not when the cabal of operators under constitutional counterfeit as Cabinet Ministers, play false. There is no alibi for diluting, distorting or making it proprietariat friendly. So this gives room for grave misgiving about why this motley body is set up *ad hoc* with no express terms of reference to focus on. The *'Hindutva'* bogey in the background of the Babri demolition, is heightened by the RSS agressiveness a la Gujarat. Secondly, the BJP election manifesto has disquieting items about constitutional changes which people suspect to be anti-secular. And suspicion is the *Upas* tree under whose shade reason fails and justice dies. There is yet another challenge to the credibility and standing of the commission".[11]

Questioning the credibility of the move Justice Iyer observed, " No doubt there are leading lights in the review galaxy; but the subject matter of the review is of the highest import and portent. Then why was Parliament not taken into confidence and the Commission sanctioned by a resolution of the Houses ? Why now and without at least consulting the opposition ? This is a 'riddle wrapped in a mystery inside an enigma'. Much misunderstanding has been caused, not totally without justification".[12]

His Lordship doubts about the real intention and bonafides of the government. He, therefore, wrote, "The facts remain that a large number of people do begin with a bias against the bonafides of the government in creating this Commission. The composition of the Commission has plus and minus points. The sole value of a public body evading constitution with the opposition in the selection of the members suffers from a political angle. The composition is debunked by the *Dalits* in the absence of a single *Dalit* crusader in the Commission; and the Backward classes have a similar grudge. Not all are carried by a former chief Justice as Chairman".[13]

Justice V. M. Tarkunde expressed that the Constitutional Review Commission is nothing but a political stunt.[14]

Advocate Rajiv Dhawan, one of the senior lawyers of the Supreme Court and legal luminary is of the view that the BJP - led NDA government should have issued a white paper before setting up the commission for review of the constitution and should have also tried for consensus.[15]

Mr. Kapil Sibbal, another senior most lawyer of the Supreme Court and spokesman of Indira Congress, said that setting up of Constitution Review Commission is the next Election Agenda of BJP.[16]

According to Prof. Madhu Dandawate, Janata Dal leader

and former Finance and Rail Minister stated, ".... There is legitimate fear in the minds of several democrats that under the cover of reviewing the entire constitution, which according to various constitutional experts, has stood the test of time, efforts will be made to destroy, what the President of India has described as 'The basic philosophy' of the constitution".[17]

Former Prime Minister V.P. Singh, while refering to Vajpayee's view that even the strongest fort needed repairs, said that, "in the name of repairs, there should be no rebuilding. Sometimes, tenants go for rebuilding in the name of repairs". He said that it was wrong to link political instability to provisions of the constitution. Inequity is the root cause", he argued.[17(a)]

Another former Prime minister, I.K. Gujaral, warned against vague and free fishing attempts to review the constitution[17(b)]

What is the reason ? Why there is so much of hue and cry against the Constitution Review Commission set up by BJP-led National Democratic Alliance government within a year of its taking over the reigns of power at the Centre? Why there was so much of urgency felt by the NDA government within a year to set up Constitutiton Review Commission? Why did the political parties, excepting NDA partners attack so severely the move of NDA government of Vajpayee for setting up Constitutional Review Commission? Why the constitutiton of the country has become so important immediatly for both the ruling partners as well as opposition? What is the constitution? What important and crucial role does the constitution play in the national life of the country? Why has this term acquired so much of importance?

We have the replies to all the above questions and that is the reason that the *Rashtriya Swayamsevak Sangh* (RSS) and its allied organisations have initiated a vicious campaign for the last several years to replace the present constitution with the one which would fulfill the long-cherished dreams of the *'Hindutva'* organisation ! The newly elected chief of RSS *(Sarsanghchalak)* Mr. K. S. Sudershan in his very first press conference at Nagpur, as the chief of the organisation, called for the new constitution for the country. "Euphemistically putting it as a suggestion, K.S. Sudershan, the new RSS Chief said the fresh constitution should be based on Indian ethos, needs and realities ...."

Negating the utility of the Constitution Review Commitee set up by the Vajpayee government, Sudershan said, "A haphazard review of the existing document would not serve any purpose. Instead thought should be given to formulating a new constitution which could address to India's needs, problems and politico-socio-cultural realities", Asked whether the RSS was for a change in the basic structure of the constitution, Sudarshan went further to advocate a totally fresh statute book.

Sudarshan, who had made his stand *vis-a-vis* the constitution clear much earlier, reiterated that the existing constitution was an improved version of the Government of India Act, 1935, framed by the British Rulers. The Independence threw up the need for a statue book and circumstances were such that the then rulers thought it fit to adopt a constitution incorporating the better part of the 1935 Act, he said. But fifty years was too big a period for a nation to get governed by a constitution drafted on temporary requirements and under alien influences, the RSS chief asserted.

The proposed review would not give the much needed Indian face and spirit to the constitution and the only option was to replace it with a new document, said Sudershan.[18]

The RSS and its sponsored organisations have continuously condemned the present constitution of the country as and when they got the opportunity. Immediately after demolition of Babri Masjid on 6th December, 1992, *The Akhil Bhartiya Sant Sammelan* (All India Saints Conference) was held at Allahabad (UP) during the *Magh Mela* where saints from different parts of country participated in the discussion on the constitution and everybody condemned it not being a Hindu constitutiton.[19]

On December 25, 1992 Swami Muktanand and Swami Vamdeo Maharaj of *Akhil Bhartiya Sant Samiti*, who have spearheaded the villainous compaign against the constitution and who have drafted a new Hindu constitution under the guidance of RSS, held a press conference in New Delhi at the residence of a Bhartiya Janata Party Member of Parliament where they called upon the countrymen to reject the "anti-Hindu constitution". Swami Muktanand said, "We have no faith in the country's laws and the Sadhus are above the laws of the land". He also blamed the word 'India' that is in the constitutiton instead of "Hindustan" and according to him that is the main reason for all ills of the country.

This very Sant Samiti also published a "White Paper" titled *"VARTMAN INDIAN SANVIDHAN"* (The Present Indian Constitution) wherein they have dealt in detail the various provisions of the present constitution and condemned them.

It is really surprising that these Saints suddenly became the authorities on the constitutional matters ! This is how the RSS initiated a debate on the constitution to know the reactions of the people. Firstly, these protagonists of *'Hindutva'* idealogy initiated the willy compaign against the constitution through *Sadhus* and *Sants* (Supporters of Hindutva ideology) so as to send a word to the innocent and ignorant Hindu masses in the country that the preachers of the Hindu religion do not have faith in the present constitution. That was the conspiracy designed, developed and carried out by RSS intellectuals to create confusion in the country about the law of the land.

Rashtiya Swayamsewak Sangh stands for *'Hindutva'* and *'Hindu Rashtra'*. Slowly but systematically and with the support of pseudo - secularists, the so-called *Mandalists* and fake socialists they are injecting in the countrymen doses of 'Hinduism' and getting everything done in their favour with the active support of those only who till few years back were their bitterest critics. That is the way of working of RSS, BJP, VHP, ABVP and all other Sangh-sponsored organisations.

It is evident that the criticism of Indian constitution by *Sangh Pariwar* is not the sudden outburst. For a long time through their various spokesmen they have raised the constitutional issues. Mr. Rajju Bhaiyya, former RSS chief, published an article in Indian Express dated January 14, 1993 wherein he observed, "certain specialities of this country should be reflected in the constitution. In place of India that is Bharat, we should have said 'Bharat that is Hindustan'. Official documents refer to the composite culture, but our's is certainly not a composite culture. Culture is not wearing of clothes or speaking languages. In a very fundamental sense, this country has a unique cultural oneness. No country, if it has to survive can have compartments. All this clarify that changes are required in the constitution. *A constitution more suited to the ethos and genius of this country should be adopted in the future"*.

The Human Resource Development Minister and the then BJP president Murli Manohar Joshi on January 24, 1993 at

Anantpur (AP) said that the present situation was due to the 'neglect of Hindutva'[20] According to *Indian Express* (January 25,1993) he harked back to what he said was the glory of India during the Vedic period and said that the need of the hour was to 'review that glory'. Joshi had then reiterated the demand for a fresh look at the constitution.

Prime Minister Atal Behari Vajpayee and Home Minister L. K. Advani, as leaders of BJP, raised the issue of failure of parliamentary form of government a number of times before coming to power and advocated presidential form of government.

In view of whatever the reactions and views expressed by political leaders and intellectuals one aspect is clear that the constitution of the country is a very important document and the only instrument through which one can acquire the political power and change not only the entire socio-economic situation of the country but also the religion and cultural scenario could even be changed. It is in this context that Prime Minister Atal Behari Vajpayee's commitment made in the presence of 108 Sadhus, as well as *"Overseas Friends of the BJP"* (including hardcore Rashtriya Swayamsewak Sangh members) and the VHP including Ashok Singhal on the foreign land where he discribed the 'temple' as part of the "India of our dreams". He also declared there himself as a proud *'Swayamsewak'* and said firmly that his right to be *Swayamsewak* could never ever be taken away and that it is dearer to him than the Prime Ministership. In an article in 'Organiser' (mouth-piece of RSS) Shri Vajpayee had written that. "The Sangh is my Soul".

These credentials of Prime Minister Vajpayee's suffice to conclude his real intentions, when he said, while addressing the august gathering in the Central Hall of Parliament on 27th January 2000 on the eve of Golden Jubilee celebration of our Republic and Constitution, that, "even mightiest fort one has to repair the parapet from time to time, one has to clean the moat and check the bannisters. The same is true about our constitution. Five decades after the adoption of the constitution, India is faced with a new situation. *The need for stability, both at the Centre and in the States has been felt acutely"*.[21]

Prior to this justifying the move to review the constitution, Mr. Vajpayee said, "the people are impatient for faster socio-economic development. The country is also faced with the pressing challenge to quickly remove regional imbalances by re-orienting the development process - to benefit the poorest and weakest".[22]

He further said that that was the purpose for which the Commission to review the constitution was proposed to be set up ....".[23]

In view of the above, it is therefore, necessary to know what does the constitution mean for the countrymen and what is that role it plays in shaping the life and destiny of the people.

What is Constitution

Dr. S. Radhakrishanan, the first vice president of the Indian Republic and who was popularly known as Philosopher King, while congratulating Dr. Rajendra Prasad on being elected Chairman of the Constituent Assembly said that, "A constitution is the fundamental law of the nation. It should embody and express the dreams and passions, the ideals and aspirations of the people. It must be based on the consent of all and respect the rights of all people who belong to this great land".[24]

Former Chief Justice of India Hon'ble Patanjali Shashtri defined, "The constitution is meant to be an instrument of permanent nature. It is meant to embody cardinal principles of democratic government and certain essential ideals for the functioning of a republic based on justice and fair play .... The constitution is not an ordinary law. It is a mechanism for the making of law. The constitution should not be treated like the Prevention Detention Act, or the Income Tax Act, to be periodically amended or annually altered"[25]

Mr. H. M. Sheerwai the former Advocate General of Maharashtra and eminent lawyer, while arguing before the Hon'ble Supreme Court in the Keshwanand Bharti case said, "A constitution is a means to an end and that end is the safety, greatness and well-being of the country and its people for whom the constitution was enacted."[26]

According to Thomas Jefferson, one of the founding fathers of American Constitution and great leader of their freedom struggle, " only a law emanating directly from the authority of the people themselves, a law binding upon the ordinary organs of government and unchangeable by them deserved to be called a constitution".[27]

Addressing the Constituent Assembly on 8th November 1948, Pandit Jawaharlal Nehru explained the importance of the basis and fundamentals of the constitution : "The constitution is after all some kind of legal body given to the ways of government and the life of people. A constitution if it is out of touch with the people's life, aims and aspirations, becomes rather empty; if it falls behind those aims, it drags the people down. It should be something ahead to keep peoples eyes and mind up to a certain high mark".[28]

Dr. Granville Austin, the American expert on Indian constitution, who has done great research on the working of Indian constitution and outcome of the same were two books : *Working a Democratic Constitution : The Indian Experience and Indian Constitution : Cornerstone of a Nation,* very simply defined that. " a constitution is like a foot-ball field—it has goal lines, it has side lines and it sets the rules. And that is all it can do. It is the human beings who have got to work it".[29]

It is evident from the above definitions that it is the constitution which creates the machinery for governance of the country and the various organs/ parts of machinary created by it are inter related with each other and responsible and accountable to the authority from which those derive the strength or power, i.e., sovereign people. It is a set of rules and regulations embodying principles and ideology. It does not work itself. It is the human beings who work it. Good or bad, it is they who are to be held responsible who work it and not the constitution.

Justice Verma has, therefore, very rightly observed while speaking on the issue of review of the constitution. He said, "The review, if any, is required only to this limited extent. But then this requirement also arises only because the country has failed in recent times to 'throw up such men in abundance who will have the interest of the country before them' and place them at all vantage points in the machinery for working the constitution as visualized by the framers of the constitution, the failure is, therefore, essentially of the men who have worked the constitution and not of the constitution itself".[30]

Justice Verma's above observation that the failure is therefore essentially of the men who have worked the constitution and not of the constitution itself is sufficient to refute the contention of Prime Minister Vajpayee that the review of the constitution is required for faster socio-economic development, because the people are very impatient for that. It is not the people who are very impatient, but it is RSS, BJP and VHP which are impatient to change this country's basic feature from Secular State to Hindu Rashtra and impose upon this country the same old Hinduism and caste based *Varnashram socio-religious system* which represents the ethos and genius of this country, as per RSS chief K. S. Sudershan.

Basics of the Constitution

There has been going on a intensive debate in the media and among the constitutional experts about the basic structure of the constitution. The debate was firstly raised with the pronouncement of *Keshwanand Bharti* epoch making judgement in 1973. Since then the debate and discussion is going on. Several times the doubts about the exactness of basic features of the constitution were raised by saffronised intellectuals and experts and they argued that the Keshwanand Bharati judgement has vaguely defined the basic features of the constitution. Their purpose behind the doubt was to facilitate them to apply their scheme of review the necessary provisions so as to enable them to have the things of their choice and requirement. Keeping this in view, Atalji and Advaniji advocated the presidential form of government. Their contention is that parliamentry democracy is not part of the basic structure of the constitution. Because it is not mentioned in the basic features illustrated in Keshwanand Bharti judgement. It is not correct.

The Keshwanand Bharati judgement has very clearly stated that, "The basic structure is not a vague concept and the appreciations expressed on behalf of the respondents that neither the citizens nor the parliament would be able to understand it are unfounded. If the historical background, the Preamble, the entire scheme of the constitution, the relevant provision thereof including article 368 are kept in mind there can be no difficulty in discerning that the following can be regarded as the basic element of the constitutional structure :

1. The Supremacy of the constitution.
2. Republican and democratic form of government and sovereignity of the country.

3. Secular and democratic character of the constitution.

4. Demarcation of power between the legislature, the executive and the judiciary.

5. The dignity of the individual secured by various freedoms and basic rights in part III and mandate to build a welfare state contained in part IV.

6. Unity and Integrity of the nation."

In addition to Keshwanand Bharati judgement which very clearly defined the basic structure doctrine, the judgement given in the S R Bommai case (commonly called Assembly dissolution case) has again reinforced that secularism is a basic feature of the constitution and it cannot be tampered with, diluted or overturned. And thus the nine member Bench headed by Justice S R Pandian has made the greatest contribution by elevating secularism to the status of a basic principle of the polity.

Analysing the various aspects of the watershed verdict, delivered by nine member constitution bench, presided over by Justice S R Pandian in the Assembly dissolution case, Sukumar Murlidharan of 'Frontline' observed that, secularism has for long been a verity all pay up lip service to some but a few choose really to abide by or practice in the political sphere. It is a concept embraced with great enthusiasm by even those whose practice negates its very essence This ideological fudge - which has lately been perfected by the Bhartiya Janata Party (BJP) and particularly by its President L.K. Advani will now no longer serve as a camouflage for communal politics. He, further, observed, "Perhaps the most valuable exposition of the concept of secularism comes from the judgement of Justice B.P. Jeevan Reddy and S.C. Agrawal. Secularism was worked into the Preamble to the constitution by the emergency enactment of the 42nd Amendment. This has been used by some as a basis for denigrating the concept. But Justice Reddy and Justice Agrawal argue that this merely made explicit what was in implicit feature of the constitution. Art. 14 institutes the right to equality before law for all within the territorial bounds of the nation. The next two articles elucidate this doctrine of equality, ruling out any discrimination on grounds of religion, race or caste. Article 25 guarantees 'all persons' the freedom of faith and belief and the right to profess, practice and propagate any religion within the bounds of public order. And Article 51(A) defines among the 'fundamental duties' the promotion of 'harmony and brotherhood' irrespective of religion, language and region ....'

How are these constitutional premises to be realised", ask Justice Reddy and Justice Agrawal unless "the State eschews the religion, faith or belief of a person from its consideration altogether while dealing with him, his rights, his duties and his entitlements"? Far from being a "passive attitude of religious tolerance", secularism is a "positive concept of equal treatment of all religions".

Justices P B Sawant and Kuldip Singh held the same view and added that the State is constitutionally prevented from "either identifying itself with or favouring any particular religion or religious sect or denomination". What emerges from this notion, they continued, is the strict prohibition of any "encroachment of religion into secular activities". The State may guarantee freedom of religion but this does not amount to any sort of explicit or implicit permission to introduce religion into non-religious and secular activites of the state.

The consequences of the BJP style of politics are dealt with at length in the Reddy - Agrawal judgement. 'If a political party espousing a particular religion comes to power', they say, then 'that religion tends to become, in practice, the official religion". This would consign all other religions to secondary status. This would 'plainly be antithetical to Article 14 to 16, 25 and the entire constitutional scheme'. From these, it follows that if the "constitution requires the State to be secular in thought and action, then the 'same requirement attaches to political parties as well'. In other words, it is impossible under the scheme of law adopted in India for an organisation to "simultaneously be a political and a religious party".

".... The business of government deals above all with secular issue such as the lives and livelihoods of the masses. It is the responsibility of the state to attend to these irrespective of religion. Where religious affiliation becomes a qualification for determining individual citizens entitlements to the attention of the state then a situation of inequity is clearly reached, calling out for constitutional correction".[31]

Originally, for a long time the RSS and its affiliates—BJP, VHP, Bajarang Dal and ABVP initiated a move against the Constitution. Vishwa Hindu Parishad and Bajarang Dal leaders quite often denounce secular provision of Indian Constitution. The Sadhu Samaj also declared a number of times that they are above the law and they are not bound by the law of the land. VHP leaders—Giriraj Kishor and Ashok Singhal have already declared that come what may, they are determined to build Ram Temple on the same very place of demolished Babri Masjid and for that they would not obey the verdict of the Supreme Court also. RSS leaders have also echoed the same sound. Thus, these Hindutva supporting organisations have created a sort of fear psychosis against non-Hindus and indirectly put under pressure the judiciary to pronounce the judgement against Babri Masjid and in favour of Ram Temple. This amounts to tampering of law of the land creating anarchy in the country and pressurising judiciary to take their side so as to avoid future consequences. This amounts to virtually dictating the judiciary to ditto their line of action or face the consequences. This is nothing but religious terrorism.

References

1. The Hindu - Daily (New Delhi Ed.) dt 15/4/2000.
2. Times of India, (New Delhi Ed.) dt 31/1/2000.
3. Times of India, (Mumbai Ed.) dt 3/2/2000.

3 (a). Frontline dt 3/3/2000 p. 27.

4. Constitution Review Commission Fruitless Pursuit by Justice Bhau Wahane p. 65, 66.
5. The Hitavada (Eng. Daily from Nagpur) dt 27/2/2000.
6. The Hitavada dt. 27/2/2000.
7. *Ibid.*
8. *Ibid.*
9. *Ibid.*
10. *Ibid.*
11. The Hindu (New Delhi) 12/4/2000.
12. *Ibid.*
13. *Ibid.*
14. Rastriya Sahara (Daily) Hastkshep dt. 12/2/2000.
15. *Ibid.*
16. *Ibid.*
17. *Ibid.*

17a. *Ibid.*

17b. *Ibid.*

18. The Hitavada (Eng. Daily from Nagpur) dt 3/2/2000.
19. Jansatta New Delhi (Hindi daily) dt 3/2/1993.
20. Indian Express dt. 25/1/1993.
21. Times of India dt. 28/1/2000.
22. *Ibid.*
23. *Ibid.*

24. Constitution Review Commission Fruitless Pursuit by Justice Bhau Wahane p. 9
25. *Ibid.*
26. Nagpur Times dt. 13/2/1973.
27. Dr. B.R. Ambedkar : Quest for Social Justice by Dr. A. M. Rajsekhriah p. 164
28. The Constitution and Constituent Assembly : A Lok Sabha Secretariat Publication p. 124
29. An interview given to The Hindu by Dr. Austin published on March 16, 1998.
30. The Hitavada dt 27/2/2000.
31. Frontline dt. April 8, 1994. p. 13 to 20.

3
Evolution of Indian Constitution

'The legacy which we (Indians) have inherited from ancient Hindu period is a very rich legacy. It is more socio-religious than political. The political institutions, built by Hindus during the period of their ascendancy in ancient days and by the Muslims when they wielded the scepter, have become a thing of the past. The British, when they became politically strong in India, built a new constitutional structure on their experiences in England to suit their political ends in India. They realised great difficulty in completely ignoring the social inheritance of India".[1]

Hindu Period

Before the advent of Britishers and lasting their 200 years rule in India, the Indian society of that time was mostly ruled by the customs, usages and traditions set out by the Hindu and Muslim rulers. During the Hindu period, "a State was called a Rashtra and its head was called the Raja. A Rashtra was divided into Deshas , Janapadas or Vishyas. The king was the head of the State. He was assisted by a large number of persons known as the Sahayas. He also sought the advice of the Parishad whose head was called the Mukhyamatya. The duty of the king was not to lay down the law of the country but merely to enforce the same. The sources of law were the Vedas, the Dharma Shashtras, Shila and Acharai. If there was any doubt regarding the law on a particular point, a council of experts, called the Parishad, was to be consulted by the king. The Kula, Jati, Shreni and the Janapada were allowed to make their own laws and it was the duty of the king not only to recognise them but also to enforce them".[2] One of the most important sources of Hindu laws was *Manusmriti* which was the instrument of regulating the inter personal relation in the Hindu society. "The *Manusmriti* divides the society into two parts. The Aryans and the Non-Aryans. The Non-Aryans were called Anarya, Dasyu and Mlechchha. The term Dasyu also included the Chandalas, Shvapakas etc. The non-Aryans moved about in the country and lived near the cremation grounds, forest and mountains. They kept a large number of donkeys and dogs. They were not allowed to enter a village at night. Even when they entered a village in day time, they had to put on a particular kind of dress. They were employed to hang people and also to carry the dead bodies. They lived by hunting.

The Aryan society was divided into two parts; Dwijatis and Ekajatis. To the former group belonged the Brahmans, Kshatriyas. The Shudras were known as Ekajatis .... The life of the people was regulated by the *Varnashram Dharma*. ... The Shudras formed the bulk of Aryan society. Their main duty was to serve the Brahmanas, Kshatriyas, and Vaishyas. They were required to remove dirt, filth and carcases .... Women were not given a place of honour by Manu. They were forbidden to study Vedas. Before marriage a girl was required to be under the control of her father or brother. After marriage, she was required to be under the control of her husband .... She was not entitled to inherit any property except Stridhana[3]

This was the life style of the people in those days when the laws made by *Manu* were in operation as stated above. In addition to *Manusmriti,* there were *Yajnavalkasmriti, Vishnusmriti* and *Naradasmriti* which governed the inter-personal relations of the people in those days. Of all the smritis the *Manusmriti* was more in operation and it alone regulated effectively the life of the people till the arrival of Britishers in India.

With the passing of time, there took place a lot of changes in socio-political and religious system of the people. The changes took place in the governing system of the country also. The *Arthashashtra* of Kautilya refers to a large number of republics. Among them were the Lichchhavikas, the Vrijikas, the Mallakas, the Madrakas, the Kukaras, the Kurus, the Panchalas, the Khombojas, the Surashtras, the Kshatriyas, the Srenis etc.[4]

According to Dr. K. P. Jayaswal, the republican form of government in India came along after Monarchy. It was Prof. Rhys Davids, who in *Buddhist India* pointed out that a republican form of government prevailed in the country of Buddha and his neighbours .... Of the many republics, that were in existence during the Buddhas time, there is a mention of the constitution of the Lichchhavis in the Atthakatha. There is also a reference to three high officers called Raja or President, Upraja or Vice president and Senapati or the Generalissima. There is also a reference to the officer of Bhandagarika or Chancellor of Exchequer in a Jataka. In fact the above four highest officers constituted the Cabinet.[5]

Thus, from the above it appears that a definite system of governance, rules and laws were in vogue during the ancient time. What we find today as parliamentary system, the same system was in practice in the republics of Buddhist era and all the rules of today's parliamentary system were observed in those days also. As such we can say with firm determination and with historical proof that we have not borrowed the parliamentry system from Britishers but on the other hand we can say that it were the Britishers who have borrowed our system of parliamentary government. In this connection Dr. Ambedkar observed in the Constituent Assembly on 26th November 1949;

" .... It is not that India did not know what is democracy. There was a time when India was studded with republics and even where there were monarchies, they were either elected or limited. They were never absolute. It is not that India did not know Parliaments or Parliamentary procedure. A study of the Buddhist Bhikshu Sanghas discloses that not only there were Parliaments - for the Sanghas were nothing but Parliaments - but Sanghas knew and observed all the rules of Parliamentary procedure known to modern times. They had rules regarding seating arrangements, rules regarding motions, Resolutions, Quorum, Whip, Counting of votes, Voting by Ballot, Censure Motion, Regularisation, Res Judicata etc. Although these rules of Parliamentary procedure were applied by the Buddha to the meetings of the Sanghas, he must have borrowed them from the rules of the Political Assemblies in the country in his time".[6]

Manusmriti was the supreme law of the land in those days i.e. during the hey days of Hinduism. One can very well imagine as to how strict, discretionary, partisan and two different set of laws were made by *Manu* for two different groups of people. If we have a look or peep into these rules/laws, we can understand that it was not less than a hell for those Shudras and Ati-Shudras, while the fruits of joy were enjoyed by the most fortunate upper classes or Brahmins.

"In the scheme of Manu the Brahmin is placed at the first rank. Below him is the Kshatriya. Below Kshatriya is the Vaishya. Below Vaishya is the Shudra and below Shudra is Ati-shudra (the untouchables). This system of rank and gradation is simply another way of enunciating the principles of inequality so that it may be truly said that Hinduism does not recognise equality. This inequality in status is not merely the inequality that one sees in the warrant of precedence prescribed for ceremonial gathering at the king's court. It is a permanent social relationship among the classes to be observed for all purposes. It will take too long to show how in every phase of life Manu has introduced and made inequality the vital force of life."[7]

Manu on Slavery and Marriage

"*Manu* recognises slavery. But he confined it to Shudras. Only Shudras could be made slaves of the higher classes. But the higher classes could not be made slaves of the Shudra. ... A Brahmin when marrying outside his class may marry any woman from any of the classes below him. A Kshatriya is free to marry a woman from the two classes next below to him, namely, the Vaishya and Shudra but must not marry a woman from the Brahmin class which is above him. A Vaishya is free to marry a woman from the Shudra class which is next below to him. But he cannot marry a woman from the Brahmin and the Kshatriya class which are above him."[8]

About the System of Punishment : Manusmriti had also defined the rules of punishment.

"(XI-127) For killing intentionally a virtuous man of the military class, the penance must be a fourth part of that ordained for killing a priest; for killing a Vaisya only a eighth, for killing a Shudra who had been constant in discharging his duties, a sixteenth part ...." (XI-128) "But if a Brahmin kills a Kshatriya without malice, he must, after a full performance of his religious rites, give the priests one bull together with thousand cows." [9]

"How strange is the contrast between Hindus and Non-Hindu criminal jurisprudence ? How inequality is writ large in Hinduism as seen in its criminal jurisprudence ?" asks Dr. Ambedkar[10]

Manu on Wages

Dealing with the question of wages to the Shudras, Manu says:

(X-124) They must allot to him (Shudra) out of their own family property a suitable maintenance after considering his ability, his industry and the number of those whom he is bound to support .... (X-125) The remnants of their food must be given to him, as well as their old cloths, the refuse of their grains and their old household furniture"

"This is *Manu's* law of wages .... It was also an iron law fixed so low that there was no fear of the Shudra accumulating wealth and obtaining economic security. But Manu did not want to take chances and he went to the length of prohibiting the Shudras from accumulating property. He says imperatively :-

"(X-129) No collection of wealth must be made by Shudra even though he be able to do it. For a Shudra who has acquired wealth gives pain to Brahmins"[11]

As regards the knowledge, the doors were kept open for Brahmins only while Shudras and women were prohibited from receiving education. They were born to be in dark and remain to be in dark always. They did not have any rights under Manu's Constitution i. e. Law of Manu. By all ways Manu made the life of Shudras and women very miserable, pitiable and unbearable !

As observed by Dr. Ambedkar, "The Smritis originally were a collection of rules relating to social traditions, customs and conventions approved of and recommended by those who were learned in the Vedas .... The authors of the Vedas were Rishis. The authors of Smritis were learned men .... While originally Hindu society was bound to the Vedas and couldn't follow any rule which was contrary to the Vedas, the new rule altered the situation and left it to the option of society either to follow the Shruti or the Smriti .... Finally came the rule according to which the study of the Smriti was recognised and a contempt of the Smriti was made a sin and a person guilty of it was declared to be condemned to be born as a beast for 21 generations"[12]

This is how the Smritis have been recognised as source of Hindu Religion and there is no doubt that, to quote Prof. Altekar, the Smritis;

"Have played a great part in determining the features of many a social and socio-religious institutions and customs and in moulding the development of modern Hinduism."[13]

Thus it is very clear from the above that the religious scriptures of Hinduism played a very important role in giving shape and content to the socio-religious institutions in India country during the Hindu period. Of the various scriptures, that played their parts, the worst and dirty role was played by *Manusmriti*, the constitutional law of Hinduism. It was this very book which was in force during the Muslim period as well as British period. The British people could not ignore the strength of Hinduism and thus they continued for several years.

Muslim Period

The Muslim period marks the beginning of a new era in India. They came in eighth century and settled down here. As long as they ruled, they did not antagonise the Hindus. Once the great country ruled by the Emperor like Ashoka the great and Chandragupta Maurya, it was really shocking that such a great country came under the rule of a few hundred Muslim invaders. But the political history of this period is full of constant struggles between a few powerful states for supremacy. 'The greatest drawback was the complete lack of political unity amongst Indian kings and the absence of the patriotic sense and lack of nationalistic spirit'.[14]

"The social system of Muslim was based on their religion, Islam, which may be described as a reformist version of current seventh century Arabian practice. The Muslims followed the principles of equality for men and they had no faith in the graded or sanctified inequality of caste system. Muslim religion places every man on an equality before God, overriding distinction of class, nationality, race and colour .... The political theory of Muslims was governed by their religion Islam. It was based on the teaching of the Quran, their religious book, the traditions of the Prophet and precedent .... The political institutions which were adopted and developed by the Muslims were based on the idea given by the Greek Philosopher. Sovereignty in a Muslim State belonged to God. The Muslim kings in India in general regarded themselves as God's humble servants. The ruler was his delegate, duly elected by the people to perform certain functions according to the legal sovereignty of the *Shara* or *Islamic Law*. The political theory laid emphasis on the fact that all Muslims formed one congregation of the faithful and it was necessary for them to unite closely in the form of an organised community. Any attempt to break away from the organised community was condemned by the religion. All the members of the community elected Khalifa or Caliph as the commander of the faithfuls. It was made obligatory on all Muslims to owe allegiance to the Caliph who was also their ruler."[15]

The Muslim ruler once in power, remained till the end unless removed by death or coup. Though he was the ruler, he was not free to make the law of the land. The entire activity of the Muslim community was regulated by Quran. He was all in all for the maintenance of interpersonal relations as well as relation between the king and people.

Among Muslim rulers, the most prominent and respected name is that of Emperor Akbar. He is known in the history as benevolent autocrat. During his period a 'Cabinet' like formation came into existence. The *"Navratna Darbar"* of Emperor Akbar was nothing but the council of ministers. "His administrative system, nevertheless, favoured the direct relations between the state and the individul peasant, the assessment and collection of revenue being controlled from the Centre and the officers having to account in detail for all receipts. It was in fact a centralised monarchy acting through bureaucratic machinery; all the strings of the government were in the Emperor's own hands and controlled by him directly".[16] However it looked like a federal state. There was central government as well as provincial governments. "The administrative agency in the provinces of the 'Mughal Empire' was an exact miniature of that central government. The Governor was officially called the Nazim but popularly known as the Subahdar"[17] Many of the official designations of these days are directly inherited from that time like - Fauzdar, Kotwal, the Amin, the Qanungo. Though the Emperor's rule directly did not contribute to the constitutional development of the country but the administrative set up, Cabinet like set up of Navaratna Darbar, Revenue system and equal royal treatment to his ministers like Raja Man Singh, Todarmal and Birbal speak about the secular character of his governance. He never imposed Islam on the Hindus and never discrimated between Hindus and Muslims. The religion, culture, customs, traditions and social system of the non-Muslim remained undisturbed during his period. There was no forcible conversion to Islam under his reign.

Today, the *'Hindutva'* supporters both in BJP, RSS,VHP and Shiv Sena blame the Muslim rulers that most of today's historical Masjids including one recently demolished - Babri Masjid, were built on the destruction of Hindu Temples. Thus these extremist Hindus are spreading the communal poison and trying to destroy the harmonious atmosphere of the country and thus are acting against the secular objective of the Constitution.

According to Catherine B. Asher, "Indeed from Akbar's time (reign - 1556 to 1605) forward Mughal rulers treated temples lying within their sovereign domain as State property; accordingly they undertook to protect both physical structure and their Brahmin functionaries. At the same time by appropriating Hindu religious institutions to serve imperial ends-a process involving complex overlapping of political and religious codes of power - the Mughals became deeply implicated in institutionalised Indian religions, in dramatic contrast to their British successors who professed a hands off policy in this respect". Thus, we find Akbar allowing high ranking Rajput officers in his service to build their own monumental temples in the provinces to which they were posted as in the case of Govid Deo Temple in Brindawan, patronised by Raja Mansingh."[18] As such citing the instances of Muhammad Ghazni, Aurangzeb or Changez Khan or for that matter Mullah Muhammad Omar of Afganistan by the extremist Hindus, who are dead-set to destabilise and destroy secular fabric of the country, must know that they are doing great harm to the country.

And Mr. Jyotirmaya Sharma in his article in *Sunday Times of India* dated March 4, 2001 has very rightly observed that 'for every Mulla Muhammud Omar in Afghanistan there is a corresponding Giriraj Kishor in India. Similarly for every felling of the Bamiyan Buddha, there is a parallel in the destruction of the Babri Masjid in India. His further remarks about the parallel he draws between felling of Babri Masjid and Baniyan Buddha in Afganistan by the Talibanised minds of self appointed saviours of Hinduism, are very pertinent and befitting." He wrote that, "It is the politics of 'friend' and 'foe' which has brought this about. And Nationalism, exclusivity, fear of complexity and plurality as well. He has again very rightly questioned the so-called protectors of *Hindutva* as to why get so hysterical over the destruction of a few statues in Afghanistan? Why not get equally charged by razing to the ground of the Babri Masjid ? Because power is an addiction and can only be attained through dividing people by sheding blood, by vitiating every gental norm in society".

It was not that the Muslims rulers alone were protectors of the Hindu temples, even some of the Hindu kings also reciprocated the same manner. Rather they did nothing to hurt the religious feelings of the Muslims.

" .... The incident suggests that mosques in Mughal India, though religiously potent were considered detached from both sovereign terrain and dynastic authority and hence politically inactive. As such their desecration would have had no relevance to the business of dis-establishing a regime that had patronised them. Not surprisingly, then, when Hindu rulers established their authority over the territories of defeated Muslim rulers they did not as rule desecrate mosques or Shrines as for example, when Shivaji established a Maratha Kingdom on the ashes of Bijapur's former dominions in Maharashtra or when Vijayanagara annexed the former territories of the Bahmanis or their successors. In fact the Rajas of Vijayanagara as is well-known, built their own mosques, evidently to accommodate the sizeable number of Muslims employed in their armed forces".[19]

This could have been a great lesson for BJP, RSS, VHP and Bajrang Dal, which on getting political power in UP, betraying the assurance given to the Parliament, Supreme Court and National Integration Council to protect the structure of Babri Masjid, they helped to demolish and destroy the dome of faith of secularism' - the Babri Masjid. And this happened in the country which is committed to secularism, where every religion has been assured to be equally respected. See the difference on the one side there is an historic evidence that Muslim rulers not only helped to build the Hindu temples for their subjects but protected the same. On the other side see the treatmant given by the communalists in India !

British Period

The British period, in the constitutional history of India dates back to the arrival of East India Company in 1600 AD for trading in India. Slowly and systematically the traders in British uniforms converted their company as the governing council and took over the reigns of India. Today's parliamentary system has grown up from the rules, regulations and acts developed, designed and implemented by them for their benefit but without causing much heart-burning to the Indians. It is a subject of detail study as to how from Regulating Act of 1773 to the Government of India Act, 1935 the changes took place in governing system of our country and how the Indians were prepared and trained to perform the parliamentary work. The *Sangh Pariwar* has bitterly criticised the present constitution for various provisions, including Government of India Act, 1935. They, however, forgot that India Act, 1935 is not a sudden outcome or imposed upon us by the Britishers at their own. It was the outcome of gradual process of giving responsible government to Indians because of ever increasing burden of maintenance and political pressures, the struggle for Independence of India launced under the leadership of Mahatma Gandhi.

The period from 1858 to 1947 was an era of direct government by the British Crown. Some major policy decisions which were taken during this period played an important role in shaping and moulding the future constitutional development of India. Three phases of development during this period which came respectively may be stated as the growth of representative institutions, self-governing institutions and dominion status. The national opinion and political situation in India were also greatly influenced by the reactions of the forces of British imperialism, nationalism and communalism".[20]

The enactment of Government Of India Act, 1858 by the British Parliament became an important land-mark in the constitutional history of India. Out of some of the main provisions of that Act, the most important provision was the creation of Indian Civil Service to which the present Indian Administration Service owes its inheritance. The Indian Council Act of 1861 laid down the foundation of the legislative system as adopted in India today. Coatman observed, " The whole effect of the Council Act was the to direct the political development of India towards the goal of democratic government by a representative legislature".[21] The main contribution of Indian Council Act of 1892 was that, Act for the first time introduced the principle of election under the garb of nomination on the recommendation, and it was the first time that the Indians were to be associated with the highest legislative function in the right manner. And its historical value in the development of constitutional law in India was that, Act had sown the productive seed of the principle of election of representatives which further developed firmly the direction of parliamentarian responsible self-government of India.

The Indian Council Act of 1909 was based on the recommendation of Sir Arundale during the period when Lord Morley was the Secretary of State for India and Lord Minto, the Viceroy of India. The political awakening of India towards the end of the nineteenth century led British administration and politicians to think in terms of introducing more reforms and gain more support of landed aristocracy and moderate elements in the Indian National Congress. The unification of India and Indians under a strong and highly centralised government was no doubt introduced and strengthened gradually but a section of the British politicians was also aware of the danger of political awakening and the unity of Indians. They foresaw danger to the British Empire and therefore, as a matter of policy resorted to the technique "to divide and rule". The vicious system of separate communal representation for the Muslims was introduced in the legislative reforms of India".[22] The Muslim League came into existence in 1906 and demanded separate representation for the Muslims in all legislatures. Perhaps the seeds of separation of Pakistan were laid in this period only through this Act.

The next move of the British Crown, from the point of constitutional development was the Government of India Act, 1919 which is known in the history of political science for introducing the new system known as "Dyarchy" in the governance of British provinces in India, in which important subjects were kept with the Governor and less important subjects were entrusted to the Indians. The other important provision of the Act was that "it made the central legislature bicameral which was to consist of the Council of States (Upper House) and the Central Legislative Assembly (Lower House). The second chamber was introduced to act as a check upon the lower house. The principle of "Separate Communal Representation", which was introduced in the Act of 1909 was retained in the composition of the Legislative Assembly and the Council of States. The elected seats were distributed among all provinces and in each province they were further distributed on the basis of communities and interests. Thus, Landlords, Depressed Classes, Muslims, Anglo-Indians and other classes were represented in the elected seats".[23] However, the reforms introduced by this Act totally failed to satisfy the Indian political leaders. Their demand for more and appropriate reforms remained as it was.

Simon Commission

The Simon Commission was appointed in 1927. The main objective of the Commision was to enquire into the working of the system of government and development of the representative institutions in India, with a view to extend, modify or restrict the degree of responsible government then existing in India. The leaders of Congress Party strongly opposed the commission, as no Indian was taken on the committee. The Simon Commission was boycotted by the Congress and other political parties. Resolutions were passed condemning the constitution of the commission. It was greeted in India, on their arrival with black flags and hartal all over the country and they shouted "Simon Go Back". However, Dr. B. R. Ambedkar, Member of the Legislative Council, Bombay and the emerging prominent leader of the untouchables, co-operated with the Commission to plead and apprise the members of the Commission about the miserable plight of his people. He also handed over a memorandum to the Commission concerning the safeguards for the protection of the interests of the Depressed classes as a Minority in the Bombay Presidency and for changes in the composition of and the guarantees from the Bombay Legislative Council necessary to ensure the same under Provincial Autonomy.

The Commission submitted its report on June 24, 1930, wherein it recommended for abolition of 'dyarchy' in provinces, there should be no interference by the Centre in the administrative and legislative work of the provinces. The franchise in the Provincial Legislature should be widened, communal electorate must be continued. It was pointed out that an All India Federation was to be set up in the distant future. The Report declared that the constitutional framework of the country could not be unitary type. It must be federal, not merely in response to the growth of provincial loyalties but primarily it must embrace all India and it was only in a Federation that

Indian states could be expected in course of time to unite with British India. Though for the time being the Report was shelved and not considered but some of its suggestions played a vital role when the Government India Act 1935 was framed.

Nehru Committee Report

"The repercussion of Simon Commission and the challenges of Lord Birkenhead, the Secretary of State for India, to produce a constitution which should be acceptable to all political parties in India, led the Indian National Congress to accept the challenge. All Parties Conference met in Delhi on February 28, 1928 and in Bombay May 19, 1928 and a small committee with Pandit Motilal Nehru as its chairman was set up to draft a constitution for India. The committee produced a memorable report which was "Masterly and Statesmanlike" and presented a Constitution, which in fact, reflected the high standard of learning in India".[24]

"The recommendations of the report were unanimous exept in regard to the basis of the Constitution. While the majority favoured Dominion Status not merely as distant goal but as "the next immediate step". It however gave liberty to all those groups and parties which made complete independence their goal.

Although the Report envisaged a future linking up of the Indian States with the rest of India in a federal polity, it confined itself to British India.... As regards the communal question, the report made many wise recommendations. It proposed joint electorates with reservation of seats for minorities on population basis with the right to contest additional seats .... full protection was to be given to the religious and cultural interests of the Muslim community.

The Report enumerated 19 fundamental rights which were to be embodied in the Statutes. It was to be declared that all powers of the Government and all authority were derived from the people. No person shall be deprived of his liberty nor shall his dwelling or property be entered, sequestered or confiscated, save in accordance with law. *Freedom of conscience and free profession and practice of religion will be guaranted to every person*. Right of free expression of opinion and the right to assemble peacefully and without arms and to form associations and or unions shall be guaranteed for purposes not opposed to public morality. All citizens shall have the right to free elementry education. All citizens shall be equal before law and possess equal civic rights. There shall be no penal law of discriminatory nature. No person shall be punished for any act which is not punishable under the law at the time it is committed .... There shall be no State religion for the Commonwealth of India or for any province, nor shall any State endow any religion or give preference to any religion. No person attending any school receiving State aid or other public money shall be compelled to attend religious instruction that may be given in the school. No person shall by reason of his religion, caste or creed be prejudiced in any way in regard to public employment, office of power or honour and exercise of any trade or calling .... Man and woman shall have equal rights.

The Report provided for a Parliament of two houses viz Senate and House of Representatives. Governor General was to be appointed by the British Government .... Senate was to consists of 200 members elected by Provincial Councils. The House of Representative was to consist of 500 members. It was to be elected on an adult franchise basis. The Governor General was to act on the advice of the Executive Council. Prime Minister was to be appointed by the Governor General and other ministers on the advice of Prime minister. The Executive Council was to be collectively responsible to the Parliament .... Provision was to be made for a Supreme Court. It was to consist of Lord President and other justices. The members of the Supreme Court were to be appointed by the Governor General in Council but were not to be removed from office except on an address from both houses of Parliament praying for such removal on the ground of misbehaviour or incapacity. The Supreme Court was to have both original and appellate jurisdiction".[25]

Now we can clearly see the base of present secular character of our Constitution in the Nehru Report also. Even during those days, 22 years back, prior to coming in to effect of present Constitution, leaders of all political parties, including Muslim League and Hindu Mahasabha had in agreement about the secular nature of the Constitution that would have come into being. One of the fundamental rights suggested by Nehru Report that 'There shall be no state religion for the commonwealth of India or for any province nor shall any state endow any religion or give preference to any religion' indicate the state of feeling at that time in the minds of countrymen and leaders of independence struggle. Independence of judiciary and checks and balances provisions were very much in the report.

'The Nehru Report was submitted on 10th August 1928 and the All Parties Conference met at Calcutta on 22nd December 1928 to consider the Report. As regards the communal question, Mr. Jinnah, on behalf of the All India Muslim League, moved amendment to the Report. He wanted to have some safeguards for Muslims in the Constitution. But all the amendments except one, moved by him were rejected. Mr. M.R. Jayakar, who represented the Hindu point of view, was opposed to the demand of Mr. Jinnah. Perhaps that was the initial sparks of incident sowing the seed of discontentment among Muslims that their emotions and sentiments were being ignored and they must have their own homeland. This was evident from the Jinnah's 14 points. However, Nehru Report was the first of its kind document prepared by Indians for Indians. That shows which type of government the Indians wanted and what type of society they desired in this country notwithstanding the hatred of Hindus for untouchables. Till that time the communal harmony of the country was intact.

EMERGENCE OF COMMUNAL ORGANISATION

The Hindu revivalism, by way of instigating the simple and innocent Hindus by the leaders of communal movement like B.S. Moonje played an important role to fan out the fire of hatred among the caste Hindus. The way had been found to unite Hindus in a movement that identified both the British and the Muslims as "oppressors". Out of this defiance emerged the Nagpur Hindu Sabha. Dr Moonje was chosen as the Vice President of the local Sabha and Hedgewar became its Secretary. The Sabha organised more protest marches and it negotiated a compromise with the government and with the leaders of the Muslim community which permitted Hindus to march in religious processions at times and in places that would not interfere with Muslim religious observances. [25A] Both Dr. Moonje and Dr. Hedgewar were interested to protect the interests of caste Hindus only. And for that they started instigating the Hindus or educating the Hindus.

We can very well understand from one of the instigations made by Dr. Moonje at Nagpur at that time:

"At that time out of 1.5 lakh (1,50,000) population of Nagpur, Muslims are only 20 thousand. But still we feel insecure. Muslims were never afraid of 1 lakh 30 thousand Hindus. So this question should be regarded here after as the question of the Hindus. The Muslims themselves have taught us to behave as Hindus while in the Congress and as Hindus outside the Congress"[26]

Such type of instigation started spoiling the communal harmony of the country and from that on the united struggle for independence of India suffered a severe set-back, culminating into creation of Pakistan.This shows that the Hindu revivalists were never in favour of secular nature of the Indian society. They wanted Hindus to have separate identity. V.D. Savarkar's thesis that the 'Hindus were a nation,' helped those Hindu revivalists and finally RSS was founded on the *VijayaDashami* Day in 1925 at Nagpur by the selected *Chittapavan* Brahmins. The history of disturbances of communal harmony of the country is very much related with the rise and expansion of RSS throughout the country. In this connection observations of some Enquiry Commissions would suffice the purpose :-

"Justice P. Venugopal, who sat on the Commission which inquired into communal flare-up in Kanyakumari district in March 1982, indicted the RSS severely:

The RSS adopts a militant and aggressive attitude and sets itself as the champion of what it considers to be the rights of Hindus against minorities. It was taken upon itself the task to teach the minority their place and if they are not willing to learn their place, teach them a lesson. The RSS has given respectability to communalism and communal riots and demoralise administration. The RSS methodology for provoking communal violence is :-

(a) rousing communal feeling in the majority community by the propaganda that Christians are not loyal citizens of this country;
(b) deepening the fear in the majority community by a clever propaganda that the population of the minorities is increasing and that of Hindus decreasing;
(c) infiltrating into the administration and inducting the members of the civil and police services by adopting

and developing communal attitudes;

(d) training young people of the majority community in the use of weapons like dagger, sword and spear;

(e) spreading rumours to widen the communal cleavage and deepen communal feelings by giving colour to any trivial incident.

The RSS shakhas include in their programmes training in lathis, swords, jevalin throw, Drills, exercises, parades and other activities are organised in play grounds and other public places. All these activities are organised in the name of physical training. The aim behind these activities appears to be to inculcate an attitude of militancy and *training for any kind of civil strife*. They often cause apprehension, fear and a sense of insecurity among the minorities. It prejudicially affects maintenance of public tranquility"[27]

Thus , Justice Venugopal has drawn complete and real picture of the RSS operation and activities.

This and other instances which prove that the *Hindutvavadis* by creating communal riots through terror tactics and spreading a message psychologically that the Hindus are insecure and they apprehend danger to their lives, they instigated the otherwise simple and innocent Hindus to commit heineous crimes and spoiled the communal harmony. In this context Justice D. P. Madon's note of Golwalkar's speeches is vital testimony as to what sort of business they - the communalists, wanted to do in this country :-

"In India there should be the rule of Hindus. There cannot be a good administration if there is the rule of various people like Hindus, Muslims, Christians, Parsis etc. If there is a head of an ass attached to the body of a monkey it will not work. Such a body will be attacked by worms and will emit bad smells. Similarly, any administration by different types of people will not work well. It will lack in morality, character and culture ...."[28]

Thus, started the minority - hate compaign by *'Hindutvavadis'* organisations. V. D. Savarkar, whom we hold in high esteem as one of the greatest freedom fighters, has also greatly contributed to fan the communal fire by way of his writings. "He wrote repeatedlly in his book *Hindutva* (1923) : *'Hindutva* is different from Hinduism'. For once he was right. Hinduism is a great religion, it is ancient. *Hindutva* is an ideology of hate. It is recent. He grouped Muslims and Christians together as ones who do not share the tie of the common homage we pay to our great civilization - our Hindu culture. He added—Christians and Mohammedan communities who were but very recently Hindus .... cannot be recognised as Hindus since their adoption of the new cult they had ceased to own Hindu civilization (Sanskriti) as a whole .... For, though Hindustan to them is fatherland, as to any other Hindu, yet it is not to them a holyland too. Their holyland is far off in Arabia or Palestine".[29]

Round Table Conference, Communal Award and Poona Pact

After publication of the Simon Commission Report and having been condemned the same by the people of India, the British Government called for the First Round Table Conference in London to know the Indian points of view on the next set of constitutional reforms that were likely to be declared thereafter shortly. As the majority of Congress leaders were in jail, other leaders representing different communities and interests were invited, including Indian States. Conference was held in November 1930. There basic principles were settled and accepted by the British Government. The form of the new Government of India was to be an All India Federation in which the British Indian Provinces and Indian States were to join, the Federal Government was to be made responsible to the Federal Legislature. Provinces were to be given autonomy in their own affairs.

In the Second Round Table Conference Mahatma Gandhi, on behalf of Indian National Congress participated. However, the Conference was totally failure. No compromise could be worked out on the issue of communal representation and hence the Prime Minister Ramsay McDonald had to declare Communal Award on 16th August 1932. According to the Award, election to the seats were alloted to Muslims, Europeans, Sikhs, Indian Christians, Anglo-Indians and the Depressed classes. In addition to these communities special seats were to be alloted to commerce and industry. Women were also given special representation on communal lines.

The most important feature of the Communal Award was the provision of *double voting power given to the depressed classes*. The members of the depressed classes who were qualified to vote were to vote in general constituency as well as they were also eligible to vote for the reserved constituencies. That was the great success achieved by the depressed classes under the able and dynamic leadership of Dr. Ambedkar. It was a totally noval experience that the people, who for thousands of years were deprived of even an ordinary life, suddenly got an opprtunity not only to decide the fate of their own leaders but also the future of those oppressors and exploiters who had subjected them to untold humiliation and exploitation for centuries.

Mahatma Gandhi had no objection to the separate electorates for Muslims, Anglo-Indians and even Sikhs but he deadly opposed the separate electorate to the depressed classes and for that he declared fast unto death in Yerwada Jail. When British Governemnt refused to move in the matter and the condition of Mahatma Gandhi became serious, the Indian leaders made lots of efforts and persuaded Dr. Ambedkar for mutual agreement which he had to do to save the life of Mahatma but with great pain for loss of right of double voting power of depressed classes.

Poona Pact : Looser and Gainers

According to the Poona Pact which was the outcome of coercive tactics of caste Hindus under the leadership of Mahatma Gandhi to alter the Communal Award to the advantage of caste Hindus, developed and designed by them to deprive the Depressed Classes of their hard-earned right to elect their deserving candidates. What they achieved through intellectual bargaining from the Britishers, had to be lost due to a political machinations. Under the Communal Award they got 78 seats while under Poona Pact they were more benefitted by number of seats, i.e., 148 seats in the Provincial Legislatures. But that very alternate arrangement worked out in the name of Poona Pact, was later on transformed into a system under which the stooges among the Depressed Classes / Scheduled Castes were created who could never be honest to the cause of the oppressed and exploited people and played their political role as the puppets in the hands of their masters. That was the outcome of Poona Pact which the shrewd Mahatma had conceived to betray the hard earned political right through logic and reasoning in the Round Table Conference. He was very much concerned with the protection of

Hinduism rather than the interests of badly suffering people which was the victim of the same system under Hinduism.

It was the outcome of the same Poona Pact, which was the main reason for the rout of the Scheduled Caste Federation candidates in the General Election held in February 1946 and the same very electoral device as agreed to by Dr. Ambedkar himself. Majority of the seats had gone to the Depressed classes candidates of the Congress persuation. Though he had won the battle in foreign land, he lost the war in his own homeland ! The Poona Pact was the greatest blow to the aspirations of the depressed classes. Right from 1919 when he first appeared before the Southborough Committee on Franchise and pleaded the cause of his fellowmen brilliantly, to the submission of a memorandum to the Cabinet Mission to include the safeguards for the protection of political rights of the scheduled castes in the new constitution, his all honest efforts were nullified by Mahatma Gandhi and caste Hindu supporters in a single stroke of Poona Pact !

The Poona Pact proved a turning point in the constitutional development of India. It was the blackest chapter in the constitutional history of India. The communalists succeeded in twisting and distorting the constitutional framework whenever the British goverment desired to initiate the reforms in favour of minorities. The trend started with the Poona Pact is still going on even today. Denial and distortion of reservation facilities in educational institutions and services independently and some time in league with the judiciary, has been going on from the day the facilities were provided in the Constitution. Political reservation has been utilised to the greatest extent by caste Hindu political parties to produce 'chamchas' to raise the hands only.

According to Kanshi Ram, president of BAMCEF "A tool, an agent, a stooge or a chamcha is created to oppose the real, the genuine fighter. Only when there are genuine and real fighters the chamchas are in demand. When there is no fight, no struggle and no danger from any fighter the chamchas are not required, they are not in demand. As we have seen that from the beginning of the 20th Century, the depressed classes had been up in arms against untouchability and unjust social order, almost all over India. Initially, they were ignored. But later, when the real leadership of the depressed classes became powerful and formidable, they could not be ignored. At this stage, the high caste Hindus felt the necessity of setting chamchas against the real leaders of the depressed classes".[29(a)]

Government of India Act, 1935

"After the Act of 1919, the Government of India Act, 1935 was the second important milestone on the road to full responsible Government in India. It played a very important role in shaping and moulding the new constitution of India 1950. The Act of 1935 is said to be the product of four diverse forces namely Indian nationalism, British imperialism, Indian Communalism and Indian Princes .... The Act marked a radical change of policy in two respects : First it introduced a federal form of Government in place of unitary form which was the British policy since long; and secondly, the provisions of the Act envisaged a federation to which the native states of India were to accede. The Act introduced partial responsibility at the centre, established provinicial autonomy"[30]

The Act provided for the division of power between the Centre and the units under three lists, namely, Federal list, Provincial list and Concurrent list. The same provision has been made in our present constitution also. One of the most important provisions of the Act was that the entire provincial administration was placed under the charge of the popular ministers who were to be appointed by the Governor, from among the members of the Provincial Legislatures on the advice of a person who commanded majority.

Though the above arrangement apparently appeared in favour of the Indians, in reality the popular government in provinces would have been a puppet in the hands of Governor, if it dared not walk out with their own measures independently.

Another important provision was the establishment of Federal Court with original and appellate jurisdiction.

Constitutional Developments from 1935 to 1947

The Government of India Act, 1935 could not be applied in totality. The provisions relating to the provinces only came into force. The Congress formed ministries in 7 of the provinces but had to resign in 1939 on account of differences with British Government.

The Second World War broke out in 1939. The international situation began to deteriorate. The British Government wanted to seek co-operation of the leaders of Indian National Congress. But they were as hostile as ever towards British Government. They wanted no less than complete Independence for India.

In March 1942, Sir Stafford Crips, the leader of the House of Commons, came to Delhi with some proposals on behalf of the British Government. The Crips proposal included among other things, the assurance for constitution - making body for India and complete transfer of power to Indian hands. Depressed classes denounced the proposals on the grounds that the necessary safeguards were not provided for their interests. The Muslim League also opposed the creation of a single Indian Union. The Hindu Mahasabhs objected to the elections on the basis of Communal Award which they were of the opinion that, from their point of view, anti-national and undemocratic. Congress also opposed the proposals. It was a total failure. This led to spread of discontentment in the country and Congress passed the famous 'Quit India' Resolution on 8th August 1942.

In 1945 Labour Party came to power in England. The Labour Government sent the Cabinet Mission to India in March 1946. Prolonged discussion took place with the members of the Mission by the leaders of the Congress and Muslim League. But there could not be mutual understanding between these two main political parties. As such finally the Cabinet Mission jointly with Lord Wavell, Governor General and Viceroy of India, issued a statement on 16th May 1946 recommending the new Constitution for India with following basic form;

"(1) There should be a Union of India, embracing both India and the states which should deal with Foreign Affairs, Defence and Communication and should have the power to raise the finances required for the above subjects.

(2) The Union should have an Executive and a Legislature constituted from British India and States representatives. Any question raising a major communal issue in the Legislature should require for its decision a majority of the representatives present

and voting of each of the two major communities as well as a majority of all the members present and voting.

(3) All subjects other than the Union subjects and all residuary powers should vest in the provinces.

(4) The states will retain all subjects and powers other than those ceded to the Union.

(5) Provinces should be free to form Groups with executives and legislatures and each Group could determine the provincial subjects to be taken in common.

(6) The Constitutions of the Union and of the Groups should contain a provision whereby any province could by a majority vote of its Legislatave Assembly call for reconsideration of the terms of the Constitution after an initial period of 10 years and at 10 yearly intervals thereafter".[31]

The Crips offer and Cabinet Mission provided for Constitution making machinery through the election of representatives based on communities quota and special interests. S. K. Biswas in his book - *Father of the Constitution of India* (Orian Books) claimed that "Mr. M.N. Roy (real name Narendranath Bhattachariya) was the Secret Agent of the British Colonial power, who used to get a colossal sum of Rs. 74,000/- per month from the Secret Fund of the Government for his spying activities prevailed over Congress. He joined Indian National Congress in 1936, soon after his release from the jail. At this juncture of Constitution-framing, it was M. N. Roy who for the first time gave the suggestion to form a Constituent Assembly with the elected members from all the political parties. This could have been the most assured way of getting rid of the unwanted person, Dr Ambedkar. All efforts were to be taken to see that he is not elected from any constitueny to enter into Assembly. This proposad came into reality in 1945-46".[32]

Dr. Ambedkar,with many others opposed the proposal of Constituent Assembly formation at a stage when almost all the provisions of the Constitution have been finalised in the form of Government of India Act, 1935. Among the prominent was EVR Periyar who opposed the move of the Constituent Assembly. Dr. Ambedkar virtually threatened :

> "The plan regarded the proposal for a Constituent Assembly as absolutely superfluous, an act of supererogation and a dangerous proposition that might involve the country in a civil war. Much of the constitution was already under the 1935 Act."[33]

Dr. Ambedkar, the Untouchables and the Constitution Making

Though the author does not agree with the version of S.K. Biswas that M. N. Roy could have influenced the British Government as well as Indian National Congress leaders like Mahatma Gandhi, Jawaharlal Nehru, Sardar Patel who were the towering personalities, however there has been no doubt that people like Mahatma Gandhi, who was the staunchest supporter of *Varnashram Social System* based on *Chaturvarnya* and who was till his last breath against the emerging of an independent leadership among the untouchables—depressed classes, could have designed differently. And it did so happen actually. Dr. Ambedkar had no safe constituency to get elected to the Constituent Assembly in his home state, i.e., Bombay or Central provinces and as such he had to finally shift to Bengal on the assurance of Jogendra Nath Mandal and the majority of the Scheduled Castes. But what was the outcome ! The Scheduled Castes of the Bengal and particularly of those areas like Jessore, Khulana, Chitgong and the adjoining areas, forming now the part of Bangla Desh and originally East Pakistan were thrown away for their having elected Dr. Ambedkar on the Constituent Assembly. They were very heavily pennalised for their daring commitment to their leader and the up-coming movement of the untouchables under the leadership of Dr. Ambedkar.

The prominent Brahmin leader of West Bengal, who later on became Chief Minister of the state alongwith top leaders of Indian National Congress were very much shocked to see emerging launching pad for the power politics of the Untouchables in Bengal in association with the Muslims. Apprehending danger to their power - politics of *Bhadralk* in that province and Brahminical power politics of high caste Hindus in Congress, that entire area of Bengal was given to Pakistan, though technically it was not logical and correct. And after 25 years, their conspiracy proved a total failure in the emergence of Bangla Desh !

Dr. Ambedkar as the recognised and popular leader of the untouchable Hindus, first appeared before the 'Southborough Committee on Franchise' on the 27th January 1919 where` he very vigorously pleaded for the rights of the untouchables for independent representation. He pleaded, ".... The untouchable is not even a citizen.Citizenship is a bundle of rights such as (1) personal liberty, (2) personal security, (3) right to hold private property, (4) equality before law, (5) liberty of conscience, (6) freedom of opinion and speech, (7) right of assembly, (8) right of representation in a country's Government and (9) right to hold office under the State. .... The right of representation and the right to hold office under the State are the most important rights that make up citizenship. But the untouchability of the untouchables puts these rights far beyond their reach. In a few places, they do not even possess such insignificant rights as personal liberty and personal security, and equality before law is not always assured to them. These are the interests of the untouchables. And as can be easily seen they can be represented by the untouchables alone. They are distinctively their own interests and none else can truly voice them. A free trade interests can be voiced by a Brahmin, a Mohamedan or a Maratha equally well. But none of these can speak for the interests of the untouchables because they are not untouchables. Untouchability constitutes a definite set of interests which the untouchables alone can speak for. Hence it is evident that we must find untouchables to represent their grievances, which are their interests and secondly, we must find them in such numbers as well constitute a force sufficient to claim redress".[34]

Dr. Ambedkar also submitted a memorandam to the Simon Commission on 29th May 1928 on behalf of the Depressed Classes Institute of Bombay concerning safeguards for the protection of the interests of the Depressed Classes as a minority in the Bombay Presidency and the changes in the composition of and guarantees from the Bombay Legislative Council necessary to ensure the same under Provincial Autonomy.

The Memorandum says that, 'the Sabha (Bahishkrita Hitkarini Sabha) respectfully protests against the non-recognition of the rights of the depressed classes in the Legislative Assembly in 1919. The Government of India is still supreme in important matters which are directly under its control or under the Reserved half of the

Provincial governments. Even in respect of the transferred subjects it continues to have the power of superintendence. It is, therefore, obvious that in the dirction of such large powers the Depressed Classes should have some voice and the Sabha would, therefore, claim that three members from the Depressed Classes of the Bomaby Presidency should be elected to the Legislative Assembly by their representatives in the local Legislative Council".[35]

Dr. Ambedkar ardently wanted that the problems of the untouchables could better be represented by the untouchables themselves. For that he demanded at least three members of the Depressed Classes be elected in the Bombay Presidency. He also demanded protection through guarantees so as to assure these clases that their case would be taken properly and their interests are sufficiently protected.

As such, 'In addition to the demand for adequate representation the Sabha (Bahishkrita Hitkarini Sabha) feels that it must also demand inclusion of clauses in the Constitution of the country and as a fundamental part thereof guaranteeing the civil rights of the Depressed Classes as a minority in the Bombay Presidency. Such guarantees must cover the recognition of the following propositions concerning the interests of the Depressed Classes :-

(1) That the education of the Depressed Classes shall be recognised as the first charge on the revenues of the province and that an equitable and just proportion of the total grant for education should be earmarked for the benefit of the Depressed Classes.

(2) That the right of the Depressed Classes to unrestricted recruitment in the army, navy and the police shall be recognised without any limitation as to caste.

(3) That for a period of 30 years the right of the Depressed Classes for priority in the matter of the recruitment to all posts, gazetted as well as non-gazetted in all civil services shall be recognised.

(4) That the right of the Depressed Classes to the appointment of a special inspector of police from amongst themselves for every district shall be recognised.

(5) That the right of the Depressed Classes to effective representation (as defined above) on the local bodies shall be recognised by the Provincial Government.

(6) That the right of the Depressed Classes to appeal to the Government of India in cases of violation of these rights by the Provincial Government shall be recognised and the Government of India shall be given the power to compel the Provincial Government to conform to the law in the matter."[36]

Dr. Ambedkar's efforts to impress upon the British Government for the adequate representation of the untouchables in the Provincial Assembly and his demand for protection of their rights through guarantees by the Provincial Government clearly conform that was the only capable leader of the Depressed Classes who could intelligently take up their problems with the appropriate authorities for their inclusion in the reforms/constitutional set-up for their betterment.

But the communalists of this country, particularly those high caste Hindus who felt that political power was their monopoly, could not digest the rise of an independent, well-educated and competent leadership of the untouchables. This was evident in the Second Round Table Conference held in London when Dr. Ambedkar participated as a leader of the Depressed Classes, Mahatma Gandhi challenged him that not he but he (Gandhi) represented the whole country, including the Depressed Classes.

Speaking in the Minorities Committee of Second Round Table Conference, on the 8th October 1931, Mahatma Gandhi said, " .... lastly, in as much as the only reason for my appearance at these deliberations is that I represent the Indian National Congress, I must clearly set forth its position. In spite of appearances to the contrary, especially in England, the Congress claims to represent the whole nation, and the most decidedly the dumb millions among whom are included the numberless Untouchables, who are more supressed than depressed, as also in a way the most unfortunate and neglected classes, known as Backward races .... It seems to have been represented that I am opposed to any representation of the Untouchables on the legislature. This is the travesty of the truth. What I have said, and what I must repeat, is that I am opposed to their special representation. I am convinced that it can do them no good, and may do much harm; but the Congress is wedded to adult franchise. Therefore, millions of them can be placed on the voters roll. It is impossible to conceive that, with Untouchability fast disappearing, nominees of these voters can be boycotted by the others; but what these people need more than election to the legislature is protection from social and religious persecution. Custom, which is often powerful than law, has brought them to a degradation of which every thinking Hindu has need to feel ashamed and to do penance.... I can understand the claims advanced by other minorities, but the claims advanced on behalf of the Untouchables, that too me is the "unkindest cut of all". It means the perpetual bar-sinister. I would not seal the vital interests of the Untouchables even for the sake of winning the freedom of India. I claim myself in my own person to represent the vast mass of the Untouchables. Here I speak not merely on behalf of the Congress, but I speak on my own behalf, and I claim that I would get, if there was referendum of the Untouchables, their vote and that I would top the poll. And I would work from one end of India to other to tell the Untouchables that Separate electorates and Separate reservation is not the way to remove this bar-sinister, which is a shame, on them but of orthodox Hindus ....

".... We do not want on our register and on our Census Untouchables classified as Separate Class. Sikhs may remain as such in perpetuity, so may Muhammadans, so may Europeans .... It hurts me to have to say this, but I would be untrue to the cause of Untouchables, which is as dear to me as life itself, if I did not say it.... It is not a proper claim which is registered by Dr. Ambedkar when he speaks for the whole of the Untouchables of India. It will create a division in Hinduism which I cannot possibly look forward to with any satisfaction whatsoever.

> I do not mind Untouchables if they so desire being converted to Islam or Christianity. I should tolerate that, but I cannot possibly tolerate what is in store for Hinduism if there are two divisions set forth in the villages. Those who speak political rights of Untouchables do not know their India, do not know how Indian society is today constructed and therefore I want to say with all emphasis that I can command that if I was the only person to resist this thing I would resist it with my life.[37]

After the Second Round Table Conference where the question of communal representation was most important and the same having been failed to be resolved the British Prime Minister declared the Communal Award to be a part of the future Constitutional reform for Indians. Under the said Communal Award, despite the threat given by Mahatma Gandhi in the Minorities Committee that he would resist the separate electorate for the Depressed Classes with his life, the Prime Minister declared the Award on 16th August 1932.

According to the Award, elections to the seats allotted to Muslims, European and Sikh constituencies were to be by votes for separate communal electorates covering between them the whole area of province.

All qualified voters who were not voters in Muslim, Sikh, Indian-Christian, Anglo-Indian or European constituencies were entitled to vote in a general constituency.

Seven seats were reserved for Maratha in certain selected plural member general constituencies in Bombay.

The members of the Depressed Classed who were qualified to vote were to vote in a general constituency. However, special seats were to be reserved for them. Those seats were to be filled up by election from special constituencies in which only the members of the depressed classes electorally qualified were to be entitled to vote. Any person voting in such a special constituency was also to be entitled to vote in a general constituency. These constituencies were to be formed in those selected areas where the depressed classes were most numerous and except in Madras, they were not to cover the whole of the area of a province. In the case of Bengal, in some general constituencies, the majority of the voters belonged to the depressed classes. Consequently no special number was to be fixed for their seats in that province. However, they were not to get less than 70 seats in Bengal. The maximum duration of the depressed classes constituencies was to be 20 years, provided they were not abolised earlier".[38]

Thus the Depressed Classes *for the first time got an opprtunity to excerise double-voting power by voting to the candidates contesting from reserved seats, where only depressed classes voters were entitled to vote, they could select the best of their candidates. In the joint electorate, where they were entitled to vote to the candidates contesting from general constituency they could vote for such a candidate who would definitly take care of them and whom they could trust.* The general contestant had always been under constant pressure not to antagonise them.

This was one of the greatest achievement made by Dr. Ambedkar in the history of Political Science. The oppressed and exploited, neglected, hated, humiliated and discarded in the socio-religious system of this country by caste Hindus, the so-called upper castes, got an opportunity for first time under the able leadership of Dr. Ambedkar to assert their real-being and exercise their political right. But unfortunately, this could not be digested by the staunch communalist caste Hindus under the leadership of Mahatma Gandhi.

Mahatma Gandhi in his letter written in March 1932 to Sir Samuel Hoare, Secretary of State for India, had warned him that he would resist with his life the grant of Separate electorate to the Depressed Classes. When the Communal Award was declared Mahatma Gandhi wrote to Ramsay McDonald, the Prime Minister that the matter was "of one of pure religion" with him and he asked : "Do you realise that, if your decision stands and the Constitution comes into being, you arrest the marvellous growth of the work of Hindu reformers who have dedicated themselves to the uplift of their suppressed brethren in every walk of life?"[39]

Mahatma's letter had no effect on the Prime Minister of England. On the other hand the reply of the Prime Minister to Mahatma Gandhi must be an eye opener for the caste Hindus of India. He wrote :

> " .... As I understand your attitude, you propose to adopt the extreme course of starving yourself to death not in order to secure that the Depressed Classes should have joint electorate with other Hindus, because that is already provided, nor to maintain the unity of Hindus, which also provided, *but solely to prevent the Depressed Classes, who admittedly suffer from terrible disabilities from being able to secure a limited number of representatives of their own choosing to speak on their behalf in the legislatures which will have a dominating influence over their future ....*"[40]

Prime Minister Ramsay MacDonald's response and reasoning was very correct and logical. He had correctly interpreted the outcome of the Communal Award and his questioning of Mahatma as to what did he want to achieve through the fast unto death except 'to prevent the Depressed Classes, who admittedly suffer from terrible disabilities from being able to secure a limited number of representives of their own choosing to speak on their behalf in the legislature which will have a dominating influences over their future".

Mahatma Gandhi's statement in the Round Table Conference that 'I do not mind untouchables if they so desire being converted to Islam or Christianity, I should tolerate that, but I can not possibly tolerate what is in store for Hinduism if there are two divisions set forth in the villages' indicates his hatred, his malice and his real intent for the Depressed Classes asserting their rights. He had no objection to giving separate electorates for the Muslims, Sikhs or Christians but he opposed the separate electorate for the Untouchables. That reveals Mahatma Gandhi's real colour and affection for the untouchables ! This was the first Communal attack on the Constitutional reforms of India, by no any other person but by Mahatma himself, the most staunchest protagonist of the *Chaturvarna Social System* and militant Caste Hindu *par*-exellence !

It was, therefore, very rightly asked by Dr. Ambedkar in his statement on Mahatma Gandhi's fast unto death on 19th September 1932 that, 'I am unable to understand the ground of hostility of Mr. Gandhi to the Communal Award. He says that the Communal Award has separated the Depressed Classes from the Hindu community. On the other hand Dr. Moonje, a much stronger protagonist of the Hindu case and a militant advocate of its interests takes a totally different view of the matter. In the speeches which he has been insisting that the Communal Award does not creat any separation between the Depressed Classes and the Hindus. Indeed, he has been boasting that he has defeated me in my attempt to politically separate the Depressed Classes from the Hindus. I am sure that Dr. Moonje is right in his interpretation of the Communal Award, although I am not sure that the credit of it can legitimately to go to Dr. Moonje. It is, therefore, surprising that Mahatma Gandhi who is a nationalist and not known to be a communalist should read the Communal Award, in so far as it relates to the Depressed Classes, in a manner quite contrary to that of a communalist like Dr. Moonje. If Dr. Moonje does not sense any separation of the Depressed Classes from the Hindus in the Communal Award the Mahatma ought to feel quite satisfied on that score ...."[41]

During the Round Table Conference only Mahatma Gandhi came to know that Dr. Ambedkar was an Untouchable. For many years he was under wrong impression that Dr. Ambedkar was a high caste Brahmin and doing some social service for the Untouchables. But when he personally saw him vigorously advocating the cause of the Untouchables, supported with high intellectual logic and reasoning it was a shock for him that an independent thinking leadership had started to emerge among the Untouchables and then he took up to the cause of those people through Harijan Sewak Sangh and patronised leaders like Jagjivan Ram who could never build up the independent movement of the Untouchables, nor was he a danger to the caste Hindu's political machinations. We can very well understand from this development that though the Congress was fighting for more and more constitutional reforms for the countrymen, they were never in favour of upliftment of the Untouchables or the Shudras and Ati-shudras. These two incidents are sufficient proof to confirm that the communalists in those days also were little different from today's but the objective was the same power should be only their monopoly by all means !

Dr. Ambedkar got elected to the Constituent Assembly from Bengal and the people of that area, who got him into the Constitution-making body had to pay a heavy price for their political venture. They had to part company with mother India to be perpetually subjected to unbearable exploitation, humiliation and torture firstly by the caste Hindus of India before partition and secondly by the military rulers of East Pakistan after partition. The reason - they formed the majority of Untouchable population and that could have helped Dr. Ambedkar to build-up his political base in the politics of India. The partition of Bengal and handing over of that particular area to the East Pakistan, even without having majority Muslim population, the criteria fixed for partition, it was a deep-rooted conspiracy of top Congress leaders of the freedom movement, who were very much afraid of Dr. Ambedkar's intellectual power and numerical strength of the untouchables, which could have mattered in deciding the destiny of democracy in India !

Constituent Assembly

India became Independent on 15th August 1947 with the partition of the country and establishment of two dominions of India and Pakistan under Lord Mountbatten's plan of June 3, 1947 as accepted by the Muslim League and All India Congress Committee.

Originally the Constitutent Assembly members were elected indirectly by communal groups of Provincial Legislatures in 1946 on all-India basis. However, after partition of the country in 1947 the representatives of the Pakistan areas went to form separate Constitutent Assembly. With formation of East Pakistan, Dr. Ambedkar lost his seat in the Constitutent Assembly. However, keeping in view his vast experience in constitutional law, his knowledge and his role in the upliftment of Depressed Classes and particulary his gesture in saving the life of Mahatma Gandhi through Poona Pact, wherein he lost and Mahatma gained, he was returned to the Constituent Assembly from Maharashatra through the efforts of Congress party. Later on, he was elected the Chairman of the Drafting Committee.

Process of Constitution-Making

Elections to the Constitutent Assembly took place in July 1946 and the Constituent Assembly met for the first time in New Delhi on December 9, 1946. The Muslim League refused to participate. After the Partition of India, composition of the Assembly completely changed. A body of about 308 members including representatives of the former princely states and those representatives of Muslim League who decided to remain in India, participated in the proceedings of the Assembly.

Initially, Dr. Sachidanand Sinha was elected interim Chairman of the Constituent Assembly on the request of Acharya J.B. Kripalani. After passing the rules of the election of the Chairman of the Assembly on 10th December 1946, Dr. Rajendra Prasad was elected as permanent Chairman of the Assembly on 11th December, 1946 and also the committees were set up to report on the issues and principles.

'The Cabinet Mission had recommended setting-up of an advisory committee on Fundamental Rights, Minorities etc. Accordingly, the Assembly constituted the Advisory Committee under the chairmanship of Sardar Patel by a resolution on 24th January 1947. The Committee constisted of 50 members in which Dr. Ambedkar was one. To facililate its work, the Advisory Committee appointed the following four sub-Committees :

(1) Fundamental Rights Sub-Committee
(2) Minorities Sub-Committee
(3) North-East Frontier Tribal Area Sub-Committee
(4) Excluded and partially excluded areas (other than those in Assam) Sub-Committee.

Dr. Ambedkar was a member of the first two Sub-Committees. The Constituent Assembly also appointed three other Committees, namely (1) the Union Power Committee, (2) the Union Constitution Committee and (3) the Provisional Constitution Committee. Prime Minister Jawaharlal Nehru was the Chairman of the first two committees while the third one was under the Chairmanship of Sardar Vallabhbhai Patel. These committees were set up by a resolution on 30th April 1947.

Dr. Ambedkar was re-elected in July 1947 from Bombay as a member of the Constituent Assembly through the efforts of Congress Party, which had earlier opposed tooth and nail his entry into Constituent Assembly and then came forward and sponsored his candidature on having been convinced that the legislation and solidification of freedom would not be easy without the services of Dr. Ambedkar. This was very much evident from the letter dated 30th June 1947 written by Dr. Rajendra Prasad, President of the Constitutent Assembly to Mr. B. G. Kher, the then Prime Minister of Bombay, to elect Dr. Ambedkar immediatly. He wrote, "Apart from any other consideration we have found Dr. Ambedkar's work both in the Constituent Assembly and the various committees to which he was appointed to be of such an order as to require that we should not be deprived of his services".

Immediatly after his re-election in July 1947, Pandit Jawaharlal Nehru invited him to join the Cabinet which he formed on 15th August 1947 on the eve of Independence. Dr. Ambedkar accepted the invitation and became India's first Law

Minister. On 29th August the Assembly unanimously elected him as Chairman of the Drafting Committee which was assigned the task of framing the Constitution"[42]

The other members of the Constitution Drafting Committee were :

(1) Shri Alladi Krishnaswami Ayyar
(2) Shri N. Gopalswami Ayyangar
(3) Shri K.M. Munshi
(4) Saiyid Muhammad Saadula
(5) Shri B.L. Mitter
(6) Shri D.P. Khaitan

In addition to the above members P. N. Krishna Mani, Asstt. Secretary, K. V. Padamanvan, Under Secretary, Jugal Kishore Khanna, Deputy Secretary, B. N. Mukherjee, Joint Secretary and Sir B. N. Rau, as the Constitutional Advisor were there to assist the Drafting Committee as members of the staff of the Committee.

The Drafting Committe first met on August 30, 1947. The Committee sat from October 27, 1947 day to day, discussing and revising articles of the draft prepared by the office of the Constitutional Adviser. The Committee met in all on 44 days till February 13th, 1948 in which Dr. Ambedkar himself conducted all the business. Fresh Draft of the Constitution, as settled by the Drafting Committee was submitted to the President of the Assembly on February 21, 1948. The Committee continued to function and dealt with suggestions for amendments suggested and mutually agreed upon from time to time. The Draft Constitution had been before the public for eight months and came up before the Constituent Assembly on 4th November 1948.[43]

It took 2 years, 11 months and 17 days for deliberations by the members before being accepted the Draft Constitution. About 7635 amendments were received of which 2473 amendments were moved. The original Draft Constitution, as prepared by the Constitutional Adviser as a text for the Drafting Committee to work upon, consisted of 243 articles and 13 Schedules. The First Draft Constitution as presented by the Drafting Committee to the Constituent Assembly contained 315 Articles and 8 Schedules. At the end of the consideration stage, the number of articles in the Draft Constitution increased to 386. In its final form, the Draft Constitution contained 395 Articles and 8 Schedules. The Constituent Assembly held 11 sessions. Out of these 11 sessions, the first 6 were spent in passing the objective resolutions and the consideration of the Reports of Committees on Fundamental Rights, on Union Constitution, on Union Powers, on Provincial Constitution, On Minorities and on the Scheduled Areas and Scheduled Tribes. The 7th, 8th, 9th, 10th, and 11th were devoted to the consideration of the Draft Constitution. These Eleven Sessions of the Constituent Assembly have consumed 165 days, out of these the Assembly spent 114 days for the consideration of the Draft Constitution'.[44]

After the Draft Constitution was presented to the Constituent Assembly on 4th November 1948, a brief general discussion followed, which was called the first reading. The second reading commenced on 15th November 1948. In the second reading Draft Constitution was discussed clause-by-clause in detail. The discussion concluded on 17th October 1949.

The Constituent Assembly sat again on 14th November 1949 for the third reading. This was finished on 26th November 1949, when the Constitution was declared as passed and thereafter the President of Assembly signed it.[45]

Important Developments in the Making of Constitution

The Constitution of free India came into effect on 26th January 1950. It completed 50 years on January 26, 2000. It was an important occasion when the Golden Jubilee of the Constitution and Indian Republic was year-long event. Taking advantage of the occasion BJP led NDA Government announced first the Review of the Constitution which was later on changed to review the working of the Constitution for the past 50 years. Tremendous opposition to the move of BJP led NDA government was raised by all the opposition parties and various non-governmental orgainsations, including prominent intellectuals.

Our Honourable President K. R. Narayanan, in his address to the nation on the eve of Golden Jubilee of the Republic and the Constitution, said:

> Today when there is so much talk about revising the Constitution or even writing a new Constitution, we have to consider whether it is the Constitution that has failed us or it is we who have failed the Constitution.

'The President was at pains to point out that great thought and delibration had gone into the choice of the appropriate form of the government for the country. Ambedkar, he reminded the audience, had explicitly drawn attention to the polarity between the notions of stability and responsibility and emphasised that he preferred to keep his faith with the latter'. In the Constituent Assembly, Dr. Ambedkar explained that the Drafting Committee in chosing the Parliamentary system for India, preferred more responsibility to more stability, a system under which the goverment will be on the anvil everyday .... The Constituent Assembly chose the system because they preferred more responsibility to stability, which could slip into authoritarian exercises of power. Another factor to be borne in mind is the immensity of India, the perplexing variety and the diversity of the country, the very size of population and complexity of its social and developmental problems. In such a predicament, described by one writer as one of 'a million mutinies', there must be in the body politic a vent for discontents and frustrations to express themselves in order to forestall and prevent major explosion in society. The parliamentary system provides this vent more than a system which prefers stability to responsibility and accountability"[46]

"The value of this system was not in any way diminished by the recent experience of instability in government', said the President, "In my opinion we should avoid too much rigidity in our system of government as in a very rigid system there is the danger of major explosions in society taking place. The possibility and facility of a change in government is itself a factor in the stability of the political system in the long term because then the people will be more inclined to tolerate a political situation they do not approve of or find difficult to cope with for long".[47]

While evaluating the strength and weaknesses of the Republic and its achievements he cautioned that justice—social, economic and political—remained an unrealised dream for millions of people. He, further, said, "The benefits of our economic growth are yet to reach the people. We have one of the world's largest reservoirs of technical personnel, but also the world's largest number of illiterates; the world's largest middle class, but also the largest number of people below the poverty line and largest number of children suffering from malnutrition. Our giant factories rise from out of squalor; our satellites shoot up from the midst of the havels of the poor. Not surprisingly, there is sullen resentment among the masses against their condition erupting often in violent forms in several parts of the country ...."

The President warned against the evils of unregulated liberalisation and the excesive focus on advertisement driven consumerism, which he claimed unleashed frustrations and tensions in society. One half of our society guzzles aerated beverages while the other has to make do with palmfuls of muddied water. Our three-way fast-lane of liberalisation, privatisation and globalisation must provide safe pedestrian crossing for the un-empowered India also so that it too can move towards 'equality of status and opportunity'. 'Beware of the fury of the patient man', says the old adage. One could say, "Beware of the fury of the patient and long suffering people".[48]

In response to Prime Miniter's justification for review of the Constitution and working of the Constitution which he did by drawing attention to the "acutely" felt need for stability both at the Centre and in the States to ensure faster socio-economic development and that the Constitution was not immutable' the President said, " The founding fathers deliberately made the amendment process of the Constitution easy so that short-comings or lacunae in the Constitution can be rectified by the Parliament without too much difficulty. There are other changes that can be brought about, like changes in the electoral law or functioning of the political parties. Whatever we may do, and we have a right to bring about necessary changes in the political and economical system, we should ensure that the basic philosophy behind the Constitution and the fundamental socio-economic soul of the Constitution remain sacrosanct. We should not throw out baby with bath water".[49]

It would be observed from the President's address to the nation that the benefits of our economic growth are yet to reach the people and his warning that whatever we may do and we have a right to bring about necesaary changes in the political and economic system, we should ensure that the basic philosophy behind the Constitution and the fundamental socio-economic soul of the Constitution remain sacrosanct, is very timely and relevant in this context.

What is the 'basic philosophy of the Constitution' and what is the 'fundamental socio-economic soul of the Constitution' that which the President desired to 'remain sacrosanct'? It is here the crux of the issue.

The founding fathers of the Constitution had a dream for this upcoming nation. Pandit Jawaharlal Nehru, the first Prime Minister of India and one of the most powerful leaders of the Indian Freedom Struggle, while moving the 'Objective Resolution' said that :

> "This Constitutent Assembly declares its firm and solemn resolve to proclaim India as an Independent Sovereign Republic to draw up for her future governance a Constitution .... wherein all power and authority of the Sovereign Independent India, its constitutent parts and organs of government are derived from the people;
> and wherein shall be guaranteed and secured to all the people of India justice, social, economic and political; equality of status, of opportunity, and before the law; freedom of thought, expression, belief, faith, worship, vocation, association and action, subject to law and public morality;
> and wherein adequate safeguards shall be provided for minorities, backward and tribal areas and depressed and other backward clases ...."

And being concerned very much with the future of India Panditji said:

> ".... We have undertaken a tremendous task and we seek the co-operation of all people in that task; because the future of India that we have envisaged is not confined to any group or section or province or other,

> but it comprises all our four hundred millions people of India .... Meanwhile, there is a duty cast upon us and that is to bear the absentees in mind, to remember always that we are here not to function for one party or one group, but always to think of India as whole and always to think of the welfare of the four hundred millions that comprise India ....
>
> 'We are all now, in our respective spheres, party men belonging to this or that group and presumbly we shall continue to act in our respective parties. Nevertheless, the time comes when we have to rise above party and think of the Nation, think sometimes of even the world at large of which our Nation is a great part. And when I think of the work of this Constituent Assembly, it seems to me the time has come when we should, so far as we are capable of it, rise above our ordinary selves and party disputes and think of the great problems before us in the widest and most tolerant and most effective manner so that whatever we may produce, should be worthy of India as a whole and should be such that the world should recognise that we have functioned as we should have functioned, in this high adventure"[50]

It is unfortunate that while the founding fathers of the Constitution had desired to forget the party-politics, sectarian politics and rise above the ordinary selves and think of not about 'the only caste Hindus or a sect of people' but they always kept before them the welfare of four hundred millions of the people of this great country. On the other hand the Bhartiya Janata Party, RSS, Bajrang Dal, Vishwa Hindu Parishad, Akhil Bhartiya Vidyarthi Parishad and many off-shoots of Hindutva supporting organisations of RSS have the only one objective and that is the supremacy of Hinduism and Hindutva cult and establishment of Hindu Rashtra, Hindu culture, Hindu education and Hindu social order ! How selfish, sectarian and limited and restricted feelings the RSS and its frontal organisations are inculcating among the innocent people of this great nation and preparing them for another division of the country wherein in one part the only *Hindutva* supporters would reign ! This is one of the worst kind of philosophy the RSS and its offshoot organisations are dedicated to. This is the most dangerous indication for those who still hope to preserve the unity and integrity of this great nation of Buddha, Mahavir, Nanak, Kabir, and Jyotiba Phule !!!

In pursuance of the great objectives set forth by the founding fathers of the Constitution, specific provisions by way of inserting part III and IV in the Constitution of India, that is, Fundamental Rights and Directive Principles of State Policy, were made obligatory on the 'would be rulers' to fulfil their long-cherished goal of a welfare and powerful state. That long-cherished goal of the founding fathers of the Constitution is still very very far away from our reach !!

References

1. Landmarks in Indian Legal and Constitutional History—By V.D. Kulshreshta p. 373.
2. History of Ancient India : By V.D. Mahajan p. 95, 96, 154, 152.
3. *Ibid.*
4. *Ibid.*
5. *Ibid.*
6. Dr. Babasaheb Ambedkar Writings and Speeches :Vol–13 p. 1214, 1215.
7. Dr. Babasaheb Ambedkar Writings and Speeches : Vol–3 p. 25, 26, 27, 30, 31, 41, 78, 79.
8. *Ibid.*
9. *Ibid.*
10. *Ibid.*
11. *Ibid.*
12. *Ibid.*
13. *Ibid.*
14. Indian Legal and Constitutional History : By V.D. Kulshreshta p. 17, 18, 19.
15. *Ibid.*
16. Mughal Empire in India : By S.R. Sharma p. 301, 302, 304.
17. *Ibid.*
18. Frontline dated January 5, 2001 p. 71, 72.
19. *Ibid.*
20. Indian Legal and Constitutional History : By V.D. Kulshreshta p. 383, 384, 385, 386, 387, 396.
21. *Ibid.*
22. *Ibid.*
23. *Ibid.*
24. *Ibid.*
25. British Rule in India and After : By V.D. Mahajan p. 364, 365, 366.

25(a) The Brotherhood in Saffron : By Walter K. Anderson and Shridhar D. Damle p. 32 and 33.

26. The Brotherhood in Saffron : By Walter K. Anderson and Shridhar D. Damle p. 33.

27. The RSS and BJP : A Division of Labour - By A.G. Noorani p. 9.
28. *Ibid* p. 38.
29. *Ibid* p. 29.
29(a) The Chamcha Age : By Kanshi Ram p. 90 and 91.
30. The Indian Legal and Constitutional History : By V.D. Kulshreshta p. 397.
31. British Rule in India and After : By V.D. Mahajan p. 404.
32. Father of the Constitution of India : By S.K. Biswas p. 106.
33. *Ibid.*
34. Dr. Babasaheb Ambedkar : Writings and Speeches Vol - I p. 256.
35. Dr. Babasaheb Ambedkar : Writings and Speeches Vol - 2 p. 441, 442, 660, 661, 662, 663.
36. *Ibid.*
37. *Ibid.*
38. British Rule in India and After : By V.D. Mahajan p. 374, 376.
39. *Ibid.*
40. What Congress and Gandhi have done to the Untouchables : By Dr. B.R. Ambedkar.
41. *Ibid.*
42. Dr. Babasaheb Ambedkar : Writings and Speeches Vol. 13 p. 25, 26, 44, 1206, 48.
43. *Ibid.*
44. *Ibid.*
45. *Ibid.*
46. Frontline - February 18, 2000 p. 26, 27, 28, 27.
47. *Ibid.*
48. *Ibid.*
49. *Ibid.*
50. The Constitution and the Constituent Assembly : Lok Sabha Secretariat Publication p. 16, 17.

4

Constitution in the Eyes of the Critics

'Every State needs some kind of order, some system by which a reasonably orderly process of government may emerge. Without such an order there is anarchy. It is here that the constitution or order comes to play its role. It is not a sudden or unexpected development. It is the outcome of and culmination of years of work. It is evolved over the years through the requirements and fulfilment of the same. It is also outcome of the struggle against the imposition of unacceptable efforts for self-development'.

'While possessing a common characterstic in content, constitutions differ greatly in type. Some writers classify them into cumulative or evolved and conventional or enacted. A cumulative or evolved constitution is the result of slowly working evolutionary changes; the product of accumulated material which has moulded and shaped political institutions of a country. Such a constitution is not made, it grows with the roots in the past. The edifice it presents is the accumulated wisdom of the past and result of numerous customs, usages, traditions, priciples, judicial decisions which has influenced its development. The conventional or enacted constitution on the other hand is the result of deliberate efforts of a man. [1]

Our constitution declares India to be a Sovereign Democratic Secular Socialist Republic. Originally, it was Sovereign Democratic Republic. The words 'secular and socialist' were inserted by the Constitution (42nd) Amendment Act, 1976 during the emergency period by Indira Gandhi's government, based on the recommendations made by Swarn Singh Committee appointed by Congress President for recommending amendments to the Constitution.

The Preamble of our Constitution runs thus :-

"We the people of India,
having solemnly resolved to constitute India into a Sovereign Socialist Secular Democratic Republic and to secure to all its citizens :
Justice, social, economic and political;
Liberty of thought, expression, belief, faith and worship;
Equality of status and of opportunity;
and to promote among them all;
Fraternity assuring the dignity of the individual and unity and integrity of the Nation;
In our Constituent Assembly this twenty sixth day of November, 1949 do hereby adopt, enact and give to ourselves this constitution"

The Preamble, thus, contains the ideals, aspirations and the objectives which the Constitution - makers intended to realise. It also points out as to what the people of this great country expect the government of India to accomplish. The government must guarantee and secure to all the people of India social, economic and political justice; equality of status, equality of opportunity and equality before law; freedom of thought, expression, belief, faith, worship, vocation, association and action.

Indian Constitution, as it is, is one of the longest and most detailed Constitution. It has like many modern constitutions, in it, the legacy of the past and destination set before it - Welfare State and justice to all-social, economic and political !

As stated in the famous Keshavanand Bharti Case by Justice Shelat and Justice Grover :

"Our Constitution is a unique, apart from being the longest in the world. It is meant for the second largest population with diverse people speaking different languages and professing varying religions. It was chiselled and shaped by great political leaders and legal luminaries, most of whom had taken an active part in the struggle for freedom from British yoke and who knew what domination of a foreign rule meant in the way of deprivation of the basic freedoms and from the point of view of exploitation of the millions of Indians. The Constitution is an organic document which must grow and must take stock of the vast socio-economic problems, particularly, of improving the lot of the common man consistent with his dignity and the unity of the nation".

"The Constitution being the Supreme all the organs and bodies owe their existence to it. None can claim superiority over the other and each of them has to function within the four corners of the constitutional provisions. All the functionaries, be they legislatures, members of the executive or the judiciary take oath of allegiance to the Constitution and derive their authority and jurisdiction from its provisions. The Constitution has entrusted to the judicatures in this country, the task of construing the provisions of the Constitution and of safeguarding the fundamental rights".

"The doctrine of parliamentary sovereignty as it obtains in England does not prevail here except to the extent provided by the Constitution. The entire scheme of the Constitution is such that it ensures the sovereignty and integrity of the country as a Republic and the democratic way of life by parliamentary institutions based on free and fair elections"

Justice Hegde and Justice Mukherjee in the same judgement observed :

"Our Constitution is not a mere political document. It is essentially a social document. It is based on a social philosophy and every social philosophy like every religion has two main features, namely, basic and circumstantial. The former remains constant but the latter is subject to change. The core of a religion always remains constant but the practices associated with it may change. Likewise, a Constitution like ours contains certain features which are so essential that they cannot be changed or destroyed. In any event it connot be destroyed from within".[2]

Justice Bhau Wahane of Bombay High Court has stated :

> "The Indian Constitution is a great social evolutionary document aiming at transforming a medieval hierarchical system into a modern egalitarian society. The majority of its provisions are either directly aimed at furthering and promoting the social revolution of attempting to further this revolution by establishing the conditions necessary for its achievement"[3]

Their Lordships have given the nature, the content and the objective set before the Constitution of India. No doubt it is a great social evolutionary document, but it is also an organic document which must grow and take stock of the vast socio-economic problems of the country. It has also to maintain the dignity of the common man and unity of the country. It declares India a Democratic Socialist Secular Republic. Democracy is the foundation of the system of governance adopted by the founding fathers on which the Secular Socialist Republic stands at large. It is committed to establish a welfare state through democratic process and without discriminating on the basis of birth, caste, creed, sect or religion. The Preamble of the Constitution commits to all citizens social, economic and political justice and also equality of status and opportunity. The liberty of thought, expression, belief, faith and worship to all citizens irrespective of their religion or race and caste and class have been ensured in the Constitution. Thus, our Constitution has ensured individual well-being as well as social well-being through Fundamental Rights and Directive Principles.

Dr. S. Radhakrishnan, 'the philosopher king' and the first Vice-President of Indian Republic, while commending the Objective Resolution, moved by Prime Minister Jawaharlal Nehru on 13 December 1946 in the Constitutent Assembly, therefore, said :

> " .... We wish to tell all those who are abstaining from this Assembly that it is not our desire to establish any sectional Government. We are not here asking for a particular community of a privileged class. We are here working for the establishment of *Swaraj* for all the Indian people. It will be our endeavour to

abolish every vestige of despotism, every heir loom of inorganic tradition. We are here to bring about real satisfaction of the fundamental needs of the common man of this country, irrespective of race, religion or community. If the trumpet gives an uncertain sound, we cannot rally the people to our support. It is, therefore, essential that our bugle call, our trumpet sound must be clear, must give the people a sense of exhilaration, must give the suspicious and the abstaining a sense of reassurance that we are here pledged to achieve full independence of India, where no individual will suffer from undeserved want, where no group will be thwarted in the development of its cultural life".[4]

That was the objective before the Constitutent Assembly when the Constitution was being framed. And when finally the document came into being, it really placed before the Indian public, the desired goals which they were expected to achieve through democratic and secular process. It was not for a particular group, sect or religion. It was for all, the entire Indian people, irrespective of their religion, race, caste, creed and sex !

Secularism Under Attack

A number of people criticise the Constitution for some or other reasons. They are upset when they miss a particular provision of their desire and choice in the Constitution. Put together all sorts of criticism and complaints against it, we can conveniently group these complaints and criticism in two sets. One set comprises the general nature of criticism. The other one is communal approach.

One of the most distinct features of the Indian Constitution is its commitment to secularism. It is neither religious nor irreligious and not also anti-religious. It is wholly detached from religious dogmas. All citizens have been guaranteed equal rights irrespective of their religion, caste, creed, class or community. Every cititzen can follow any religion or practice no religion. The State has no religion of its own or it is against no religion.

The Fundamental Right to Freedom of Religion, under Article 25 of the Constitution states :

(1) Subject to public order, morality and health and to the other provisions of this part, all persons are equally entitled to freedom of conscience and the right to profess, practice and propagate religion.

(2) Nothing in this article shall affect the operation of any existing law or prevent the state from making any law -

(a) regulating or restricting any economic, financial, political or other secular activity which may be associated with religious practice;

(b) providing for social welfare and reform or the throwing open of Hindu religious institutions of a public character to all classes and sections of Hindus.

Explanation I. The wearing and carrying of *Kirpans* shall be deemed to be included in the profession of Sikh religion.

Explanation II. In sub clause (b) of clause (2), the reference to Hindus shall be construed as including a reference to persons professing the Sikh, Jain or Buddhist religion and the reference to Hindu religious institutions shall be construed accordinglly.

According to this Article 'every person in India shall have the freedom of conscience and also shall have the right to profess, practice and propagate religion, subject to restrictions, imposed by the state on the grounds - (i) public order, morality and health (ii) other provisions of the constitution; (iii) regulation of non-religious activity associated with religious practice; (iv) social welfare and reform; (v) throwing open of Hindu religious institutions of a public character to all classes of Hindus.'[5]

In Bommai vs Union of India, the Nine Judges Constitution Bench of the Supreme Court has founded their conclusions as to the contents of 'secularism' under the Indian Constitution on its various relevant provisions such as Articles 25-28, 30, 14-16 and 51A :

> "Drawing from the foregoing provisions, the majority of the 9 judge Bench has laid down the following ingrediants of 'Secularism' under our Constitution, which must be taken as conclusive :
>
> (i) The Constitution prohibits the establishment of a *Theocratic State.*

(ii) Not only the State is prohibited to establish any religion of its own, but it is prohibited further to identify itself with or favouring any particular religion because the State is enjoined to accord equal treatment to all religions and religious sects or denominations.

(iii) On the other hand, Secularism under the Indian Constitution does not mean an anti- God or atheist society.

It only means the equal status of all religions, without any preference in form or discrimination against any one of them.

Under a Secular State, the existence of a legal right or public duty does not depend on the profession or practice of any particular religion. The State attempts to secure the good of all citizens irrespective of their religious beliefs or practices.

(iv) Secularism as comprising the foregoing ingrediants

(a) is a basic feature of our Constitution and

(b) any State government which violates any of the foregoing mandates, or pursues any 'unsecular policy' or course of action renders itself amenable to action under Art 356"[6]

Immediately after demolition and destruction of Babri Masjid by the *Karsevaks of VHP, Bajrang Dal, RSS, Shiv Sena* and other off-shot organisations of RSS, including some of the top BJP leaders, under whose leadership and presence the shameful act of criminal violence and historical blunder was committed; the three BJP ruled State governments were dismissed by the President under Article 356. The dismissal was challenged in the Supreme Court and the apex court while upholding the dismissal of three BJP led states ruled that 'secularism is a basic feature of the Constitution and any State government seen to be acting against the secularist ideal can be dismissed by the President'.

Reacting to the Supreme Court verdict Soli Sorabji, present Attorney General of India and a legal luminary, then gave his own analysis behind the action of the Centre and judgement of the Court. In the article published in the Times of India dated March 23, 1994, he observed :

> " .... What was the material before the Centre in the present case? Firstly, the BJP manifesto on which elections were contested and won in three states which *inter alia* declared that " the party is committed to build Shri Ram Mandir at Janmasthan by relocating superimposed Babri structure" and similar speeches by the leaders of the BJP. Secondly, some of the Chief Ministers and Ministers belonged to the RSS which was a banned organisation at the relevant time and the extreme improbability of implementation of the ban by these ministers. Thirdly, the exhortation by BJP ministers in these three states ministries to join *'Karsewa'* in Ayodhya on December 6, 1992, the public sent off to the *Kar Sewaks* and the subsequent welcome on their return after the destruction of the mosque. One BJP MLA in Himachal Pradesh had publically admitted his participation in the destruction. Fourthly, at least in two states, viz. Madhya Pradesh and Rajasthan there were atrocities against the Muslims and loss of lives and destruction of property"

While taking note of the Supreme Court verdict, Mr. S. Sahay, emminent journalist and former editor of 'Statesman' in his article in The Hindustan Times dated 23/3/1994 wrote :

> "The zealous pursuit of the Constitutional culture by these judges is indeed praise-worthy. One can not but unhesitatingly admire the ruling on secularism which strengthens the constitutional base of our democracy. However, there is a chasm between the constitutional and political culture of this country. The sad fact is that India, that is Bharat, has never evolved beyond family, caste and communal lines. And there has been not one general election ever since independence which has not been predominantly fought on caste and community lines. Well there are parties and communities for which religion is a whole way of life".

He did not stop here. He, further, commented on the halfway verdict of the Court and also blamed the Centre for playing the role of a mute spectator till the structure was demolished completely. He wrote :-

> "By making secularism a basic feature of the Constitution but taking a rather limited view of justiciability, the Court has left the Central Government free to undo state Governments though in much more sophisticated way than it has done so far. Whatever the material placed it is well-known that the dismissal of three state governments in which BJP was in power was unfair act intended to hide the Centre's own shortcomings in preventing the demoliton of the Babri Masjid".

Mr. Ram Jethmalani is another prominent legal personality of the country, who has also been known as a person creating confusion and double speak, challenging the very concept of secularism in the Constitution, he raised a bogey of the concept in his article published in The Sunday Observer (weekly newspaper dated 24-30 January 1993). According to him :

> " .... Though the secularism and its variations figured prominently in the Constituent Assembly debates, the Assembly did not nick-name the Constitution as secular. Even the aims and objects of resolution of December 6, 1946 moved by Jawaharlal Nehru, did not use the word "Secular". It did promise that the Constitution shall guarantee and secure to all the people of India justice/social, economic and political - equality of status and opportunity before the law, freedom of thought, expression, belief, faith, worship, vocation, association and action subject to law and public morality. These words supposed to contain the special brand of non- western secularism which the Indian Constitution was expected to embody.
> Many of these words became the preamble in the final Constitution but the preamble itself refrained from using the ambiguous and dubious word "secular".
> Only Mrs. Gandhi introduced it during the Emergency while horrors of Turkman Gate were being perpetrated on the minorities".

Thus, Mr Jethmalani tried to make it very clear that Constitution was never committed to secularism. On the other hand its very concept of secularism was ambiguous and open to be interpreted in any way to the conveniece to the person.

But to remove the clouds of doubt from the mind of Jethmalani and many others Justice Ahmadi in his judgement in the Bommai case traces, "The notion of secularism before independence and until the framing of the Constitution. He says that eventhough the word secularism did not initially figure in the Constitution, the concept of secularism was very much embedded in it. All that the 42nd Constitution (Amendment) Act has done is to formalise it".

Justice B. P. Jeevan Reddy, who was also on the same bench, did not see any argument that secularism was a vague term, as mentioned by Mr. Ram Jethmalani. His view was that in the context of the Indian Constitution, and he said he was only concerned with the constitutional context and not with the general meaning of the word, secularism is more than a passive attitude of religious tolerance. It is a positive concept of equal treatment of all. He was not much bothered about the fact that whether the concept was originally Western or Indian. What mattered to him was that, that was the constitutional goal and a basic feature of the Constitution. Thus, according to him, the founding fathers had proceeded to create a state which was secular in its outlook and egalitarian in action.

In the same S. R. Bommai case, Justice P. B. Sawant and Justice Kuldip Singh along with Justice Pandian, who presided over the nine members Constitutional bench observed : "The Preamble and Art 25, 26, 29, 30, 44, 51-A, 14, 15,16 by implication prohibit the establishment of a *Theocratic State* and prevent the state either identifying itself with or favouring any particular religions or religious sect or denomination. The State is enjoined to accord equal treatment to all religions and religious sects and denominations. Under our Constitution whatever be the attitude of the State towards the religion, religious sects and denominations, religion cannot be mixed with any secular activity of the State. In fact the encroachment of religion into secular activites is strictly prohibited. The State's tolerance of religion or religions does not make it either a religious or theocratic state."[7]

In view of the above judgement and its having been confirmed that the 'secularism' is the basic feature of the

Constitution, the *'Hindutva-vadis'* or protagonists of *Hindu Rashtra* are very much agitated over the issue and as such they have designed different strategy to counter this fact. Setting up of Constitutional Review Commission is one of those strategies. *Jalabhishek* Programmes in Kashi-Vishwanath temple in Varanasi, organisation of *Mahakumbha* on a very large scale, enchroachment on Safdarjung shrine in New Delhi and claiming each and every Muslim / Islamic monument allegdly built-up on the destruction of Hindu temples and many more similar activities in North- India tentamount to creating a psychological social climate so as to pressurise the poor innocent and ignorant Hindus to fall in the trap of extremist Hindutva-wadis. The RSS Chief's repeated call at Nagpur, New Delhi and Agra to scrap the present Constitution is nothing but a part of the conspiracy to destroy the secular fabric of the Constitution and impose upon this country the long-cherished concept of *Hindu Rashtra*.

The blatant repudiation of judiciary by VHP leaders, declaring that "Ram Temple issue was not within the purview of the judiciary" by Pravin Togadiya, International Secretary General of VHP is nothing but the contempt of the judiciary and an insult to the Constitution of the country.[8] Acharya Giriraj Kishore, Senior Vice President of VHP in an interview given to Frontline July 7, 2000 said, "We have made it clear right from the beginning that as far as we are concerned the construction of the Ram Temple is not a matter of adjudication. No Constitution, no laws, no government and no Prime Minister can stop our work ...."[9]

Mahant Ramchandra Paramhans, Chairman of Shri Ramjanmabhumi Nyas told Frontline July 7, 2000 that "no Constitution, no laws, no government and no Prime Minister can stop our work" and that Shri Ramjanmabhumi Nyas was committed only to the Dharma and Dharmacharyas.

However, the *Hindutvawadis* and protagonists of orthodox Hinduism could not digest the concept of secularism. They had in mind and even today they have their goal of Hindu Rashtra. Ram Jethamalani, a Rajya Sabha Member with the support of Shiv Sena and BJP and till few months back a Cabinet Minister in the Vajpayee Government, when doubt about the concept of secularism for the sake of chair and calls it ambiguous we can understand the plight of so-called intellectual Hindus and legal luminaries. The so-called moderates and pragmatists also are not better than Jethmalanis and Advanijis ! What to talk of the poor Sadhus and Saints whose level of understanding, depth of study and outlook are always shaped by their patrons whose dictates they are bound to obey and capable of enjoying the comforts and luxuries of life sitting in Rishikesh, Hardwar, Mathura or Mansarovar.

The word secular or secularism in the Constitution has come under severe attack by the Sangh Parivar and its cohorts. The most strong arms of the Sangh, i.e., Vishwa Hindu Parishad and Bajrang Dal are the most vocal on the issue. However, the organisations of Sadhus and Saints of Hinduism do not lag behind.

The Akhil Bhartiya Sant Samiti, Vrindavan Mathura under the Chairmanship of Swami Muktanand Saraswati prepared a commentary on the Indian Constitution and the same was published in 1993 under the title - "Vartman Indian Sanvidhan" (The Present Indian Constitution). 'The word "Indian" was used in the Hindi title with a purpose to categorically denounce the same'.

This commentary on Indian Constitution by Sadhus, was a glaring phenomenon on the word secular. According to that :-

> " The third word in the Preamble is 'secular' which, again has not been interpreted. In Hindi version it says sect, secular whereas, the word is commonly used for religious secularism, Panth and Dharma (sect and religion are two different words), sect and community have separate identities as compared to Dharma. Of all the available interpretations of the word Dharma, this is most widely accepted, "a system in which a human being's welfare is taken care of in this and the other world".
>
> Later, we saw the rise of many sects and communities. There is but one truth and our greatmen have described in various ways. Article 30 states all minorities, whether based on religion or language, shall have the right to establish and administer educational institutions of their choice. This encourages divisive forces. Article 16 states "there shall be equal opportunity for all citizens in matters relating to employment or appointment to any office under the States". Part four is a contradiction of

> the same article and states, nothing in this article shall prevent the State from making any provisions for the reservation of appointments or posts in favour of any backward class of citizens which in the opinion of the State is not adequately represented in the service under the State".[10]

This is evident from the above observation that the Sangh Parivar is not in agreement with intent of the concept of secularism and, secondly, provision of the reservations for backward class citizens also does not find favour with them. As such we can understand their apathy when the same "Commentary" concluded -

> "The Constitution destroys our heritage and tradition by adopting religious secularism as its foundation. India is a country known for its Dharma. Here Dharma does not imply community or cult (Panth). Here Dharma means international brotherhood. Therefore our policies would be cult secular"[11]

The term 'Secular' has also come to acquire the most important and significant place in the debate and discussion among the academicians and social scientists of the country. Right from its literal meaning to its contribution to the religious relationship in India's multi-cultural society and the role played by it to harmonise inter-religious understanding.

Dr. Ashish Nandy castigates secularists by observing that, ".... An idea of secularism, an import from 19th contury Europe into South Asia has acquired immense potency in the middle class cultures and state sectors of South Asia, thanks to its connection with and response to religious ideology". Hence, Nandy rejects Secularism because it is Western and it legitimises the power of the state. Partha Chatterjee, takes three abstract principles of the Secular State like "liberty", "equality" and "neutrality" and finds the practice of Indian Secular State flawed on all the three levels of secularism .... Chatterjee and many others castigate Nehruvian version of Secular India because Hindu social reforms were undertaken but Muslim Personal Law was not reformed by Nehru's Secular Government. For this Nehru has been criticised by several social scientists.

According to Pt.Nehru : "Communalisn is the badge of a backward nation, not of the modern age. People have their religion and they have a right to hold firmly to it, but to import religion into politics and to break up the country is something, which was done in Europe 300 to 400 years back. We in India have to get rid of it. We have declared that we will fight communal organisations in every way, whether they are Muslim organisations or Sikh or any other". A clear message of Nehruvian Secularism is that every Indian has freedom to pursue his/her religious beliefs because India is neither Hindu, nor Muslim, nor Sikh, nor Christian".[12]

Thus, Dr. C. P. Bambhari of Jawaharlal Nehru University, while reviewing the book of essays written by prominent social scientists under the title - *Secularism and its Critics,* observed:[13]

" .... Neutrality of the State is a myth and such theory is fallacious and flawed. Even as an ideal it is not relevant. The forces of *Hindutva* are struggling to capture the Indian State for establishing *"one nation, one people and one culture"*. - Even an elementry understanding of the essence of State system tells us that some groups occupy clear controlling power within the State and the contest is to capture the power of the State. This is the struggle which is being waged by secularists on the one hand, and the enemies of secularism on the other. What is the whole conflict about secularism ? Marx had alerted us about the social essence of the State and the forces of *Hindutva* or Christianity in the West or Muslim majority in Pakistan understand the significance of state power much better than democratic theorists of a secular state.

> "Further, the issues of minority cultural rights get linked with religion and every secular State should be sensitive enough to deal with the problem. A secular State is always involved in maintaining a balance because as human agency, it can hurt the religious feelings even unwillingly. Nehru as head of a secular government made every effort to provide a sense of security to Muslims in the aftermath of partition of India. Minorities expect that a secular state will provide them security of life and property and a Hindu or fanatic Christian state can not be entrusted with such a task. Secularisation of society

> is a very large project and involves many other areas of social and economic transformations. The first and foremost duty of a secular state is to protect religious minorities and not show any discrimination against them in public life on the basis of religion. Citizenship irrespective of religion should be the basis of an individual's relationship with the State. This is the goal of any Secular State worth its name, and religious movements are directed primarily against a Secular State System because they believe in official religion-based states of the majority community. It is fundamental struggle between modernity and feudal theocracy and inspite of critics, this struggle is worth undertaking because liberated citizenry is able to build human society in their own image ...."

The 1994 Supreme Court verdict in S. R. Bommai vs Union of India or popularly known as the State Assemblies Dissolution Case, had given a big blow, for the time being, to the increasing communal extremism propounded by Sangh Parivar and its off-shoot militant organisations. The trend could have further erased the communal intensity and also arrested the further growth but for the lack of a unified and country–wide strong and well-knit network of any social or cultural organisation. Everything and anything can not be fought on the political platforms only. The people joining political platform are mostly motivated with the selfish and personal interests. Otherwise changing of colour / flags or caps from time to time, after having failed to secure the desired ticket would not have been visible. It is irony of political philosophy of that persons like George Fernandes, Ram Vilas Paswan, Sharad Yadav and Karunanidhi, who have all along been projected as secularists, socialist and anti-Brahminist, are today at the feet of communalists.They are neither able nor capable to fight these communalists through mass-movements and as such their surrender before the communalists is their fate !

Justice K. Ramaswamy, in his judgement written in S. R. Bommai case, has observed very correctly that "Rise of fundamentalism and communalism of politics are anti-secularism. They encourage separatist and divisive forces and become breeding grounds for national disintegration, and fail the parliamentary democratic system and the Constitution".

And we must not forget what the apex court in Ziyauddin Burhanuddin Bukhari vs Brijmohan Ramdas Mehra (AIR 1975 SC 1788) held that :

> "The Secualr State rising above all differences of religion, attempts to secure the good of all its citizens irrespective of their religious beliefs and practices. It is neutral or impartial in extending its benefits to citizens of all castes and creeds".

Presidential vs Parliamentry Form of Government

In 1998 no sooner did he become Home Minister, L.K. Advani selected as the topic for the Thakur Prasad Memorial Lecture at Patna on April 26, 1996 "Need for a Commission to Review the Constitution". He explained in so many words that, "the basic structure doctrine does not bind us to parliamentary democracy".[14]

Why there has been so much of crying by the communalists and also by the capitalists for Presidential Form of Government ? The reasons in that, with the socio-political awakening among the Dalit-Shoshit Samaj (the oppressed and exploited people) and asserting of their political rights, the political scenario of the country is fast changing. The power of vote has completely changed the political equation of the country. The Dalit-Shoshit Samaj has started to exercise their right to vote caustiously and intelligently. Consequently the balance of power started getting tilted unexpectedly in every election. Laloo Prasad Yadav, a backward in Bihar with less than majority number of MLA's to support, could become Chief Minister of Bihar in 1995 and Miss Mayawati, an untouchable-scheduled caste of Delhi, with 43 MLA's at her command, could compel even *Manuvadis,* to whom she blamed, criticised and cursed day in and day out for the last more than 10 years, to support her Chief Ministership for six months in the first instance and, secondly, again for six months. And the most unique and surprising phenomenon of this vote power was that H.D. Devegowda, a backward from Karnataka could also become Prime Minister of India with only 43 M.P.'s of his Janata Dal. That all could be possible because of parliamentary form of system provided in our Constitution. Otherwise an untouchable Shudra woman and touchable Shudras could never have dreamt of weilding a political power in the chairs of Chief Minister or Prime Minister. This was possible and this is possible even today under Parliamentry system of government. And this very thing / provision of the Constitution has irked very badly the *Hindutva* supporters who are custodians of the 'Status-quo' in socio-political system of the country of *Varnashram Social System* and also committed to bring back the bad-old days though with a changed face.

For centuries these *Manuvadis - Brahminical Society*, enjoyed fruits of all powers and kept the Shudras and Ati-Shudras deprived of all powers - educational, social, cultural, economic and political and made all designs and conspiracies under the disguise of religious scriptures, and wanted to perpetuate that very same power in their own hands. But the political scenario of Bihar and U. P. as well as at the Centre in person of Laloo Prasad, Mayawati and Devegowda shocked those 'status-quoists' to such an extent that they had to bear with their bare issues. This opened their eyes and this political situation strengthened their original intention to further reinforce the presedential form of system.

The *Manuvadis* never lose an opportunity and find a way out to their advantage even in the adverse/critical situation. They never lose the hope. They never get disgusted, disllusioned and disappointed, though temporarily they move backward, they do it to speed up and move forward. They did the same thing in Uttar Pradesh.

In 1993 U. P. Vidhan Sabha elections BSP and Samajwadi Party fought the Assembly elections jointly and came to power under Mulayam Singh Yadav. That was the first time in the political history of India that the Backwards, Scheduled Castes and Minorities came under one roof and on one platform. That was the perfect political equation in the Indian political scenario to rule over this country. But the equation could not last long. It was a short lived experiment ! They parted company shortly and in such way never to meet again. On this historical break-down, the reaction of the *Manuvadis* was really worth noting (?) BJP leader Atal Behari Vajpayee, then leader of Opposition in Parliament, said in Rajat Sharma's *"Aapki Adalat TV show"* of Zee TV that, "they have removed a big thorn with the help of small thorn and finally both the thorns were thrown away in the dust". That was the Brahminical conspiracy to destroy the unity of the Scheduled Caste, Scheduled

Tribes, Other Backward Classes and Minorities. Both, the Samajwadi Party of Mulayam Singh and Bahujan Samaj Party of Kanshi Ram fell into the cleverly prepared trap of Brahmincal society and their ill-designs and lost. The destiny must have laughed at this short-sightedness and lack of vision of these leaders ! That is how, for centuries these *Manuvadis* could rule over this country and enjoy the political power, the master key of all locks, through such machinations and conspiracies. And Shudras and Ati-Shudras have always fallen into their traps and lost for their ego, short-sightedness, lack of vision and greed for immediate and limited gains.

That was really a great blunder committed by those who had come together. The history would never forgive both Kanshi Ram and Mulayam Singh that they have betrayed the Bahujans and also demand of time and situation. And now the BJP is ruling over Uttar Pradesh for the last four years. And it was Uttar Pradesh again, which could make Atalji reach the Centre through coalition politics. Even today if the votes of SP and BSP are totalled both in Assembly and Lok Sabha elections - constituency-wise, the BJP and Congress stand no where, even nearby ! And if the same experiment and strategy is repeated elsewhere the day would not be far off when the dream of Dr. Ambedkar, the architect of the Constitution and messiah of the millions of down trodden could be fulfilled. Dr. Ambedkar had advised the Scheduled Castes and the Backward Classes on 25th April 1948 at Lucknow Conference of Scheduled Caste Federation :

> " .... I then turned to the question of unity between the scheduled castes and the so-called Backward Classes. This I did at the request of the leaders of the Backward Classes who were present at the conference. I said it was a pity that the two classes whose needs were common did not join together. The reason was that the Backward Classes did not like to associate themselves with the Scheduled Castes because they were afraid that such an association will bring themselves down to the level of the Scheduled Castes.
>
> "I said that I was not anxious to establish interdining and inter-marriage between the Scheduled Castes and the Backward Classes. They may well remain separate social entities. There is no reason

why they should not join hands to form a political party to remove their backward condition. I pointed out how the Scheduled Castes have improved their condition by playing their part, in the politics of the country and there is no reason why the Backward Classes should not do the same.

"If I said that the Scheduled Castes and the Backward Classes form majority of population of the country, there is no reason why they should not rule this country. All that is necessary is to organise for the purpose of capturing political power - which is your own because of adult sufferage. People do not seem to pick up courage because they are overwhelmed by the belief that the Congress Government is there for ever. I said this is a wrong impression. In a popular democracy no Government is permanent and not even the Government established by the two of the tallest Congressmen, Pandit Nehru and Sardar Patel. If you organise, you can even capture that Governemnt".[15]

Dr. Ambedkar's advice given 52 years back to these people is most relevant and useful even in today's circumstances. He was well aware about the difficulties of the touchable and untouchable Shudras of the country and he wanted to remove those difficulties through the law of the land. He was, therefore, of the view that these miserable people must have their say in the formation of the government. This was possible under adult sufferage if the government is responsible and accountable to the voters from time to time. This situation was possible only in the parliamentry form of government, in which the political executive or the government in power could be removed any time through No-confidence motion. This is the great and very powerful instrument to hold the Govt. always resposible and accountable to the people. Under presidential form of government it was not possible. Though there was stability in the system, there was less accountability and there was also possibility of its turning into authoritarian rule. Dr. Ambedkar's advice to the Backwards and Scheduled Castes at Lucknow Conference to expand their domain of political power by joining hands to form the majority must be viewed in this perspective. Because in the parliamentry system majority is the rule and Scheduled Castes alone or Backward Classes alone would not be able to form the majority or for that matter minorities also would not be able ! Dr. Ambedkar was more concerned with the responsibility and accountability than stability. He dealt in very details about the merits and demerits of the presidential as well as parliamentary forms of system. He clarified his point of view in the Constituent Assembly on 4th Nov. 1948. Thus :

> "The Presidential system of America is based upon the separation of the Executive and the Legislature. So that the President and his Secretaries can not be members of the Congress. The Draft Constitution does not recognise this Doctrine. The Ministers under the Indian Union are members of Parliament. Only members of Parliament can become Ministers. Ministers have the same rights as other members of Parliament namely, that they can sit in Parliament, take part in debate and vote in its proceedings. Both systems of Government are, of course, democratic and the choice between the two is not very easy. A democratic Executive must satisfy two conditions - (1) It must be a stable executive and (2) it must be a responsible executive. Unfortunately it has not been possible so far to devise a system which can ensure both in equal degree. You can have a system which can give you more stability but less responsibility or you can have a system which gives you more responsibility but less stability. The American and the Swiss system give more stability but less responsibility. The British system on the other hand gives you more responsibility but less stability. The reason for this is obvious. The American Executive is a non-Parliamentry Executive which means that it is not dependent for its existence upon a majority in the Congress, while the British system is the Parliamentary Executive which means that it is dependent upon a majority in Parliament. Being a non-Parliamentry Executive, the Congress of the United States can not dismiss the Executive. A Parliamentry Government must resign the moment

> it loses the confidence of a majority of the members of Parliament. Looking at it from the point of view of resposibility a non-Parliamentary Executive being independent of Parliament tends to be less responsible to the Legislature, while a Parliamentary Executive being more dependent upon a majority in Parliament become more responsible. The Parliamentry system differs from a non-Parliamentry system in as much as the former is more responsible than the latter but they also differ as to the time and agency for assessment of their responsibility. Under the non-Parliamentry system, such as the one that exists in the USA the assessment of the responsibility of the Executive is periodic. It takes place once in two years. It is done by the Electorate. In England, where the Parliamentary system prevails, the assessment of responsibility of the Executive is both daily and periodic. The daily assessment is done by members of Parliament, through Questions, Resolutions No-confidence Motions, Adjournment Motions and Debate on Addresses. Periodic assessment is done by the electorate, at the time of the election which may take place every five years or earlier. The Daily assessment of responsibility which is not available under the American system is, it is felt, far more effective than the periodic assessment and far more necessary in a country like India. The Draft Constitution in recommending Parliamentary system of Executive has preferred more responsibility to more stability".[16]

It was felt at that time that the British system of Executive, which would provide a strong democratic executive, which would suit the country. K.M. Munshi and Alladi Krishanaswami Iyyar, both the members of Drafting Committee were the staunch supporters of Parliamentry Executive but for different reasons. Munshi said in the Constituent Assembly.

> " .... Between the two Executives, one on the American model and the other on the British Model, there can be no question of preference.... During the last 100 years, the Indian pubilc life has largely drawn upon

> the traditions of the British Constitutional law. Most of us .... have looked upto the British model as the best. For the last thirty or forty years, some kind of responsibility has been introduced in the government of this country. Our constitutional traditions have become parliamentary and we have now all our provinces functioning more or less on the British model. As a matter of fact, today, the Dominion Government of India is functioning as a full-fledged Parliamentary Government. After this experience why should we go back upon the tradition that has been built for over 100 years, and try a noval experiment ...."[17]

Alladi Krishanaswami Iyyar, another member of the Drafting Committee, was no less the supporter of parliamentary system of government. He observed,

> " .... An infant democracy can not afford, under modern conditions, to take the risk of a perpetual cleavage, feud or conflict or threatened conflict between the Legislature and the Executive and to promote harmony between the different parts of the Government system .... These, then are the reasons which influenced this Assembly as well as the various Committees in adopting the Cabinet system of Government in preference to the presidential type".[18]

The *Swarn Singh Committee,* appointed by Congress President Devkant Barua in 1975 for recommending amendments to the Constitution of India was also of the view that it was unnecessary to abandon the parliamentary system in favour of the presidential system. The Committee further observed that, in a federal set-up with the kind of regional diversity as we have, the parliamentary system is the best suited to preserve the unity and integrity of the country. It also ensures greater responsiveness to the voice of the people.[19]

Dr. Granville Austin, a leading American scholar, who has worked extensively on the Indian Constitution rejected out right the view that parliamentary democracy in India had failed and said he was "not convinced" that a Presidential system would be more effective. He was also of the firm opinion that even after 200 years the U.S. Presidential system was far from perfect.[20]

Constitution : An Instrument of Change Rigidity vs Flexibility

Smt. Indira Gandhi as a political head of the government during her hey-days tried to introduce absolutism through imposition of emergency and twisted the Constitution to suit her likes so as to perpetuate her family rule in 1975. But after a year or so she began to realise that she was on the wrong side. By the time she realised her mistake she was out of power. The people of this country could never tolerate the tyranny and torture of emergency. Consequently both the mother and son were thrown away from the seat of power. Smt. Gandhi used the same very provisions of the Constiution to convert the democratic rule into a dictatorial rule and the outcome is an eye-opener for those who intend to venture to use this risky and double-edged instrument !

No doubt there might be some lacuna in the constitutional provisions but that does not mean that the entire constitution needs to be replaced. 'As repeatedly made the point by Dr. Austin that no constitution was perfect and his own understanding of the Indian Constitution was that conceptually it had withstood the test of time. Finally, a constitution was as good as the people who "worked it". He seemed to be against making a constitution too rigid. For he felt that if you lay down too many rules, you might end up curbing the role of individuals in running a democracy.[21]

Rigidity vs Flexibility

The Indian constitution is not a rigid constitution. It is a flexible constitution. The constitution can be amended easily. The method of amendment is not so rigid and difficult as that of the USA. But every care has been taken by the founding fathers that it would not become so easy that any political party could change any provision convenient to implement their own designs. That would have destroyed the very basis of the constitution. Even then the amendment procedure has come under severe attacks.

Regarding the method of the amendment of the constitution, Dr. B.R. Ambedkar observed. " .... What is said to be the absurdity of the amending provisions is founded upon a misconception of the position of the Constituent Assembly and of the future Parliament elected under the constitution. The Constituent Assembly in making a Constitution has no partisan motive. Beyond securing a good and workable Constitution it has no eye on getting through a particular measure. The future Parliament, if it met as a Constituent Assembly, its members will be acting as partisans seeking to carry amendments to the Constitution to facilitate the party measures which they have failed to get through Parliament by reason of some articles of the Constitution which has acted as an obstacle in their way. Parliament will have an axe to grind while the Constituent Assembly has none. That is the difference between the Constituent Assembly and the future Parliament. That explains why the Constituent Assembly though elected on limited franchise can be trusted to pass the Constitution by simple majority and why the Parliament though elected on adult sufferage can not be trusted with the same power to amend it".[22]

Dr. Ambedkar's fear of misusing some provisions of the constitution by some political party for their selfish and partisan motive was not totally unfounded. In 1976 Smt. Indira Gandhi and her hand-maid Indira Congress Party, through 42nd Constitution Amendment Act, sought to do away with the power of the court to invalidate a Constitution Amendment Act, even where it is not in accordance with the procedure laid down in Art. 368, by the use of the words 'On any ground' in cl (4) and the words 'no limitation whatever' in cl (5). The prime motive behind this move was to control that part of Keshavanand decision that though the Fundamental Rights constituted no limitation on the amending power, there were other 'implied limitation', namely, that the power to amend could not be used to alter the 'basic features of the Constitution or to make a new Constitution. This latter view in Keshavanand's case was superseded by cl (4), (5) providing that (a) there were no limitations, express or implied, upon the amending power under Art 368 (1) which is a 'Constituent power' and that (b) a Constitution Amending Act would not, therefore, be subject to judicial review on any ground".[23]

It was, however, in the Minerva Mills vs Union of India case that the Supreme Court Constitution Bench declared cl. (4), (5) to be invalid on the ground that these clauses, which removed all limitations upon the power of Parliament to amend the Constitution and precluded judicial review of a Constitution Amendment Act, on any ground, sought to destroy an 'essential feature' or 'basic structure' of the Constitution".[24]

Similarly, the recent move of Bhartiya Janata Party led NDA government to review the Constitution is not without ulterior motive. The Bhartiya Janata Party for many years has been criticising the Constitution for not reflecting their desired ideals, ethos and aspirations of imposing the concept of *Hindu Rashtra* on the people of India. But they have kept nothing hidden. Their agenda of *Hindu Rashtra,* free market economy, Hindu religion oriented education, supremacy of Sanskrit language and raising mosque and mandir issues from time to time and disputing the genuine mosques allegely built on the destruction of Hindu temples etc. and the whole Hindu agenda is very much open. Those who criticise BJP for their hidden agenda are living in the 'fools dome'. Their's nothing secret or hidden. Those who have joined them from time to time either to form the State governments or Central government, it is their helplessness or rather their total and utter incapability and bankruptcy of intellectual powers that they could not build up a third alternative without *Hindutva* support. Even those who till few years back were barking at BJP as *'Manuvadis'* and *'Kamandalist'* party are today licking their boot and finding them comfortable and convenient to form a joint front or government to enjoy the comforts of power. They forget that they were the very same people who once and again criticised them being communalist.

The Bhartiya Janata Party and even *Sangh Parivar,* time and again, declared as to what they had in their mind for the people of this country, what type of social and religious system they want to establish, what type of economic and industrial policy they want to pursue and what sort of educational system they would like to introduce in India. Despite all that being known the so-called fake socialists, half-hearted Mandalists and even the so-called Ambedkarites have joined them to form the governments and helped them to expand their sphere of influence and power directly and indirectly. And, in fact, it is they who are gaining day by day and not those who joined them. With merely two Members of Parliament in 1984, today they are 182 and dictating the terms. They have entirely changed the face of Indian economy, educational curriculum has been under drastic changes and entire religious atmoshphere of the country has been communalised. The minorities and SCs/STs are feeling totally insecure and deprived due to various policy decisions taken in service matters under the pretext of Second Generation Economic Reforms. Anti-Congressism of Dr. Lohia could not build-up a viable third alternative of Secular Socialistic Democratic parties either during his life-time or thereafter by his political heirs but provided free gound to weaken the Congress party and strengthen communalist forces. It was anti-Congressism of Lohia which came as a blessing in disguise to enable the communalists to consolidate and strengthen their sphere of political influence through the politics of joint fronts and alliances.

The BJP has never declared that they have entirely discarded their original agenda. They have only said that temporarily they have kept the same in abeyance. The day, they get total majority they shall implement their original policies including construction of Ram Temple at Ayodhya, Uniform Civil Code and many other things.

And for all that they want to replace the present Constitution with that Constitution which they have in mind. Knowing fully well that today even not being in a position to amend the present Constitution as they desire or replace it, neverthless they got the Constitution Review Commission appointed so as to confuse the innocent people about the various provisions of the Constitution and to mobilise the masses later on to support their point of view. And the so-called anti-communalists are sitting like spectators on their fence enjoying the ministerial comforts and the bags full of future comforts.

The BJP and its allies do not have requisite majority in the Rajya Sabha. They also don't have requisite State Assemblies to ratify the desired amendment. And it is not that they are not aware of the technical difficulty in getting their amendmends passed. Despite that appointment of Constitution Review Commission is their long term planning which their allies are unable to foresee and understand. This is not the first instance, during the JP movement, the RSS activists and BJP leaders very systematically infiltrated into the movement and high-jacked the whole movement to their advantage. They did not even hesitate to join the Janata Party though they were well-aware that they entirely differ with all other political parties but to come out of isolation, they temporarily sacrificed their brand-name and symbol. They were very much sure that that *Tamasha or conglomeration* of different political parties under the name of Janata Party would not last long. And the same thing happened. After 18 months of 'One Act Play', the ego and greed of prime ministerial crown demolished and destroyed the trust and hopes of the millions of voters who first time after 37 years of one party Congress rule voted for change. They totally betrayed the public. But BJP benefitted immensely out of this destruction. Their isolation and 'touch me not' brand came to an end. It became the mainstream political party. During the 18 months rule they consolidated their solid political grounds. Even RSS and its other front organisations benefitted enormously in terms of money and bureaucratic patronage. And who were at loss ? The entire remaining lot excluding BJP ! That was the long term planning, the vision those leaders had, the patience they had !

The present situation is also not very different from that. Leaders like Karunanidhi known for his strong opposition to Brahminical ideology and who has spearheaded Anti-Brahmins movement in Tamil Nadu with Annadurai and Periyar has forgotten the motive and objective of the movement which he had led. BJP, which was till few years back a non-entity in Tamil Nadu, has made entry in Parliament with four number of Members of Parliament, firstly through Jayalalitha and now through Karunanidhi.

Other allies of BJP - like NC, AGP, BJD, Samata Party, Telugu Desam etc. have no basic ideology. Their limited and only objective is to safeguard their power interests in their respective States irrespective of who are at the Centre. To protect their own power interests, they can go to the extent of sacrificing their interests of the people. Their ideology is power ideology. They do not have any other base, other than political organisation. And as such these political outfits are unable and helpless to counter the moves of BJP and RSS, which as one of the largest and biggest network of organisations catering to all sorts of moves, i.e., political, social, religious, economic, cultural, legal, educational, women, students, labour and several other fields. They all work under one unified command of RSS, though they speak from different platforms, ultimate aim is to establish *Hindu Rashtra* in place of Secular Bharat, that is India !!

Who is the Real Architect of Indian Constitution ?

Our Constitution has been under continuous attack for one or other reasons by the conservatives as well as communalists of this country. Arun Shourie, now the Minister of State for Disinvestment in the Vajpayee Government and who was earlier associated with World Bank, has written a book under the title - Worshipping False Gods - Ambedkar and the Facts which have been erased. Mr. Shourie, through this book, tried his best with instances and documentary evidence to prove that Dr. B. R. Ambedkar was not the real architect of the constitution. His efforts to prove that Dr. Ambedkar was not the real architect of the constitution started sometime in 1996 firstly through syndicated articles in various newspapers in English as well as language newpapers and finally culminated in the shape of the above controversial book. Even before that the Sangh Parivar had also started finding faults with the constitution and for the same the constitution has come under their severe attack from different angles and for different reasons. Their efforts jointly with Shourie coincided with the manifesto of BJP declaring the review of Constitution if elected to power. And finally, NDA Governemnt appointed the Constitution Review Commission soon after within a year of their taking over the reigns of power at Centre. That was the urgency for them. Arun Shourie also got his reward in the shape of ministerial berth in the Vajpayee Governemnt for his loyal and committed service to the Sangh Parivar in the nature of his denouncing Dr. Ambedkar's contribution through his writings. He had also criticised reservations for SC/ST through his syndicated articles in various newspapers, - English as well as language newspapers.

Ever since Dr. Ambedkar came to be recognised and honoured as the architect of Indian Constitution, this was very difficult for *Sangh Parivar* and *Brahminical* society to digest that an *Untouchable Shudra* has been regarded as the architect of Indian constitution in this country of *Manu - Maharaj*. The preparations were afoot for a long time to displace Dr. Ambedkar from the seat of architect of the Constitution !

The first ever opportunity the *Sangh Parivar* could search out was in the demolition of Babri Masjid on 6th December, 1992. This was the 37th Mahaparinirwan Day (Death Anniversary) of Dr. Ambedkar. The *Sangh Parivar* wanted to protest against the Constitution of Ambedkar on his very Death Anniversary and send a message to the followers of Dr. Ambedkar and other secularists in the country that they did not respect or accept Dr. Ambedkar's Constitution. Later on K. S. Sudershan, Sarsanghchalak of RSS demanded at Nagpur to scrap the present constitution. And for that they selected the 6th December, the Day for denouncing the Doctor's Constitution ! As a law giver they do not accept any other than their Manu Maharaj !! In the same way the Vajpayee Government selected 11th May, the Buddha Jayanti Day for Atomic Explosion and termed it *"the Buddha smiled"*. On the very same Birth Anniversary of Buddha, the apostle of peace, love, compassion and whose message of international friendship and brotherhood has been the corner-stone of our foreign policy; the BJP led Vajpayee Government guided and managed by the *Sangh Parivar* struck the whole world by nuclear explosion on Buddha Jayanti and the entire world got a different message ! That was the treatment meted out to Buddha and Dr. Ambedkar by the communalists. Both the acts conceived, planned, designed and executed at proper occasion with a view to send a message to the Indian people that they do not accept the Constitution of Dr. Ambedkar or they don't have any regards for his contribution.

There is much relevance in the demolition of the Babri Masjid and burning of *Manusmriti* by Dr. Ambedkar on 25th December, 1928. Through burning of *Manusmriti,* the so-called sacred scripture of communalists, Dr. Ambedkar had sent a message to his peopple that he did not believe in the rules of Manu Maharaj as the same were partial, discriminatory and deny the Shudras and Ati-Shudras their dues. To retaliate and repudiate the same attack, the *Hindutvavadis* selected the 6th December, the Mahaparnirwan Day of Dr. Ambedkar not hurly-burly, but with a definite purpose and after full thought given to it !!

The demolition of Babri Masjid was a symbolic attack on the Constitution of India and on its architect. The Kalyan Singh Government of BJP-Sangh Parivar, despite their giving an assurance to the Supreme Court of India, Parliament of India and the National Integration Council, to protect the Babri Masjid structure, they demolished it. That was one of the chapters of big conspiracy of *Sangh Parivar.*

Arun Shourie's story is another chapter of Sanghi conspiracy. He was entrusted with the job of defaming Dr. Ambedkar in context to his contribution to the freedom struggle of the country and through such insinuations to denounce and challenge his authorship of the Constitution.

He was also associated with the World Bank as an Executive before he joined Indian Express as an Executive Editor. As an Executive Editor of Indian Express during the struggle of Ramnath Goenka with Indira Government, when he wrote a number of investigative stories he came into the limelight. Afterwards, his colleagues in the Express exposed that the entire material was collected by them and he used the same in his own name ! He has been closely associated with the *Sangh Parivar* as their intellectual spokesman propagating their view points through his writings. Not directly but indirectly, his job is to defend the *Sanghi* intellectual thinking.

Arun Shourie in his book - Worshipping False Gods made it a point that there was no contribution of Dr. Ambedkar in the Constitution making. He has given large number of instances, incidents and contexts to support his point of view. However, all those incidents, contexts, and instances have been interpreted by him with the biased attitude. All those who question the contribution of Dr. Ambedkar to the national freedom struggle must keep in mind that there were two parallel freedom struggles being fought in this country in those days.

One was to liberate our country - India i.e. Bharat from the clutches of British Government. The other one was to set free the millions of downtrodden from the slavery of *Varnashram Social System* of Hinduism under which they were suffering for thousands of years. One was the struggle for political power, the other one was to liberate the oppressed and exploited humanity. The one was to enjoy the political power and luxuries. The other one was to make them at least to live like human beings, who were compelled by *Chaturvarnya social system* to live like less than animals. The one was to assert all the powers and prove one's supremacy. The other one was for equality, self-respect and humanitarian life. One was led by the Brahmins and Banias of this country. The other one was led by the Shudras and Ati-Shudras for their emancipation from the slavery of Brahmins and Banias.

Dr. Ambedkar was the leader of Shudras and Ati-Shudras Lokamanya Tilak, Mahatma Gandhi and Jawaharlal Nehru were the leaders of Brahmins and Banias. For Brahmins and Banias there was only one enemy - the Britishers. But for the Shudras and Ati-Shudras there were two enemies - the High Caste Hindus who were their oppressors and exploiters for centuries and secondly, the Britishers, who were ruling over them through the same very Brahmins and Banias.

There was nothing wrong when Dr. Ambedkar opted to lead the struggle of millions of Shudras and Ati-Shudras - touchables and untouchables. The reason, at least, at that time, the enemy of the enemy was in power and there was nothing wrong to seek the help of the enemy of the enemy for liberation of his own people who were neglected, deprived, oppressed and exploited by the same Brahmins and Banias for thousands of years. And for their emanicipation whatever Dr. Ambedkar could do by whatever the means and methods available to him at that time, all that was justifiable and in the best interests of Dalit Shoshit Samaj. As such to brand Dr. Ambedkar as a "stooge of Britishers or blame him for joining the Viceroy's Executive Council is sheer foolishness and it reflects their indignition, callous and biased attitude of those who never missed an opportinity to criticise him on this or that count. To Dr. Ambedkar the upliftment of the Untouchables - the Shudras and Ati-Shudras and to make them live the honourable life with self-respect like any other human being, was the most important task. It was definitely more important than the struggle of independence. It was no less than the struggle of independence for the Depressed Classes people - the neglected lot, who were deprived of all their human rights. They were not allowed to take education, to bear arms and had no property. By all means this Hinduism had made their life more than miserable and pitiable. No community, no people or no society in the world has been subjected to such terrible subjugation as the untouchables were subjected to in this country !!

If Mahatma Gandhi, Jawaharlal Nehru and Subhas Chandra

Bose are the heroes of freedom struggle for political power, Dr. Ambedkar had a place in the socio-political history of India as the liberator of millions of untouchables - Shudras and Ati-Shudras. Thus, his contribution to the liberation of this country can not be minimised. And he never hid his real intention, his only and the only goal was liberation of untouchables from the slavery of *Chaturvana Social System.* When he was elected the Chairman of the Drafting Committee, it was undoubtedly a great honour bestowed upon him as an untouchable by caste but he did not hide his real intention and said:

> "I came to the Constituent Assembly with no greater aspiration than to safeguard the interests of the scheduled castes. I had not the remotest idea that I would be called upon to undertake more responsible function. I was, therefore, greatly surprised when the Assembly elected me to the Drafting Committee. I was more than surprised when the Drafting Committee elected me to be its Chairman"[25]

This statement of Dr. Ambedkar must be sufficient counter reply for his critics. But it was not that much only. When he was pushed to the wall to break his head by the 'Fast-unto-death' by Mahatma Gandhi and his life was in constant danger by the communal and criminal conspiracy of Mahatma Gandhi to win the lost war, after declaration of the Communal Award by British Prime Minister in favour of the Depressed Classes, he very clearly and firmly told all those who pleaded with him on behalf of Mahatmaji to save his life and accede to their proposal:

> "But I tell you I shall not deter from my pious duty, and betray the just and legitimate interest of my people even if you hang me on the nearest lamp-post in the street. You better appeal to Gandhi to postpone his fast about a week and then seek for the solution of the problem".[26]

Dr. Ambedkar, all through his life had only one motto and that was how to uplift his people and how to make them live the life of honour and self-rspect. For that, by whatever scheme and method he could benefit his people, he did it. His main attempt, however, was to get political rights for his people in order to bring about a fundamental change in the existing social system. As such he said to Mahatma Gandhi :

> "If in my endevour to secure human rights for my people, who have been trampled upon in this country for ages, I do any disservice to this country, it would not be sin; and if any harm does not come to this country through my action, it may be due to my conscience. Owing to the promptings of my concience I have been striving to win human rights for my people without meaning or doing any harm to this country".[27]

But he was not unfaithful or disloyal to his country. Otherwise, he could have thought of a separate and independent State for the untouchables ! Like Jinha, he could have also planned a separatist movement. But he was rank nationalist. He was the most committed to the ideals of this country. The ideals of Buddha, Kabir and Jyotiba Phule. Therefore, speaking in the Constituent Assmebly on 25th November 1949, he said:

> " .... But my mind is so full of the future of our country that I feel I ought to take this occasion to give expression to some of my reflections thereon. On 26th January 1950, India will be an independent country. What would happen to her independence ? Will she maintain her independence or will she lose it again ? This is the first thought that comes to my mind. It is not that India was never an independent country. The point is that she once lost the independence she had. Will she lose it a second time ? It is this thought which makes me most anxious for the future. What perturbs me greatly is the fact that not only India has once before lost her independence, but she lost it by the infidelity and treachery of some of her own people. In the invasion of Sindh by Mohammed-Bin-Kasim, the military commanders of King Dehar accepted bribes from the agents of Mohammed-Bin-Kasim and refused to fight on the side of the king. It was Jaichand who invited Mohammed Ghori to invade India and fight

against Prithvi Raj and promised the help of himself and the Solanki Kings. When Shivaji was fighting for the liberation of Hindus, the other Maratha noblemen and the Rajput Kings were fighting the battle on the side of Moghul Emperors. When the British were trying to destroy the Sikh Rulers, Gulab Singh their principal commander sat silent and did not help to save the Sikh kingdom. In 1857 when a large part of India had declared war of independence against the British, the Sikhs stood and watched the event as silent spectators.

"Will history repeat itself? It is this thought which fills me with anxiety. This anxiety deepened by the realisation of the fact that in addition to our old enemies in the form of castes and creeds we are going to have many political parties with diverse and opposing political creeds. Will Indians place the country above their creed or will they place creed above country ? I do not know. But this much is certain that if the parties place creed above country, our independence will be put in jeopardy a second time and probably be lost for ever. This eventuality we must all resolutely guard against. We must be determined to defend our independence with the last drop of our blood".[28]

Mr. Arun Shourie's agony is that despite all the best efforts made by *Manuvadis* and *Brahminism* to defame Dr. Ambedkar, firstly as the stooge of Britishers and secondly, his non-involvement in the national freedom movement, there was no adverse effect on the increasing popularity and numbers of Ambedkar's followers. That was really a great blow to their conspiracy ! As such Arun Shourie was entrusted with the job to finally counter Dr. Ambedkar's claim as the architect of Indian Constitution. This was another severe ecommunal attack on the Indian Constitution.

Arun Shourie's charge against Dr. Ambedkar's being the architect of Indian Constitution can be summarised as follows :

(1) Dr. Ambedkar opposed the constituting of Constituent Assembly;
(2) Though Dr. Ambedkar was the Chairman of the

Drafting Committee, it was B. N. Rau and not Ambedkar who prepared the Draft Constitution;

(3) The provisions of the Constitution were approved by voting and that confirms that it was no free hand for Dr. Ambedkar. Therefore, his question - 'Who is the author when decision are by votes ?'

(4) It was the joint efforts of all leaders and not by Dr. Ambedkar alone.

(5) During the freedom struggle all along Dr. Ambedkar was on the side of Britishers.

In his book—*Worshipping False Gods,* at one place he wrote :

"But I am not on the amnesia that would be natural to a person who had been with the British all those decades during which the others were struggling for preciously those very rights, I am not on his version of his history either. I am only on the texts of those successive reports and resolutions and lists they had incorporated of the rights which Indians must have.

And, please remember the antecedents of the provisions on Fundamental Rights are just one set of examples, the geneology of other parts of the constitution - in particular, as we shall see, of the structure itself - can be traced just as easily. That being the case, is one person the author or what the Constitution contains ?"[29]

At another place he stated :

> "When this is how proposals were considered, recommendations finalised, and decisions taken - by discussion, by repeated revisions and reconsideration by votes - who is to be annoited as the author of the Constitution ?"[30]

Shourie is also upset that there are more and more statues of Dr. Ambedkar coming up in all corners of the country than any of the leaders of the freedom struggle. He is also very much upset that the Govt. of Maharashtra has published Dr. Ambedkar's all the writings and speeches in consolidated way. He is also terribly upset by the increasing say of Dr. Ambedkar's followers in the Indian politics. It is also really a heart-burning for these Gandhians that no more he could command the political dictates single handedly as they did during independence struggle and exploit the situation in their favour.

As explained earlier as to why Dr. Ambedkar did not participate actually in the freedom struggle and why did he opt to lead the movement of the untouchables, the oppressed and exploited people of this country. As far as the question of authorship of the Constitution is concerned, there needs hardly any other explaination than what T. T. Krishnamachari, who was also in the Constituent Assembly and who observed highly about the contribution of Dr. Ambedkar in the making of Indian Constitution : He Said, :

> "Sir, I am one of those in the House who have listened to Dr. Ambedkar very carefully. I am aware of the amount of work and enthusiasm that he brought to bear on the work of drafting this Constitution. At the same time I do realise that that amount of attention was necessary for the purpose of drafting a Constitution so important to us at this moment has not been given to it by the Drafting Committee. The House is perhaps aware that of the seven members nominated by you, one had resigned from the House and was replaced. One died and was not replaced. One was away in America and his place was not filled up and another person was engaged in State affairs and there was a void to that extent. One or two people were far away from Delhi and perhaps reasons of health did not permit them to attend. So it happened ultimately that the burden of drafting this Constitution fell on Dr. Ambedkar and I have no doubts that we are grateful to him for having achieved this task in a manner which is undoubtedly commendable ...."(31)

Though people of India recognised his services and his contribution and showered the praises and compliments upon him, he never boasted that he was the architect of the Constitution. Responding to the compliments and praises showered on him, he said :

> "The credit that is given to me does not really belong to me. It belongs partly to Sir B. N. Rau, the

> Constitutional Advisor to the Constituent Assembly who prepared a rough Draft of the Constitution for the consideration of the Drafting Committee. A part of the credit must go to the members of the Drafting Committee, who as I have said, have sat for 141 days and without whose ingenuity to devise new formulae and capacity to tolerate and to accommodate different point of view, the task of framing the Constitution could not have come to so succesful a conclusion. Much greater share of the credit must go to Mr. S. N. Mukherjee, the Chief Draftsman of the Constitution ...."[32]

India got freedom in 1947. Thousands and thousands of people sacrificed their lives for the independence of India. But why only the name of Mahatma Gandhi is recognised as undisputed leader of freedom struggle ? Indian Army defeated Pakistani soldiers in 1971 Bangla War and made 95,000 Pakistani soldiers to surrender but why Bharat Ratna was awarded to Smt. Indira Gandhi alone? Why Motilal Nehru Committee is known as Nehru Committee? Why Sarkaria Commission is known as Sarkaria Commission? Mr. Shourie is not a child that he does not understand that always organisation and team is recognised by the name of his head. But in this case it was not the mere name. Dr. Ambedkar laboured very hard. Mr. TTK, who himself was associated with the Drafting Committee has accepted his tremendous work in the Constitutent Assembly. And then it was left to the people of India to decide who is the real architect of Indian constitution and not to Arun Shourie or RSS !!

References

1. Principles of Political Science : A.C. Kapoor p. 325.
2. Keshwanand Bharti vs. State of Kerla (1973) 4-SCC-225.
3. Constitution Review Commission - Fruitless Pursuit : Justice Bhau Wahane p. 15.
4. The Constitution and the Constituent Assembly : A Lok Sabha Secretariat Publication p. 28.
5. The Shorter Constitution of India : Durga Das Basu p. 217
6. *Ibid.*
7. S.R. Bommai vs Union of India - AIR (1994) SC - 1919.

8. Hitvada (English Daily from Nagpur) dt. 22/3/2000.
9. Frontline : dt 7/7/2000 Interview with Venkitesh Ramkrishnan
10. Frontline dt. May 7, 1993.
11. *Ibid.*
12. The Hindu, Sunday June 7, 1998 (Secularism And its Critics - edited by Rajiv Bhargava, Oxford University Press - Review).
13. *Ibid.*
14. Frontline, March 3, 2000 p. 30.
15. The Oppressed Indian (monthly journal from New Delhi) January 1982.
16. The Constitution and the Constituent Assembly : A Lok Sabha Secretariate Publication p. 108, 109.
17. B.R. Ambedkar : Quest for Social Justice : A.M. Rajsekhriah p. 192.
18. *Ibid.*
19. The Times of India (Mumbai) dt. April 13, 1976.
20. The Hindu (New Delhi) dt. March 16, 1998.
21. *Ibid.*
22. The Constitution and the Constituent Assembly p. 122, 123.
23. Shorter Constitution of India : Durga Das Basu p. 1142, 1143.
24. Minerva Mills vs Union of India - AIR (1980) SC - 1789.
25. Thus Spoke Dr. Ambedkar - Vol. II p. 173.
26. Dr. Ambedkar : Life and Mission, Dhanahjay Keer p. 208, 167.
27. *Ibid.*
28. Dr. Babasaheb Ambedkar : Writings and Speeches Vol - 13, p. 1213 and 1214.
29. Worshipping False Gods : Arun Shourie p. 484, 485, 466.
30. *Ibid.*
31. Dr. Babasaheb Ambedkar : Writings and Speeches Vol. 13 p. 72, 1208, 1209.
32. *Ibid.*

5
Indian Culture Under Hindutvawadi Attack

Professor K.N. Panikkar, who teaches history at prestigious Jawaharlal Nehru University of New Delhi and who has also authored several history books, while addressing a meeting, organised by Safdar Hashmi Memorial Trust on 13th April, 2000 in New Delhi, observed that "the Sangh had been trying to acquire social power through cultural avenues". However, on a optimistic note, he said, the attacks on cultural front had seen a "spontaneous secular reassertion which is an important way of resisting the march of Hindu communalism".[1]

Nobel laureate Amartya Sen, speaking at the 61st and 'Millennium' Indian History Congress on 2nd January, 2001 at Kolkata launched a subtle, and scathing attack on the Sangh Parivar and the rightist forces for "trying to misguide and brainwash the people", and attempting to "rewrite history and destroy the very entity that is India".

Prof. Sen's message to those arguing that Lord Rama was born at the exact spot where the Babri Masjid stood was clear : "It is not history that they are misusing but fables, myths and legends that are being called 'history' and then misused".[2]

Prof. Panikkar and Dr. Amartya Sen's scathing attack on the initiative by the RSS and its off-shoot organisations to distort India's composite culture to their communal advantage and project it as they see to it is nothing but a step towards creating a fascist state.

What is Culture ?

According to E. B. Taylor, one of the early anthropologists, 'culture had a meaning more immaterial and less utilitarian. It is that complex whole which includes knowledge, belief, arts, morals, law, custom and any other capabilities and habits acquired by man as a member of society'.[3] C.C. North defines it as 'consisting in the instruments constituted by man to assist him in satisfying his wants'. Among these instruments, in which culture is taken to consist, Folcom includes material elements and skills, symbolic elements of social structure and sentimental elements or social values'.[4]

"The satisfaction derived by man from the interplay with his environment are not only confined to the objects produced therefrom; but they also extend to the ways and patterns in which they have been produced. Hence together with the objects and things that man applies to his own personal uses there is the great variety of customs, folk ways, traditions, ideologies, institutions and techniques which, though in some ways derived from the interplay of man with his environment, in their turn facilitate, hinder, or otherwise modify this very interplay. This complex whole of objects and ways of behaviour of material and immaterial interests and satisfaction, has been designated by early and modern anthropologists by the name of culture".[5] This idea of culture does not imply that it is an artificial accomplishment of man. On the contrary, many of man's needs, aspirations and institutions are but the spontaneous expressions of his nature, realised in time and space, seeking to satisfy these needs in a multiplicity of ways. Hence the radical universality of the fundamental trails of culture together with the diversity of their manifestation. Thus, for example, appetite for food is natural to man, though the kind of food, the way of preparing and taking it is conventional and artificial; similarly, language is natural to man but the particular language that one speaks is the product of history and circumstances. Culture itself is natural, but its type and manifestations depend on certain conditions environmental as well as social and psychological".[6]

Further, 'Culture is the direct expression of our nature; in our ways of thought and action in art, religion, morality, and recreation. It deals with interests and values conceived as ends, to which various actions and objects are directed as means'.[7] In Mathew Arnold's words, 'Culture is the study of perfection, and of harmonious perfection; general perfection and perfection which consists in becoming something, rather than in having something, in an inward condition of the mind and spirit, not in an outward set of circumstances'.[8]

Thus, it would be observed that culture is related with the outward relations of man with man, society with society and community with community. It denotes what we are and what we must have. "The cultural activities of man are in the last resort the spontaneous and free expression of his personality manifest through his valuations and are ultimately directed to the possession of truth, goodness, and beauty in whose pursuit man realises himself. Thus, man's cultural interests thrive better in a free than regimented society; better where there is security and mobility than where there is fear and strife".[9]

Judged on the basis of above statement and explanation, we can simply say that culture is the outcome of man's outward reflections urged and regulated by inner voice. Man desires to look better by dress, postures and what he speaks. That shows his efforts how best civilised he appears. Rites, rituals, customs and traditions are important factors to shape the cultural activities. A society, a community, a nation is also recognised by the culture, the people or the constituents of that society project.

Individual Culture *vs* Composite Culture

The Right to Freedom of Religion is one of the fundamental rights. Art 25 of our Constitution guarantees every citizen of India the freedom of conscience and right to profess, practice and propagate religion of his choice subject to certain conditions.

"Subject to the restrictions which this Article imposes, every person has a fundamental right under our Constitution, not merely to entertain such religious belief as may be approved of by his judgement or conscience but to exhibit his belief and ideas in such overt acts as are enjoined or sanctioned by his religion and further to propagate his religious views for the edification of others".[10]

According to Article 29 of the Constitution, -

(1) Any section of the citizens residing in the territory of India or any part there of having a distinct language, script or culture of its own shall have the right to conserve the same.

(2) No citizen shall be denied admision into any educational institution maintained by the State or receiving aid out of State Funds on

> grounds of religion, race, caste, language or any of them".

It could be observed from clause 1 of the Art. 29 that if there is a cultural minority which wants to preserve its language, script and culture , the State shall not impose upon it any other culture which may be local or otherwise. Thus, every community, tribe or society having distinct existence has a fundamental right to manage its own affairs in matters of religion, language, culture etc.

Culture of any community or society is very important factor indicating its status in socio-religious context and it also works like a barometer of development of that community. Anything, right or wrong, existing in that society is their personal problem and only they - as community, have right to set it right provided such problem does not spoil or become a national hurdle : customs, traditions, ideologies, rites and rituals and institutional bindings though in some ways derive from the interplay of man with his environment facilitate, hinder or modify whole of his objects and behaviour, neverthless it is their own prerogative, fundamental right to fashion their ways and behaviour. And when this prerogative or previlege, right to have their own ways, their distinct existence is threatened, there is bound to be spontaneous reaction visible in the form of mass movement or peaceful agitation.

As long as the affairs of the community or a particular society are concerned, it is their domain. But when it comes to national scenario, it reflects the whole-sum total of all communities or societies. To outside world we are known as Indian culture. It is immaterial for outside India as to how a particular community behaves within the country. But when somebody looks at it as Indian affairs, it is recognised as Indian.

We in India are different communities, different religions, following different rites, customs, traditions, languages. But beyond the borders we are one-united, only Indians - *Bhartwasis*. It is unique example in the world that despite so many deversities in language, religion, caste, creed and rites, we are best known as unity in diversity. No language, no religion or no caste and class has ever come in the way of our unity as and when we had to face problem beyond the border. No Jaichand nor Mir Jaffer has ever emerged on such occasion. For thousands of years,

India - that is Bharat, could maintain its distinct identity, a nation united and strong. That is the strength of Indian culture.

Mosques and Mandirs were never the problem in our country. Ram and Rahim were two sides of the same culture. Hindus as well as Muslims have the same regard and respect for Kabir and Sai Baba. The Mazar of *Malang Shah Baba* (Kalyan - near Mumbai) was equally a place of importance and worship for both Hindus andMuslims till few years back. Muslims maintained their independence and distinct identity. They have their own rites and rituals, customs and traditions. There was no interference in their religious affairs. So did the Sikhs, Hindus, Jainis, Buddhists and Parsis. The Constitution never came in their way to put the hurdles in their personality development. Our's has been a cosmopolitan culture - all inclusive - the Indian culture - *Bhartiya Sanskriti* ! Indian art, theatre, music, dance and all that make Indian culture rich, vivid and wholesome, has never been a subject of controversy. Bharat Ratna Bismilla Khan commands the same respect and regard of all those Indians who also regard and respect Bharat Ratna Lata Mangeshkar ! Indian audience is equally enthralled by the Ghazals of Mehendi Ali Khan as well as Pankaj Udhas. Cine star Dilip Kumar alias Yusuf Khan, Dev Anand and Raj Kapoor have been loved and applauded immensely by the cinegoers for the last more than 50 years. They did not find any difference between trajedy queen Meena Kumari and ever charming Madhuri Dixit. Film producers Sanjay Khan and Rakesh Roshan performed marriage of their daughter and son (Hritik Roshan) both as per Hindu as well as Muslim rituals. This is the Indian culture- our culture ! It has thousands of years legacy ! Never it was in dispute !!

Indian Culture Under Communal Attack

It was on 6th December 1992 when India's composite culture : Hindu-Muslim Bhai-Bhai slogan came to be torn into number of pieces. More than four hundred years old dome of Hindu-Muslim cultural unity and integrity was demolished at one stroke in the presence of BJP and RSS leaders, the guardians of Bhartiya Sanskriti- L.K. Advani, M. M. Joshi and thrown to pieces. And Shiv Sena Chief Balasaheb Thakre exclaimed - *I am proud of my boys !* Instead of feeling shame-shame, sorry and regret he poured out the poison of hate-divide in our great Indian culture! That was the darkest day in the history of Hindu-Muslim unity! *Ram* became the tool in the hands of so-called protagonists of Hinduism to divide India into two segments. Hundreds and hundreds of Hindus and Muslims became the targets of bullets as well as bombs. The dome of Hindu-Muslim unity fell, falling many a number of human-beings!!

Emboldened by the excessive assertion in the aftermath of Babri Masjid demolition, the *Fascists* elements, in the persons of protagonists of Hinduism or saviours of Hinduism, begin to zoom like victors in the war. After1989-Riddles of Hinduism episode, when Shiv Sena staged a big protest march against the publication of Riddles and more than equally counter offensive by the Ambedkarites in Mumbai in support of Riddles, it was another episode that shook Mumbai terribly. Vengeful action of *Hindutvavadis* in 1992 was countered with equal force by way of bomb-blasts killing thousands of innocents !

The repeated hooliganism of the so-called protagonists of Hinduism and Hindutvavadi culture and in-action of the *Saffronised Sarkar* of U.P. had proved beyond doubt the real intention of the State Government.

The *Ved Parayan Kendram* and *Kashi Sanskriti Raksha Sangharsh Samiti* which had compelled the owner of local cinema hall in Varanasi to remove two scenes from Yash Chopra's *Mohabbatein* was yet another fascist move after disturbing the shooting of Deepa Mehta's controversial film *'Water'*. Why? Because in the first incident the recitation of *Gayatri Mantra* by Amitabh Bachchan with his shoes on was being viewed as an affront to Bhartiya (Hindutva) Sanskriti. Forcing to comply the others as per the dictates of Dharma and arrogating to compel for the same is nothing but violation of the law of the land.

Disturbing of shooting of 'Water' (film) on the banks of Ganga at Varanasi is another rowdy example of extremists of the so-called Hindutvavadi culture. 'Although Deepa Mehta obtained Centre's clearance, the Uttar Pradesh government denied her permission to film in Varanasi'. The 500 strong mob under the banner of the *Kashi Sanskriti Raksha Sangharsh Samiti,* which includes members of *Sangh Pariwar* - tore down and later burnt a part of the wooden set erected at Tulsi Ghat. Chanting slogans like - *'Tirthsthan ka aapman nahi sahega Hindustan'* (India will not tolerate the insult of holy places), the demonstrators vowed to halt shooting"[11]

The reasons, the protestors say that the film on the widows of Varanasi of the 30's vilifies Indian culture by presenting some widows as prostitutes. For many protestors, the film title itself was an insult : Water, they felt, was too simplistic a term for the holy Ganga river.[12] "There are many things which even if true, should not be talked about", asserted Giriraj Kishore (of Vishwa Hindu Parishad). The film is a deliberate attempt to defame Hindu institutions. In the name of communal harmony, such films should neither be made, nor screened"[13]

Seshadri Chari of *Organiser*, English mouth piece of *Sangh Pariwar* and advisor of Sanskar Bharati, one of the off-shoots of RSS, concerned exclusively with culture, declared on the occasion that, "Film makers, writers and artists should not transgress the limits of what the society, they are working within consider permissible".[14] Though on the one hand he says that - "RSS does not believe in laying down any cultural policy and creativity arises out of inner convictions, which cannot be dictated by policy", on the other hand his version that, "we have to live with the fact that our society is very sensitive on certain matters" must remind him that why that very society is averse to see what do they do and what does happen in the society. Literature is the mirror of what happens in the society. We should not forget that, that is an opportunity to introspect when we view a particular incident being performed by the artists on the stage or in film. This helps to mend and correct what we committed against the normal humane and moral values.

In Maharashtra what *Krantijyoti Savitribai Phule* did for the orphaned babies born to the young widows of Brahmin community, who were forbidden for remarriage after the death of their husbands at young age, see the heineous crimes committed by the people of the so-called high caste society of that time. The number of children born out of illegitimate sexual relations with the young widow Brahmin girls, took shelter in the orphanage of Savitribai - Jyotiba Phule. Even one of the prominent social leaders of the time Justice Ranade remarried a young girl comparatively of his daughter's age after the death of his wife. But he, too, could not dare remarry a widow. This happened in the same very society to which Giriraj Kishore and Sheshadri Chari represent.

If the film makers or the writers project such stories

through their writings, novels, dramas or films, what is wrong with that? Why are we afraid to see the sins committed by our own fore-fathers? Sexual misuse of widows in the Ashrams of many a number of known Sadhus and Sanyasis is not new. The columns and columns of national news papers are full of such stories. So, should not the writers / dramatists and film makers have the right to expose such dubious and heineous systems? How long to allow such things to operate in the society? Its exposure is the best way to put an halt to such incidents or create awakening and reduce the incidence.

Our Constitution has given us the right to Freedom of Speech and expression.

(1) According to Article 19 (1) (a)[15] Freedom means the right to express one's convictions and opinions freely, by word of mouth, writing, printing, picture or electronic media, or in any other manner (addressed to the eyes or the ears). It would thus include not only the freedom of the Press, but the expression of one's ideas by any visible representation, such as by gesture and the likes. Expression, naturally, presupposes a second party to whom the ideas are expressed or communicated. In short, freedom of expression includes the freedom of propagation of ideas, their publication and circulation and the right to answer the criticism levelled against such views; the right to acquire and import ideas and information about matters of common interest. It would not, however, include every concomitant right except where, in a given case, it forms an integral part of the exercise of the named fundamental right.

2. It is indespensable for the operation of the democratic system.

3. Like the other freedoms cl (1) (a) referes to common law right of freedom of expression and does not apply to any right created by statute, e.g., the right to contest an election, which is to be excercised subject to the restriction imposed by the statute.

4. In order to be justified as a valid restriction upon any of the rights guaranteed by cl (1) not only should such restrictions be related to any of the permissible ground

enumerated in the relevant limitation clause, but it must be reasonable.

5. Freedom of expression is a preferred right very zealously guarded by the Supreme Court. A citizen has a right to produce movies or to exhibit films on the Doordarshan which is part of the freedom of expression.

The relevant provisions of the Constitution have been interpreted by the highest court of the land accordingly. Despite such abundant constitutional support the extremist actions of the so-called *Hindu (Kashi) Sanskriti Raksha Sangharsh Samiti* or many other off-shoot organisations of RSS in the name of and for the cause of Hinduism and *Hindutvavadi* culture is doing nothing but to terrorise and destroy the sanctity of the Constitution and rule of law.

Film *Mohabbatein* is not an isolated example, misused by the so-called saviours of the *Hindutvavadi* culture to comply with their designs. There are many more examples. The *Chaddi-Banian* (Nicker-Banian) protest march in front of the house of cine star Dilip Kumar by the Shiv Sainiks of Balasaheb Thakre crossed all the limits of decency. His fault? He spoke in favour of 'FIRE' purely in artistic way, and only in support of art. For Bollywood is not short of anecdotes relating to the forceful deletion of scenes or dialogues, alteration of names like Radha and Sita, modification in the title Kaliyug Aur Ramayan worse still is intervention of ministers and politicians .... The problem with all such protests, according to writer Kamleshwar, is that the fringe elements get vocal and seem to articulate public opinion,, because the majority remains silent and does not bother to make a noise ...."[16]

As per the ruling of the Supreme Court of India in Rangarajan vs Jagjivan (1989) S.C.J. 128, "A citizen has a right to produce movies or to exhibit films on the Doordarshan which is part of the freedom of expression". Ever since the Centre has been taken over by the BJP led NDA Govt. the *Sanghi* paratroopers have started jumping on each and every issue in the name of *Hindutva* culture and arrogated to themselves the role of concious-keeper. This has totally destroyed the fabric of rule of law and it is an indicator of the future plan of things to come.

Education: Changing Colour and Concept Under NDA Government

'The term education comes from the Latin *educare* which literally means *bring up* and is connected with the verb *educere* which means to bring forth .... Plato held that the end of education was 'to develop in the body and in the soul (of the pupil) all the beauty and all the perfection of which they are capable or to develop in short 'a sound mind in a sound body'[17] According to Aristotle, education meant 'to develop man's faculties, especially his mind so that he may be able to enjoy the contemplation of the supreme truth, goodness and beauty in which perfect happiness essentially consists'.[18]

According to Radhakrishan Report on University Education, "The purpose of all education, it is admitted by thinkers of East and West, is to provide a coherent picture of the Universe and an integrated way of life', and this cannot be a collection of distracting scraps but should be a harmony of pattern .... As regards the education of any man as a member of a particular nation or society, he must be not only acquainted with its history and traditions, but also identified with what is good in its aspirations, hopes and way of life .... The education of an individual as member of his society, is not independent from his condition as a member of human race and of international society.... Besides the pertinent knowledge of international conventions or rules, with which particular persons may be concerned everybody needs a special training as man; by which he may develop the best that is in himself, his intellectual, volitional, social, moral and asthetic powers, so that in future contacts between nation and nation may no longer be similar to the clashing of two conflicting but to the meeting of two friends parties"[19]

The original idea of education during the period of Plato and Aristotle was 'to bring up' and 'develop in the body and soul all beauty' or 'sound mind in sound body'. If mind is sound, automatically the body takes sound shape. Sound means to develop all faculties of a person so that he is capable of taking the sound decision - right or wrong.

The concept of education from 'sound mind in sound body' developed into an advanced stage of to understand and interpret 'coherent picture of the Universe and integrated way of life' so that the human relations becomes harmoneous. The basic purpose of education as it was interpreted by the great thinkers, not only to develop sound mind in sound body or understand the coherent picture of Universe, but 'man as a member of particular nation or society, he must be acquainted with its history, sociology, politics and what is good and what is bad, as well as what is in the national interest. Knowing fully well that man does not live in isolation or independently, he needs to interact with the persons in the similarly situated nations and for that he must know the international rules not for conflicts and confrontation but for mutual understanding and reciprocal responses.

According to Cardinal Newman, it is education which gives a man a clear conscious view of his own opinions and judgements a truth in developing them, an eloquence in expressing them, and a force in urging them. It teaches him to see the things as they are, to go right to the point to disentagle a skein of thought, to detect what is sophistical and to discard what is irrelavent. It prepares him to fill any post with credit and to master any subject with facility. It shows him how to accommodate himself to others, how to throw himself into their state of mind, how to bring before them his own, how to influence them, how to come to an understanding with them, how to bear with them.... he knows when to speak and when to be silent, he is able to converse, he is able to listen, he knows when to be serious and when to trifle and he has a sure fact which enables him to trifle with gracefulness and to be serious with effect ...."[20]

Speaking of the spirit that the citizens of modern India should develop in the present circumstances the necessity of training Indians in the democratic way of life to which India is fully committed; the Mudliyar Report on Secondary Education (1952) stresses :

> "Citizenship in a democracy is a very exacting and challenging responsibility for which every citizen has to be carefully trained. It involves many intellectual, social and moral qualities which connot be expected to grow of their own accord. *In any kind of regimented social order, the individual does not need to indulge in the travail of independent thinking....* But in a

> democracy - if it is more than the thoughtless exercise of the vote - an individual must form his own independent judgement on all kinds of complicated social, economic and political issues and to a large extent, decides his own course of action".[21]

One of the basic objectives of education in India according to Mudliyar Commission Report, is the necessity of training Indians to meet the challenges of democratic way of life to which we Indians are committed fully. This is possible only when an individual is prepared in such a way, right from his childhood, that he is able to form his own independent judgement on all sorts of issues including social, political and economic. This is not possible in such a system where his entire being is regulated in some sort of regimented order. That is what happened in Hitler's Germany and Mussolini's Italy.

Our Constitution has declared a Secular Democratic Socialist Republic for us.That is why Mudliyar Commission Report has suggested such sort of education for our people which can meet the challenge of demoratic way of life. It must also be a secular education. For us, in our Constitution, as pronounced by Justice K. Ramaswamy of the Supreme Court, writing the judgement in S. R. Bommai vs Union of India, 'Secularism is part of the fundamental law and basic structure of the Indian political system to secure to all its people socio-economic needs essential for man's excellence with material and moral prosperity and political justice'.[22]

Justice P.B. Sawant, along with Justice Kuldip Singh and Justice Pandian, in the same matter observed that :-

"The Preamble and Articles 25, 26, 29, 30, 44, 51-A, 14, 15, 16 by implication prohibit the establishment of a theocratic State and prevent the State either identifying itself with or favouring any particular religion or religious sect or denomination. The State is enjoined to accord equal treatment to all religions and religious sects and denominations. *Under our Constitution whatever be the attitude of the State towards the religion, religious sects and denominations, religion cannot be mixed with any secular activity of the State.* In fact, the encroachment of religion into secular activities is strictly prohibited. The State's tolerance of religion or religions does not make it either a religious or a theocratic State".[23]

Justice B.P. Jeevan Reddy for himself and on behalf of Justice S. C. Agrawal and Justice Pandian ruled in the same matter, refered to above :

> ".... In matters of State, religion has no place. No political party can simultaneously be a religious party. Politics and religion cannot be mixed. *Any State Government which pursues unsecular policies or unsecular course of action acts contrary to the Constitutional Mandate and renders itself amenable to action* under Art 356".

It could be observed from the above that no State activity would bear the colour of any religion or religious sect. Religion cannot be mixed with any secular activity of the State. Education is a State activity in India. It is responsibility of the State to plan, design and regulate all the educational activities right from pre-primary stage to the post-graduation level and all professional courses.

"As the educational system is so influential in the life of society it is not surprising that the State has always taken a special interest in it, though that has sometimes gone too far. As soon as a totalitarian regime gains control over a nation one of the first things it does is to bring under its sway the whole educational system and to transform the teachers into paid agents of the regimes".[24] That is what the present BJP-RSS led NDA Government has initiated to do.

Saffronisation of Education

Immediatly after taking over the reigns of power at the Centre, the NDA's Human Resource Development Minister Murli Manohar Joshi, a hard-core and conservative RSS functionary took over the charge of Education. The first and foremost task he did was that he replaced top-brasses of NCERT, which is the sole planning, designing and controlling agency of education at the Centre.

'The National Curriculam Framework for School Education released by Mr. Joshi on 14th Nov. 2000, on the eve of 'Bal Divas', Pandit Jawaharlal Nehru's birth day, has attracted widespread criticism, especially those relating to spirituality, religiosity, value education and indigestion of education .... The document pre-supposes an almost jingoistic superiority of India's tradition and culture over other's and seeks to reemphasise this all along. It also contains an uncritical study of globalisation. ... Inherent in the document is a sort of admiration for the rigid caste system that characterised agrarian India. It does not contain an iota of criticism of the repressive and exploitative structure that the system essentially represents.... The most damaging portions appear in the section on "social sciences", where there is a blatant attempt to do away with the study of history. The document states that in order to make the social sciences more meaningful, relevant and effective, the concerns and issues of the contemporary world need to be kept in the forefront. To this end, the quantum of history may have to be substantially reduced. Academics aver that this idea is so ludicrously epochal that it must have been the first time in the world that such a suggestion has been made. Past developments could be studied as a 'backdrop for understanding the present', the document says. This implies that history need not be studied for its lessons and its intrinsic worth.... In contrast, the 1988 document, National Curriculam for Elementary and Secondary Education - A framework, had implicitly stated that the teaching of history should be objective and free from any communal, parochial and other prejudices. It did not suggest any reduction in the quantum of history taught in the schools; in fact, it had highlighted the importance of the subject"[25]

"Teaching of social sciences ought to promote a human and national perspective and inculcate a sense of pride in the country and in being an Indian, states the new document. It is irrelevant to note that no such 'being an Indian' sentiment was mooted in the 1988 document, which in measured doses talked about the scientific study of social phenomenon and events to develop a genuine interest in, and an urge for, the preservation of what was good in Indian Culture and the improvment of the existing socio-economic cultural set-up".[26]

'NCERT's second document released on the same occasion under the title - *Journal of Value Education,* is the brain-child of the Education Secretary, M. K. Kaw, who has authored a chapter that leaves little doubt about the political inclinations of the author as also of the document .... The document laments that a "sizeable section of Indian society seems to have distanced itself from the religio-philosophic ethos, the awareness of the social design and the understanding of the heritage of the past. In the very first section titled - Context and Concerns, the sub-section 'Education for Value Development', states that another significant factor that merited urgent attention is religion.... It goes on to recommend a comparative study of the philosophies of all religions, which need to be inculcated at appropriate stages in education right from the primary school. The school academics have always maintained, is not the right place to teach the philosophies of various religions.... Given the secular and democratic polity of India all Education Commissions were aware of the dangers of over emphasising religion in any manners".[27]

The New Document prepared under the stewardship of Education Secretary M. K. Kaw has been totally an over-hauling attempt of educational system of the country. *Its main objective is to regiment the tender and young minds to subscribe to the saffron philosophy of Hindutva ideology at the later stage when they perform as the citizens of India. Every care has been taken to formally introduce Saffron soft corner for the coming generations. Denouncing other religions and highlighting the only Hindutvawadi religion, by writing that the greatest damage to our intellectual freedom has been caused by traditional religions, especially by those which have a single holy book from which they derive their authority. Here by pointing out single holy book indication the intention seems to single out Muslims and Christians for attack.*

Praful Bidwai, eminent writer and journalist, has, therefore, very rightly observed in his article "Prejudice as 'education' (Frontline, dated December 24, 1998) that, "If Human Resource Development Minister Murli Manohar Joshi has his way, our children and grandchildren will grow up believing that 'Hindu culture', as the *Sangh Pariwar* defines it, is the sole influence that has shaped India since the Vedic times. This culture, they will learn, has remained unchanged since time immemorial. All other cultures, civilizational influences and traditions are extraneous, 'impure', alien, not part of the Indian 'heritage'. They are at best only marginal to the values relevant to us. In this view, 'Bharatiya culture' is mankind's highest achievement. It is at once all encompassing but also infinitely tolerant".

Mr. Bidwai, further, commented that these 'discussion papers are reminiscent of the fatwas issued in Hitler's 'nationalism' among school children and to specify in the minutest detail what constitutes authentic 'German culture', why the idea of racial purity and the sacred nature of the Aryan 'master race' must never be questioned'.

And finally he concluded, 'It is of such stuff that Hindutva's education and culture project is made. This project is far more dangerous and insidious than the construction of the Ram temple. It involves manipulating minds, infiltrating hatred into them, encouraging them to think smugly in stereo - types, and making people's self-identity dependent on bigotry and false pride. Ultimately, the project means yoking the mind to a hateful, communal, nationalism - for generations to come'.

Perhaps, it was in that context that Pascual Gisbert, in his book - *Fundamentals of Sociology,* alerted that, *"As soon as a totalitarian regime gains control over a nation one of the first things it does is to bring under its sway the whole educational system and to transform the teachers into paid agents of the regime"*.... This unhealthy tendency is spreading in various forms even in democratic countries, though the phenomenon is not new". So also Praful Bidwai has timely warned the secular Indians that, *"This project is far more dangerous and insidious than the construction of the Ram temple"*.

The off-shoot of the RSS organisation—"Vidya Bharti, aim of which is to evolve an alternative model of education, to sensitise young minds to the cause, has already under its wing - 13,000 schools, 74,000 teachers and 17.5 lakh students right from the 'balwadi (kindergarten) to high school and where the emphasis is on Hindu culture, Sanskrit exams, quiz programmes and painting competitions on Hindu mythology and leaders like Hedgewar, Golwalkar and Subhash Chandra Bose—are the norms".[28]

No other organisation except RSS has done such an enormous planning to capture the political power at the Centre and State level. Today, most of the educational institutions and universities are headed by the RSS activists and even heads of the departments are under them. No other political party or socio-cultural organisations have ever thought of such a big planning. They have only immediate target of political power and becoming the minister, cabinet minister or chief minister. Their short-sightedness or selfish power-hunger has catapulated BJP into power at the Centre. And they are dead-set to completely change not only the face of the polity but the structure and content also, so that NRIs would not be able to recognise it, when they visit their Hindustan, say, after a period of 5 to 10 years !

It is not out of context when Teesta Setlwad, Editor, *Communalism Combat*, a Mumbai-based magazine, says '*institutions like NCERT are vulnerable because education has not been a priority for other political parties. Nor has the quality of education been debated by parents, teachers and politicians'.* "Which party other than the BJP has made education and its context a consistent issue for mobilisation and campaigning" ? She askes.[29]

This is true. More than 100 per cent true. No other political party has such a huge network other than BJP - RSS. RSS has entered into every section of human activity. They are aware and they were very well aware that if they wanted to have *Hindustan* of their dream, safe for Hindus and for the welfare of Hindus, they must organise and mould every human activity in such a way that in the long run that accounts for their total outcome - Hindustan for Hindus ! Today not only they have a strong political outfit in the name of Bhartiya Janata Party (original Bhartiya Jana Sangh) but in other walks of life also they have equally strong well-disciplined and ideologically on strong footing other off-shoot organisations which operate under unified direct command of RSS, but works in different areas. Their students organisation and labour organisation are one of the strongest organisations. Jawaharlal Nehru University was once the exclusive domain of Left student organisations for many years since its inception. But now Akhil Bhartiya Vidyarthi Parishad has made the inroads and ousted leftists. The Labour wing of RSS - Bhartiya Mazdoor Sangh has left behind the number one trade Union—INTUC/AITUC in membership. Vanvasi Kalyan Ashram founded in 1952 to trap the tribals has to its credit today the BJP rule in Jharkhand. Their's long term planning - for complete socio-economic and political power and not for only political power like other short-sighted political parties.

Indian History Under Historical Attacks

"In a bizarre case of a *mea culpa,* (NCERT) National Council for Educational Research and Training has launched an attack against its own history text books, pointing out alleged 'biased and Kurtful sentiments', claiming that the area of 'history has resisted moderation, revision and modification'. The author of this 'Critique' is none other than NCERT Director J. S. Rajput and the historians under attack include Romila Thapar, Satish Chandra and R. S. Sharma.

Though Prof. Rajput's four- page note does not identify who has raised the objections some of them ludicrous, the NCERT director himself seems to subscribe to them, when he says they were brought to notice by those 'really concerned with the children, the future of the Indian society etc'.

An example is a paragraph on Akbar in Romila Thapar's description of Akbar's marital alliances with Rajput royal families. The note states :

> There are those who find that this was a one sided policy which Akbar continued and which really caused great humiliation, to other communities who were never allowed to do what Akbar was doing to them'.

Challenging the charges made in Prof. Rajput's note, Arjun Dev, a former Professor of History and Head of the Department of education in social sciences and humanities of the NCERT, states that "there have been new editions every few years and existing text books (have been) re-written and revised ! Prof. Dev, who has been associated with the writing of history text books published by the NCERT since 1963, also points out that the NCERT has always incorporated new findings and new course content, making necessary changes even while 'defending itself from attackes on the basis of obscurantist, communal and sectarian prejudices on unacademic grounds'.

Terming Prof. Rajput's charges as 'disgraceful' Mr. Dev says, 'Deliberate distortion is not to be expected from the head of an educational institution'.

Noting that the NCERT has always incorporated necessary changes even while the institution including its director had always defended its own books against similar attackes in the past, Mr. Dev says in this case the NCERT had not consulted its own faculty let alone have the books evaluated by experts before condemning them. Mr. Rajput's views, he states, confirms that the NCERT has decided to withdraw the books without consulting the NCERT faculty".[30]

Ever since the hardcore *Sanghi* functionary, Murli Manohar Joshi took over the Human Resource Development Ministry under BJP led NDA Government, the socio-cultural environment of the country has started to undergo total over-hauling. The education, arts, film, history, culture and every thing the RSS had desired to change to suit their colour, taste and set-up i.e. Hindutvawadi socio-religious order has been deliberately and systematically, through their own ways of working and system, being changed. This they did even during the Congress rule through their hardcore activists working on the top of the departments. Today there is no hurdle in their way. They want to change the colour of India. Total saffronisation of education, culture, arts, history, science and all that matters in the socio - religious set-up. Murli Manohar Joshi proved to be one of the most deserving and the true son of RSS motherland !

The Congress ruled this country for 40 years or so at the Centre and States, but except propagating the views of Gandhi and Nehru, or highlighting the Nehru family and imposing dynastic rule through dynastic democracy, they did no harm to education, arts, culture or history and science, though Smt. Indira Gandhi also used the Hindu trump-cards from time to time to grab the political power. The damage caused to this polity by Congress would be repaired. But the damage being caused to polity by RSS - BJP - VHP - Bajrang Dal would be beyond repairs. As Partition of India in 1947 is beyond repairs !!

Of all the RSS functionaries Murli Manohar Joshi alone has been very forceful in implementing the RSS agenda. During the last 2½ years he has made more than 250 key appointments to institutions as varied as the Indira Gandhi National Centre for the Arts, University Grants Commission, the Indian Council for Historical Research, National Council for Educational Research and Training and Indian Council for Social Sciences Research. All the hardcore RSS cadres have taken over the charge. But the most controversial appointment is that of NCERT chief J.S. Rajput and B.R. Grover, ICHR chief. And the most controversial issue is that of"withdrawal by ICHR of two volumes of documentary history by Profesors K.N. Panikkar and Sumit Sarkar. The reason given by ICHR authorities for withdrawal of the volumes is that those were sent directly to the Oxford University Press without authorisation and they wanted to subject them to fresh perusal. However, the real reason, as Prof. Sarkar himself has given at Kolkata while speaking to Times of India News Service after attending the 61st Session of Indian History Congress, is that—"The Rashtriya Swyamsevak Sangh had collaborated with the British Raj during the historic Quit India Movement of 1942. A secret report sent to British intelligence head-quarters from Mumbai in September that year mentions that the British Raj had 'no reason to worry about the RSS' since it was 'completly loyal to the Raj ....' It is the presence of these kinds of official documents and reports in the *'Towards Freedom'* volumes that had prompted an apprehensive *Sangh Pariwar* and the BJP dominated Indian Council of Historical Research to withdraw the last two volumes hurriedly from the press". Mr. Sarkar further said, "The Sangh Pariwar is scared that if published the 'Towards Freedom' series of books - a compilation of secret documents from the last years of British Raj - will expose their true colours .... The BJP government and the RSS - VHP combine do not want their carefully cultivated image of true patriots to be tarnished. They had to prevent scholars and students from gaining access to these documents. The attacks have been inspired by a sense of fear that the real face of the RSS might emerge from these documents. It is part of the over all attacks by Hindu Chauvinist forces and the right wing government to suppress the academic freedom".[31]

What Prof. Sumit Sarkar said about the Sangh people is not incorrect. "Dr. Shyama Prasad Mukherjee, the founder President Bhartiya Jan Sangh and patron saint of the BJP was quite clear in his mind as to how the Government should respond, if the Congress gave a call to the British rulers to Quit India. In a letter to the Governor of Bengal, on July 26, 1942 - less than a fortnight before the All India Congress Committee passed the Quit India resolution on August 8 - he wrote : *'Let me now refer to the situation that may be created in the province as a result of any widespread movement launched by the Congress. Anybody, who during the war, plans to stir up mass feelings, resulting in internal disturbunces or insecurity, must be resisted by any government that may function for the time being'.*[32] This was their patriotism to the motherland Bharat and Freedom struggle ! And, they are proud to say - Vande Mahtaram !!

The story of V. D. Savarkar - the so-called *'Swatantrya Veer'* (Freedom Fighter) is not very different about his patriotism. Sangh and Savarkar were two sides of the same fake coin.

Savarkar accepted such humiliating conditions for his own release from the jail that he did not deserve to be called a real *'Swatantryaveer'*. And his attitude and movements even after his release from the jail was not fitting to the honour of *Swatantryaveer*.

"The release order issued by the Governor exercising the power conferred on him by section 401 of the Code of Criminal Procedure 1898, read as follows :

(1) That the said Vinayak Damodhar Savarkar will reside within the territories administered by the Governor of Bombay-in-Council and within the Ratnagiri district within the said territories, and will not go beyond the limits of that district without the permission of Government or in case of urgency, of the District Magistrate.

(2) That he will not engage publically or privately in any manner of political activities without the consent of Government for a period of five years, such restriction being renewable at the descretion of Government at the expiry of the said term.

Savarkar accepted these conditions without any compunction. The Government suggested that he should state that his trial was fair and the sentence awarded was just. At the same time, it told him this was 'in no way made a condition of his release'. Yet he went ahead and made this statement : "I hereby acknowledge that I had a fair trial and just sentence. I heartly abhor methods of violence resorted to in days gone by, and I feel myself duty bound to uphold Law and the Constitution to the best of my powers and am willing to make the Reform a success in so for as I may be allowed to do so in future".

It was only in May 1937 that the newly elected Congress Government of Bombay removed completely the humiliating conditions to which Savarkar had submitted in order to secure his release from prison"[33]

Despite such begging and kneeling down before the British Raj, he is adored as the 'Swatantraveer' and equated with Martyr Bhagat Singh, Rajguru and Chandrasekhar. This is a great insult to these patriots if he is compared to them.

The story of this patriotism and service to motherland does not stop here only. As a Hindu Mahasabha President Savarkar issued an edict in September 1942 :

> "I issue this definite instruction to all Hindu sabhaites in particular and all Hindu Sangathanists in general .... holding post or position of vantage in the Government services should stick to them and continue to perform their regular duties".[34]

That was his services to the motherland when Gandhiji had given the call of Quit India and thousands of people went to jails for freedom struggle.

These instances of documentary proofs and many such others, which form the part of the two disputed volumes, 'Towards Freedom', withdrawn by ICHR. These volumes would definitely expose the true face of patriotism of people like Savarkar and organisations like RSS. This will make them naked in the public eyes.

Arun Shourie and his likes who have condemned Dr. B. R. Ambedkar for joining Viceroy's Council in 1942 should have read these documents of RSS patriotism and then questioned Dr. Ambedkar's yeoman's services to the nation as a real patriot. Dr. Ambedkar never missed an opportunity to criticise and condemn the actions of British Raj as and when the Raj acted against the interest of the motherland.

It was also rumour during Emergency in 1975 - 76, when majority of the political leaders were put into jails, the RSS had made a compromise with Smt. Indira Gandhi and Atal Behari Vajpayee had opologized ! And despite all that, they say proudly Vande Mataram !!

The BJP - RSS - VHP and Bajrang Dal have their own designs of writing of Indian history. Some of the examples would suffice the cause.

(1) **"From the NCERT text book - Sanchayika (vol -II)**

** The Bhartiya Congress was founded in 1885. Its first session was held in Bombay in 1889.*
Fact: The Congress was founded in 1885 and the first session took place the same year.
** In 1748 some European traders started coming to India. They included the Portuguese, the English and the French.*
Fact: Vasco da Gama reached Calicut in 1498; Albuquerque conquered Goa in 1510, the East India Company was formed in 1600 and the French East India Company in 1690.
** Chandrasekhar Azad took into his hands "the leadership of the revolutionary party" after the execution of Bhagat Singh on March 23, 1931.*
Fact: Impossible. Azad was shot dead on February 27, 1931 a month before Bhagat Singh was hanged.
** Subhash Chandra Bose led a revolutionary movement in Andhra.*
Fact: Bose's movement had an all-India character.
** All of Indian History till Ghori's invasion in the 12th century AD called the Vedic period.*
Fact: The Vedic period coincides with the centuries in which the four Vedas and Upanishadas were written and ends several centuries before the birth of Christ.
* Chanakya wrote a book called Kautilya Ka Arthashahtra
Fact: It was called Arthashashtra
* Vedanta is a book written by Shankaracharya
Fact: Vedanta is a system of philosophy

(2) **Education in RSS Vidya Bharati Schools**

The Sanskrit Jnan Course teaches :
* The first people to inhabit China were Indians.
* The first people to inhabit Iran were Indians.
* Thousands of opponents of idol worship, the followers of Islam, go to the pilgrimage centre of the Islamic community at the Kaaba to worship the Shivlinga.

Some Questions with Answers

Q. Why is the Babri Masjid not a Mosque ?

A - Because Muslims till today have never offered namaz there.

Q. Between 1528 to 1914 how many devotees of Rama laid down their lives to liberate the Rama temple ?

A - Three lakh fifty thousand

Education in Gujarat State (BJP Government)

From the Social Studies Book for Classes

* The Varna system was a precious gift of the Aryans to mankind.

* Apart from Muslims even Christians, Parsis and other foreigners are recognised as minorities. Yet, in most States Hindus are in minority and Muslims, Christians and Sikhs are in majority".[35]

If the things are allowed the Vidya Bharti way, then the next generation of Hindus shall be full of hatred, vengeance and animosity against the minorities and it would not take much time for India to be again divided between majority and minority Indians. RSS - BJP also have the same designs. They want India - that is, Bharat for Hindus and Hindus alone. The efforts, therefore, where ever possible and visible to them, they do it to remove the imprint of their short coming and highlight the *Hindutvawadi* culture whenever and where ever they get an opportinity.

"In 1977 when the Janata Party, of which the Jan Sangh was a key constituent, came to power, it quickly withdrew R. S. Sharma's Ancient India because it spoke of beef eating in ancient India and attributed the settlement of Rama's Ayodhya to 700 B. C."[36]

The Right wing scholars are not prepared to digest the charges levelled against them. At the 61st session of Indian History Congress at Kolkatta they were more virulent in defending the RSS - VHP attempt to saffronise history.

"For centuries the Mughals, the British and finally our own scholars have deliberately misguided people by their one-sided writings. Men like Babar and

> Aurangzeb have been praised even though they destroyed our ancient monuments and killed our brothers. And true heroes like Lord Rama, Chhatrapati Shivaji and Golwalkar have been deliberately ignored".[37]

It seems there is a tough fight going on between the Leftist and Rightist historians to project the history of this country in their own perspectives. A student of the tender age of 10 to 18 has been left with no choice but to move Left or Right. He is most likely to lose his right to freedom - to be informed rightly and correctly without bias. However, the RSS has already launched in 1973 the Bhartiya Itihas Sankalan Yojana with the aim of re-writing Indian history of the last 5000 years - to prove that the Aryans were indigenous people of Bharat and not invaders; and that there is sufficient archaeological evidence for Ram Janmabhoomi.

Professor K. N. Panikkar, in an interview given to Frontline–March 17, 2000, has cautioned the people that, :

> "....Historical scholarship in India is very strong and it has a very good record of adhering to the methods of discipline. Now I feel that the discipline is in danger for two reasons. One, though historians in this country are largely secular and have great regard for the methods of history writing, there has been a slow erosion .... today an over-whelming majority of young historians who were very secular before, have gone over to communal view. This is actually an indication of how this kind of ideology is creeping into the university departments .... More important there is a popular history that is being created by Hindu communalists, which has nothing to do with the professional history being produced in the universities. I some times wonder whether this popular history will completely overwhelm the professional strain .... And I understand there is a huge project undertaken by the RSS, through an organisation known as Itihas Sankalan Samiti, to write the history of each district of the country. So if these histories are published,

they will become the accepted or the most easily accessible history for the mass of the people, which is going to influence the popular understanding. So this danger of popular history replacing professional history is really very strong. Once that happens, the historical consciousness in society might also be influenced".

Sangh Pariwar does not believe in the secular history or historians. They are dead set against the secular word. Naturally, they will have their own colour of history which would suit them best. It is upto the leaders of all sorts of political, social, religious thinking and so on to get ready either to face *Hindutvawadi* attacks and get immersed in the Saffron colour for ever or forget about the short-sighted selfish political gains and build up a vast, strong and perpetual socio-culture, network to sustain the onslaughts of ever growing saffron ...forces to hold on its fort to retaliate with equally forceful counter attack in the same manner !!

References

1. The Hindu - April 14, 2000 (New Delhi Edition).
2. Times of India, (Bombay Edition) dt 03/01/2001.
3. Fundamentals of Sociology - By P. Gisbert p. 256
4. *Ibid.*
5. *Ibid.*
6. *Ibid.*
7. Fundamentals of Sociology - P. Gisbert p. 287.
8. Culture and Anarchy - Mathew Arnold p. 9.
9. Fundamentals of Sociology : P. Gisbert p. 290.
10. Shorter Constitution of India : Durga Das Basu p. 217.
11. The Week - dated 13 Feb 2000 p. 33-34, 37.
12. *Ibid.*
13. *Ibid.*
14. *Ibid.*
15. Shorter Constitution of India : Durga Das Basu p. 119, 120.
16. An article by Ratnottama Sengupta in Sunday Times of India dt. 9/12/2001
17. Fundamentals of Sociology : P. Gisbert p. 219, 225, 223.
18. *Ibid.*
19. *Ibid.*
20. *Ibid.*
21. Government of India Ministry of Education, Report of the Secretary Education Commission (1952–53) p. 23.

22. AIR (1994) SC 1919 - S. R. Bommai *vs* Union of India.
23. *Ibid.*
24. Fundamentals of Sociolgy : P. Gisbert p. 234.
25. A Biased Agenda - Frontline, December 22, 2000 p. 92, 93, 94.
26. *Ibid.*
27. *Ibid.*
28. Outlook - Dt. April 27, 1998 p. 17.
29. The Hindustan Times - New Delhi (Ed) Dec. 19, 1999 (An article : Saffron Generation by Akshaya Mukul).
30. An Article : NCERT attacks its own history books by Aunohita Mojumdar—The Times of India dt. 24/5/2001.
31. The Times of India dt. 6/1/2001.
32. The RSS and the BJP - A Division of Labour : A. G. Noorani p. 42, 44, 45
33. *Ibid.*
34. *Ibid.*
35. The Hindustan Times - New Delhi dt. December 19, 1999 p. 15.
36. *Ibid.*
37. The Times of India - Bombay dt 4/01/2001.

6
Indian Economy Under Capitalist Attack

While moving the Objective Resolution in the Constituent Assembly of free India on the 5th Day of the First Session, Pandit Jawaharlal Nehru, first Prime Minister of India, said:

> ".... We have given the content of democracy in this Resolution and not only the content of democracy but the content, if I may say so, of economic democracy in this Resolution. Others might take objection to this Resolution on the ground that we have not said that it should be socialist state. Well, I stand for Socialism and that India will go towards the constitution of Socialist State and I do believe that the whole world will have to go that way. What form of Socialism again is another matter for your consideration. But the main thing is that in such a Resolution, if, in accordance with my own desire, I had put in, that we want a Socialist State, we would have put in some thing which may be agreeable to many and may not be agreeable to some and we wanted this Resolution not to be controversial in regard to such matters. Therefore, we have laid down, not theoretical words and formulae, but rather the content of the thing we desire ...."[1]

Pandit Jawaharlal Nehru had a very clear idea and thinking about the nature of economy that the free India should pursue soon after departure of the British. He could have imposed his own thinking and like on the Constituent Assembly and subsequently in the Constitution, being the tallest personality of the freedom struggle and the most dominant figure in the Congress Party. But he did not. The matters of controversy, he wanted to keep away. And, therefore speaking on the merits of the Resolution Sir Alladi Krishnaswami Ayyar, one of the members of the Drafting Committee made it very clear that, :

"…. It has to be remembered that the main object of this Assembly is not the fashioning of a Constitution of a Local Board, a District Board or making changes in the present constitution of this or that part of the country but to give concrete expression to the suffering aspiration of a people yearning for freedom by framing a constitution for free and independent India or the good of the people, one and all, of this great and hisorical and, irrespective of caste, class, community or creed, with a hoary Civilization going back to several centuries …."

Despite the biased and ill-willing charge of *Saffron Saints of Hindutvawadi* civilisation, the leaders sitting in the Constituent Assembly were men of high-standing national stature, deeply devoted and dedicated to the motherland - Bharat, and totally free from all negative isms of caste, class, community, colour and religion. Their dedication, their devotion and their high-morale and integrity towards the motherland was beyond doubt. They did not work for some selfish motive, for certain communities. In the words of Dr. Ambedkar, the architect of the present Constitution,--

"…. The Constituent Assembly in making a Constitution has no partisan motive. Beyond securing a good and workable Constitution it has no axe to grind …."[2]

Pandit Jawaharlal Nehru, Dr. Ambedkar, Sir Alladi Krishnaswami Ayyar, Dr. Rajendra Prasad, K.M. Munshi and all those associated with the work of constitution- making were never the persons of partisan characters. They had none of their own selfish motive. Good of the country and good of all was the only objective for which they worked and for which they lived !

To avoid the controversy and dispute in the constitution-making, Pandit Nehru did not insist for a particular form of economic model of development for the country. However, after coming into being of the Constitution of free India, the policy decision was taken to that extent through-, "the Industrial Policy Resolution of 1956, which had its objective the acceleration of the rate of economic growth and the speeding up of industrialisation as a means of achieving a socialist pattern of society.---the 1956 Industrial Policy Resolution gave primacy to the role of the State to assume a predominant and direct responsibility for industrial development ...."[3]

India opted for planned economy, without which all round development was not possible. Through the Five Year Plans, industrial development was based on domestic protection and was inward looking. Public Sector had the commanding heights. Nevertheless, a solid infrastructural base was created to run the economy. Priority and strategy of the Second Five Year Plan (1956-57 to 60-61) was to establish a socialistic pattern of society. And thus, started the wheels of economic-development of country. Special importance was given in the two Resolutions of 1948 and 1956 Industrial policy to the development of steel, heavy engineering, machine tools and heavy chemical industry. The total number of Central Public Sector Undertakings as in 1960-61 was only 26 which increased to 241 in 1994-95 giving profit after tax 72.2 billion rupees and paid to Central Government Rs. 47,000/- crores in the form of dividend, tax and interest. The total strength of the employees is more than 22 lakhs. These undertakings have played a very important role in the development of national economy during the past 50 years.

Economic Planning

When India became free, we had two options, either to go the Anglo- American way of capitalist society or Russian way to build-up socialist economy through Russian model of planning with dominant role for the State to plan, regulate and mobilise resources for the purpose. Without the lead role of the State, the very objective of the founding fathers of the Constitution and freedom fighters to endeavour for establishment of Welfare State was impossible. People's well-being was the prime motive of the State and not partisan motive for profit which is the basic feature of capitalist society. Speaking about socialism and socialist state Justice Chandrachud, Chief Justice of India in Nakara Vs Union of India (AIR 1983-SC-130) observed:

> ".... This is not mere semantic. The edifice of our Constitution is built upon the concepts crystallised in the Preamble. We resolved to constitute ourselves into a socialist state which carried with it the obligation to secure to our people justice-social, economic and

political. We, therefore, put part IV into our Constitution containing directive principles of state policy which specify the socialist goal to be achieved ..... At a later stage it was observed that the fundamental rights are not an end in themselves but are the means to an end the end is specified in part IV .... The principal aim of a socialist state is to eliminate inequality in income and status and standard of life. The basic frame-work of socialism is to provide a decent standard of life to the working people and especially provide security from cradle to grave...."[4]

Chief Justice Chandrachud's observation made it clear that the objective of the founding fathers of the Constitution, though originally not put into the Preamble, through the provision of part IV of the Constitution, was to make this country a Socialist State. And basic frame-work of the socialism is to provide a decent standard of life to the working people. Is it possible in the capitalist society where the motive of profit and only profit, and nothing else, is the sole objective?

Dr. B.R. Ambedkar, also said that their object in framing the Constitution was two fold : (i) to lay down the form of political democracy, and (ii) to lay down that our ideal is economic democracy and also to prescribe that every government whatever it is in power, shall strive to bring about economic democracy. He says :

" There are various ways in which people believe that economic democracy can be brought about; there are those who believe in individualism as the best form of economic democracy; there are those who believe in having a socialist state as the best form of economic democracy; there are those who believe in the Communistic idea as the most perfect form of economic democracy". But "it is no use giving a fixed rigid form to something which is not rigid, which is fundamentally changing and must having regard to circumstances and the times, keep on changing ", observes Dr. Ambedkar and believes that the directive principles incorporated in the Constitution of India have great value, for they lay down that our ideal is economic democracy.[5]

Economic democracy is a pre-requisite of socialism which stands for a socialistic pattern of society. It is a state of economically classless society wherein ownership of the instruments of production should be vested in the State. But control over the State (and thus, indirectly over what the State controlled) would have to be vested in everyone alike. No group or class of society could have any special advantage as against other groups or classes in controlling the State ....[6]

It is in practice observed that, those who control the economic life, those in whose favour the property relations are organised, those who stand to benefit by the organisation of forces of production, they ultimately decide the character of the State ....[7]

That is why Dr. Ambedkar very rightly observed that, " If the party to which they have supported financially comes into power, they will naturally try to extract concessions for themselves either by modifying the present legislation or by influencing the party in power to legislate in such a manner as would be beneficial to their interests ...."[8]

And, that is what is happening today in our country.

The Outlook, a English Weekly News magazine has carried a fantastic and eye-opening cover story in their March 5,2001 weekly issue as to how by their brazen manipulation of the Prime Minister Atal Behari Vajpayee's (The so called most liberal among the Saffronised faces and self less Swayamsewak of the country, who does not have his own family and has no property or lust for wealth) Office, a clutch of powerful business houses is forcing critical economic decisions on key ministries and making mockery of the reform process.... It is not level playing field. The business of governance is subverted by a group of industrial houses,.... Key economic decisions are being thrust on the nation, to the comforts of a few business lobbies.... Much of the favours shown to the industrial lobbies are passed off as economic reforms...."

The News Magazine has pointed out 5 to 6 instances wherein as to how Reliance and Hindujas have been favoured and for their benefit only the rules and policies have been twisted in the name of reforms. As Dr. Ambedkar had pointed out above, those who invested in the party to elect them would definitely extract their share of flesh. The reforms under the name of liberalisation and globalisation are meant for those industrial houses and persons and not for general masses. What to talk of the poor and needy!

Socialism to Capitalism under Globalisation

Smt. Indira Gandhi, though acted like a democratic dictator during the period 1975-76 after crowning the victory of Bangla Desh war, nevertheless she had taken a bold step by inserting two words- *socialist* and *secular* in the Preamble of the Constitution (42 nd Amendment) Act, 1976 and this has empowered the Supreme Court to strike down a statute which failed to achieve the socialist goal to the fullest extent or which adopts a classification which is not in tune with the establishment of a welfare society ....[9]

Thus, the judiciary has on a number of occasions interpreted the various statutes in the light of the objective and the inherent intent of the Preamble. S.R. Bommai case is a classic example, when the Supreme Court of India justified dissolution of Assemblies of BJP ruled states for acting contrary to the secular spirit of the Constitution.

The concept of socialism is doctrine and movement which advocates establishment of society on the basis of common ownership of some or all the means of production, distribution and exchange and holding of them for the equal benefit of all. No doubt Pandit Jawaharlal Nehru hoped that India will go towards the constitution of socialist state but he was also not sure or clear in his mind at that time as to what form of socialism should India adopt. Because, the concept is not only of various types but it is also changing and developing. The USSR, once the leader of world socialist states failed to expand the corridors of socialist pattern of economy even after 75 years successful experiment. Why did Russia fail to sustain the socialist pattern? That could have been the subject of intensive and thorough debate and discussion for the researchers of socialism. However the main reason behind the failure seems non-involvement of masses voluntarily in the movement. Dictatorship would not be able to sustain for a long time. It is, therefore, Dr. Ambedkar's concept of State Socialism with Parliamentary Democracy the best alternative suited to this country as well as to all those Socialist States world over which failed to sustain the system.

The "failure of socialism as demonstrated by the disintegration of the Soviet Union as also by the collapse of the erstwhile Socialist States in the Eastern Europe is treated as the triumph of democracy based on capitalist economy. As a logical corollary to this belief, there is observed an unqualified and unquestionable faith in the superiority of the institution of market which is sought to be held as panacea for all the economic problems facing the contemporary world including, of course, developing countries like India...."[10]

And, this failure is not because of the intent and content of the system but the use of the system and the methods adopted are the reasons. "Dr. Ambedkar's Democratic Socialism, therefore, stands for liberty, equality and justice in all spheres of life and attainment of the same through democratic ways. He advocated the State Socialism with a view to put an obligation on the State to plan the economic life of the people on the lines which would lead to the highest point of productivity without closing every avenue to private enterprise, and also provide for the equitable distribution of wealth..... He was against monopoly in very shape and form but, he favoured state ownership in the field of agricultural land, industry and insurance with due provision to safeguard socio-economic interests of all the people...."[11]

Dr. Ambedkar, when failed to provide the concrete shape to his concept of State Socialism in the constitution, he found out the alternative in the name of Directive Principles of State Policy which were, though not enforceable in the courts, nevertheless those provisions came to be regarded as " instruments of instructions" for the policy-makers as well as the judiciary. Many a number of judgements of the Supreme Court and High Courts are ample testimony to that effect.

Now, the very concept of socialistic pattern of society is under drastic change in the country. Pandit Nehru's brain-child concept of Mixed Economy is also, being replaced firstly and initially by his own Congress Party and then BJP led NDA government. When India became free it was thought that for the country like India, Mixed Economy was the best alternative, if not socialist economy. "Having adopted a 'mixed economy' where the public and private sectors could co-exist with the former dominating the core sectors of the economy, the Government has articulated its industrial policy through various Industrial Policy Resolutions. The key features of all these resolutions included a dominant role for the public sector (where the Government has a majority share-holding), demarcation of priority and non-priority sectors by the Government, encouragement to the small-scale sector industries with a specified maximum investment in plant and machinery, prevention of concentration of economic power, control of foreign investments in India, encouragement of domestic entrepreneurship and balanced regional growth."[12] However, all these high-sounding commitments finally proved not upto the mark or expectation when the "Statement of New Economic Policy of 1991 (under P.V. Narasimha Rao's leadership) and under the stewardship of Dr. Manmohan Singh (a World-Bank trained theoretician and economist)" was presented to Parliament on July 24, 1991. The New Economic Policy - known as *Man-Mohanomics*, was destined to entirely reverse what the founding fathers of the Constitution had dreamt for this great country and that also destroyed the Nehruvian Mixed Economy. It was clear-cut capitalist conspiracy against the logic and spirit of the Preamble of the Constitution. It was definitely violation of the Preamble- which declares India a 'Socialist' Republic. And the Supreme Court has ruled in Atam Prakash Vs State of Haryana (AIR 1986. SC 854 (864) in the light of the Preamble-read with Arts. 14,16 to strike down a statute which failed to achieve the socialist goal to the fullest extent or which adopts a classification which is not in tune with the establishment of Welfare Society.

Indian economy conceived, planned and carried out for the past forty years from 1950 onward through successive Five Year Planning, did not fail in itself but could not give better results due to political curruption and excessive bureaucratization. Even public sectors could not give very best results due to corruption in high levels in league with politicians in power. Otherwise, inherently there is no defect in the concept of public sector system. The Indian worker is not less than any other worker in his dedication, devotion and performance but it is the top-management which has been mostly corrupt; and cause for losses to the establishment.

How best the employees of public sector undertaking could contribute to the nation-building and national development could best be observed from the statement made by Mukesh Ambani, Vice-Chairman and Managing Director of Reliance Industries. In fact, Ambani attributed his Group's achievement in commissioning Rs. 25,000 crores refinery complex at Jamnagar to the contribution made by the employees who joined his Group from the PSUs:

"....I have no hesitation in saying that Reliance has been built on the back of the calibre of PSU employees. Nearly 40 per cent of our employees are from PSUs" Ambani admitted while de-livering a lecture on the success of Reliance Petroleum under thze series "Ideas that have worked...."[13]

It is really a great surprise that employees of PSUs could change the fate of Reliance but the same very employees made government efforts futile, and finally Government had to sell out many of the PSUs at throw away prices for the reasons of receiving heavy losses. The decision for disinvestment of many a number of PSUs, and to off-load the government holdings is also directly related with continuous losses. Sometime, there appears a doubt about the honesty of the top management, who in conspiracy with the politicians and prominent Industrial Houses in the country, are playing fraud on the Constitution !

A decade of globlisation, liberalization and privatisation is over. The much publicised targets and achievements are still beyond the reach of those who propounded the alternative to Mixed Economy/Socialistic Planned Economy. Five-lakh jobs a year announced in 1991-92, have proved a mirage beyond doubt ! On the other hand, '*according to a member of the BJP think-tank 10 millions lost jobs in the past five years, while 7 lakh small units shut, 7000 medium and large industrial units closed down*'.[14]

The growth rate of 8 per cent could never be achieved, despite all big and bold promises by the successive Finance Ministers and supporters of globalisation and liberalisation!!

Globalisation : Instrument of Imperial Capitalism

The 1990s witnessed momentous changes in the world. The international political and economic order was getting restructured to suit and benefit to the capitalist countries to the maximum extent. Western political powers, though professing and practising democracy, they always managed to their own advantage and benefit the political and economic relations. The developed economies were always in search of the markets to sell their products and services so as to enable them to save from impending excess production and maintain the economic equilibrium both in economic and political sphere of influence.

We in India after independence, instead of creating and building a new socio-economic order and our own model of economic development free from corruption, nepotism and favouritism, our leaders, wielding political powers involved in increasing their own wealth and property as a price of their so-called sacrifices during the freedom struggle. No leader, no statesman could put an ideal before the Indian public so as to adore them. The foundation of corruption, favouritism and dynastic democratic system was laid during this period only. The high-sounding objectives of the Preamble of the Constitution and provisions of directive principles promised and assured in the Constituent Assembly, remained mere messages to read. Despite eight Five Year Plans, we have still more than 50 per cent population below poverty line. Health care and clean drinking water to a large number of people is yet to be arranged. Free and compulsory education upto the age of 14 is still a dream project !

Why did it so happen ? Why the one party rule of one family for such a long period could not build-up ideals for others ? The reasons could be different, clarification and explanation would also be different. But the reality is that those empowered and powerful wanted to retain all the powers with them perpetually so as to prevent the oppressed and exploited people from asserting their legitimate role in the Indian polity. This wretched and deprived humanity, neglected and exploited for centuries should not raise their heads. The best way for that was to deprive them of the developmental benefits. To keep them backwards, to keep them ignorant and to keep them always dependent was the conspiracy the rich, the powerful and the high-caste people played in the name of developmental politics.

What Indian ruling classes adopted for retention of their powers of oppression and exploitation, the same methodology and scheme of things have been adopted by the powerful and rich Western countries through Globalisation and liberalisation of the developing countries or under-developed countries. Zbigniew Brzenzinski, former National Security Advisor in the Carter Administration (of USA) and who credits himself for having bought down the Soviet System, describes 'globalisation as a three-tiered hierarchy, with barbarians at the bottom and a single super power at the top'.[15] He then recommends :

> "The three great imperatives of geopolitical strategy are to prevent collusion and maintain security dependence among the vassals, to keep tributaries pliant, and to keep the barbarians from coming together."[16]

What Aijaz Ahmad, in his essay—Globalisation: A Society of Aliens? (Frontline- October 13, 2000) has observed about globalisation in the international context is equally applicable in our country to the socio-economic system operating under *Varnashram Social System*. He observed;

"As full-fledged imperialism, globlisation is an integrated system of economic, political, military and ideological powers and geopolitical arrangements supervised by real people in the real board rooms.... The whole edifice is upheld in a complex system of law, and regulation which has two overlapping aspects. There are first of all the regulatory regimes of the IMF, the World Bank, the International Financial Institutions (IFIs), and so on which are, together fast emerging as a new world government for imposing uniform policies, obligations, and conditionalities around the world, especially the imperialised world.... But an equally crucial aspect of this globalisation of law and sover eignty is that national legal systems are being constantly pressed into altering their own laws to make them more compatible with—often mere facsimiles-American law.... It is the selling that is universal, while production is always local.... Meanwhile, globalisation unites the market and divides human-beings because human-beings can best be used for the purposes of global marketing if they act as individual consumers and not as a people in solidarity with each other."[17]

The main objective behind Globalisation and Liberalisation is nothing but the exploitation of weak by the strong. It is exploitation of powerless by the powerful. It is again the same philosophy - survival of the fittest and elimination of the weak! What Darwin had propounded years back !!

Chandrashekhar, former Prime Minister of India and once known as 'Young Turk', during Indira Gandhi's regime, recently, on the conclusion of his PURI to PORBANDAR Car Journey Programme at Porbandar criticised severely the economic policy of BJP led NDA government. He said, "If no move is initiated unitedly forgetting our party differences against the globalisation and liberalisation, the day is not far off when this country would again become the slave of economic imperialism"[18]

The former Prime Minister's concern about economic slavery of the country is not unfounded. Founding fathers of the Constitution never anticipated that their sacrifices and hard work would go this way and our own people, our own leaders would mortgage our own freedom for the sake of economic comforts and luxuries of life. It seems, by resorting to globalisation the present BJP led NDA Government have two objectives in view- firstly, to allow the capitalists of the country and abroad to loot the Indian people in any way and in any manner to the maximum and accumulate the wealth in the hands of few business houses and industrialists. In other words to create supremacy and domination of those, who were once the all powerful and dominating. Alternatively, when wealth is accumulated in the hands of few, welfare would be dictionary word. This will take the Indian society to bad old days of *Varnashram Social System* in which *Brzezinski's 'barbarians'* (Shudra and Ati-shudras- oppressed and exploited) would take their place at the bottom of the system and super powers- the high-caste people would direct and dictate the Barbarians!

Praful Bidwai, the eminent writer and columnist, in his regular column- Beyond Obvious, in the Frontline dated October 13, 2000 has very rightly observed about the probable effects of liberalisation, privatisation and globalisation upon the under—previleged, oppressed and exploited people. He wrote:

> "The BJP is also strongly right-wing; pro-rich and anti-poor. It has mindlessly promoted LPG (liberalisation, privatisation, globalisation), systematically undermined public services and food security, and greately widened inequalities. No other party has attempted such wholesale transfer of public wealth into private hands, further disempowered the poor. None of these speaks of liberalisation, even in the political sense. Indeed, the effect of these policies is to weaken and disenfranchise the vast majority of the people, especially the most underprivileged and vulnerable, thus weakening their citizenship rights. In all this, Vajpayee's BJP is as conservative as the RSS, which is

deeply hostile to full participatory democracy based upon the empowerment of the under privileged."[19]

In a Democratic Socialist State, participation of underprivileged is a must and for that only it becomes the duty of the State to empower them so as to enable them to contribute through democratic participation in the national development. Changing the model of development from Mixed Economy to liberalisation and privatisation under globalisation is nothing but to issue the licences to the rich industrialists and few industrial houses to exploit and oppress the poor and deprived to that extent that 'No Mayawati, No Laloo or No Devegowda emerges again!

Secondly, and most importantly, the real conspiracy behind this policy is to deprive Bahujans (SC/ST/OBC/Minorities) of their reservations.

NDA Government's Economic Policy and Bahujans

In 1991, when the P.V. Narasimha Rao's Minority Govt. Finance Minister Dr. Manmohan Singh unfolded Rao Govt's. Economic policy, BJP leader L.K. Advani, congratulated Prime Minister Rao for adopting their party's economic agenda and he was happy that finally Indira Congress had taken U-turn. Dr. Singh had, then, declared that New Economic Policy would create five lakh jobs every year and Indians would enjoy the economic prosperity. Despite tremendous protests by NGOs. India had signed WTO Agreement. Slowly and systematically during the last ten years, the track of Indian economy has changed the route from Mixed Economy to Capitalist Economy and surrendered before the American Economic Imperialism.

Though, Indira Congress lost the next election, the new Finance Minister did nothing extraordinary but followed the suit. It was in continuation of that policy that Vajpayee Government initiated further reforms. In consonance with Budget 2000-2001 commitment to House by the Finance Minister Yashwant Sinha that ' the process of disinvestment / privatisation has been hastened.' Ministry of Railways and Tele-communications had separately declared that they were open for privatisation. AIR India and Indian Airlines are already on the verge of privatisation. Govt.'s stake in public sector banks has been brought down to

33% and thus public sector banks are also on the way of privatisation. BALCO has already been sold away at throw-away-prices!

Ban on recruitment in government services for the last many years, especially in the lower cadre, retrenchment, VRS, privatisation of public sector undertakings, banks, many of the departments of various Central ministries, unrestricted entry of MNCs and their products, reduction of duties/ taxes on imports and many other measures taken since 1991 by the successive governments have changed the face of Indian economy completely. One decade of experiment with Liberalisation and Globalisation is over. The Promised Sun and Moon are still very very far away from the reach of Indians. But one thing happened. Tonnes and Tonnes of employees have been rendered jobless. 'Five lakhs of job promise' proved a mere empty promise. Why? What is the reason? Why the Govts. at Centre and States have resorted to such Anti-labour and Pro-capitalist policies?

Finance Minister Yashwant Sinha in his third budget speech on 28th Feb.,2000 had announced in the Parliament that " Government's Policy towards the public sector is clear and unambiguous. Its main elements were :-

> Restructure and revive potentially viable PSUs; Close down PSUs which connot be revived; Bring down Government equity in all non-strategic PSUs to 26 per cent or lower, if necessary; and Fully protect the interests of workers"

Mr. Sinha in his next budget, i.e., 2001-2002 has again given numbers of concessions and exemptions to the industrialists so that they would loot the poor and wretched which ever manner they could. He had also declared in his budget speech that 27 more PSUs would be privatised. That means the entire Public Sector Units would be sold out irrespective of whether these are sick units or not.

The Government have also established New Deptt. for Disinvestment under Arun Shourie, who is the most Anti-Scheduled Caste/Scheduled Tribes, to establish a systematic policy approach to disinvestment and privatisation. NDA Agenda for governance had indicated the journey of Indian economy from

Socialism to Capitalism. Thus BJP or NDA are dead-set to revive and impose upon this country not only capitalism but through capitalism they have planned to perpetuate orthodox Hinduism, Communalism and finally Fascism-the Superiority of *Hindutvawadi* religion!

Indian Constitution and Indian Economy

Our Constitution through its Preamble, declared our resolve to constitute India into a Sovereign Socialist Secular Democratic Republic.... and thus the objective of the founding fathers of the Constitution was to establish a Socialist Secular Democratic Republic and not capitalist society, the way BJP led NDA Govt. and earlier P.V. Narasimha Rao and Manmohan Singh had started. Though the words 'Socialist and Secular' have been added to the Preamble by 42nd Amendment in 1976 by Indira Gandhi Govt. Part IV of the Constitution i.e. Directive Principles of State Policy and more particularly Articles 38, 39 (b) (c), 41,42, 43, 46 emphasise the need, necessity and urgency of implementation of those provisions for realising our cherished goal of 'welfare state' - the long cherished dream of our Constitution. But the economic policies initiated by Rajiv Gandhi Govt., adopted by Narasimha Rao-Manmohan Singh's minority Govt. and further concretised and implemented within a short span of 2½ years by Vajpayee's 23 parties coalition Govt., has totally shattered the dream of our Constitution and founding fathers. It is also against the spirit and sentiments of Constitution and needs to be condemned/rejected.

According to Supreme Court, "Though the *Preamble* does not add to or substract from the enacting provisions of the Constitution, the Supreme Court has been reading the enacting provisions in the light of the *Preamble* and thus it has been held that the word 'Socialist' read with Art. 14 could strike down a statute which failed to achieve the Socialist goal to the fullest extent. Though the word Socialism is vague, our Supreme Court has observed in *Randhir Vs. Union of India* (AIR 1982 SC 879—Para–13) that its principal aim is to eliminate "inequality of income and status and standards of life, and to provide a decent standard of life to the working people."

It is very illogical, unreasonable and out of context that-despite the firm commitment of our founding fathers of the

Constitution, the present BJP led NDA Govt. have started changing the face of Indian Economy from socialistic society to capitalist society, so that the working class, the oppressed and exploited people of this land would never raise their heads against exploitation and oppression they had been subjected to for centuries.

Five Decades of Indian Economy : 1947-1997

"Any economy has to deal with three kinds of prices - that of agricultural goods, industrial products and the wage rates. In a market economy prices of these goods always move in conformity. In a controlled economy (Socialist economy) they have to be adjusted by the policy-makers who are either politicians or bureaucrats. In a completely liberalised economy, planning has no role to play. It is the market forces, which play their vital role to shape the economic outcome.'

Pandit Jawaharlal Nehru, the first Prime minister of free India, who was very much under the influence of Russian Socialist Economy after his visit to USSR, initiated Five Year Planning for economic and industrial development of the country. It was under P.C. Mahalanbois with Nehru that the strategy of industrialisation started in the country and Second Five Year Plan period had laid the foundation for a strong, diversified, complex industrial structure in post-independence India. It was during this period, the Public Sector Undertakings started taking shapes under the Centre as well as States. Emergence of PSUs in large number to serve the cause of public was greatly motivated with the nationalist dedication. No doubt, the founding fathers of the Constitution did not intend to bind people of India to any particular economic 'isms', but nevertheless various provisions inserted in Part - IV of the Constitution i.e. Directive Principles of State Policy and the Preamble, are ample proof and indication as to what was their real intention the rulers should follow.

1947 to1997 - Fifty years period is enough period to assess the outcome. We opted for planned economy and implemented eight Five Years Plans .... Starting from a growth rate of around 3.5% during the First Plan, we have acquired strength enough to achieve around 7.8 per cent growth now.... In five decades, we have achieved food self sufficiency and production has kept pace with the demands. Through the Five-Year Plans, solid infrastructure base to run the economy was created. Bhilai, Bokaro, Rourkela and now Visakhapatnam on the one hand and HMT, BHEL, ONGC, IOC and many other public sector undertakings have played a very important role during the past five decades. But despite that today BJP led NDA government have decided for disinvestment and privatisation. The Process had started under P.V. Narasimha Rao of Indira Congress in 1991 in full scale. Even before that under Rajiv Gandhi a preparation were in full swing. Why? After all, there has always been a big question - Why Disinvestment and Privatisation ? Where did we fail ? What is wrong with Public Sector ? What is wrong with Labour ? Why did and how did the management fail to pick-up loopholes and black holes emerging in the system ? PSUs were created with a view to serve the large purpose of welfare society benefiting both the people as well as labour.

Today after fifty years experiment with PSUs the Government have come to this conclusion that PSUs are not fit to serve the people. There are people in the country, who say that planned economy or Socialist economy does not suit this country or rather ills of economy are due to that. Shri Balasaheb Deoras, the former Chief of RSS once, while addressing the gathering of intellectuals in New Delhi, observed that the real reason for backwardness of the country was the socialist economy. He staunchly supported the free market and capitalist economy. It was in 1967-68 or so, the Bhartiya Jan Sangh's Dr. Subramanyam Swamy had drafted a Swadeshi Five Year Plan for India, which propounded the economic policy of then BJS and the same very policy has been propagated and advocated for a long time. Now, they got an opportunity through the power-hungry and opportunists coalition partners - so to say - the half-hearted Socialists, dejected the demoralised Lohiyaiats and baseless and rootless Mandalists. It is not the NDA economic policy but the BJP/RSS commitment to capitalist society that is on.

Again the question is why this programme ? Why this policy ? The answer is not simple. The answer is not easy.

Employment Opportunities in Governments and PSUs

According to the 1991 Census there were 306 million workers in our country and about 10 per cent of which were marginal workers. The work force of the nation accounts for 37.4 per cent of total population. And according to the Planning Commission, India had a labour force of 339.22 million (37.4 per cent of the total population) at the end of March 1995. Out of the total force, 52 million are educated, and 1.52 million are well trained technical manpower. During the period 1991-95 about 27.07 million persons entered the labour force at an annual rate of 2.1 per cent. Job opportunities generated during the same very period was around 22.77 million. Thus, 4.30 million persons out of the 27.07 million entered the labour force during the period, were left without any job. It was estimated in 1952 that if full employment was to be reached by the year 2002 A.D., 94 million jobs may have to be created in the aggregate. With this target in view, the First Five Year Plan generated employment for 5.5 million while during the year 1992-93 to 1994-95 per year it was 6.3 million. As on 31.12.1995 367 lakh educated persons are registered with Employment Exchanges. And during the last 5 years 20-25 lakhs must have added to make it around 40 millions jobless. As on date the Central Govt. and State Govts. are the biggest and largest employers. If not taken all together the major strength of employees in Rly., Defence, P&T, Port, Banking etc. put together is not less than 50 lakhs, of these Railways alone count 17 lakhs employees. The way disinvestment and privatisation has started this strength would go down to much lower. During the last ten years the strength of public sector employees has gone down from 22 lakhs to 19 lakh....[20]

Reservations and Economic Policy

In a meeting held on 29th March 2000 the Central Cabinet decided to amend the Constitution proposing to increase the scope of quotas to bypass the Supreme Court judgement of August 1997 which had put a ceiling of 50 percent on SC/ST reservations in goverment jobs in any given year to clear the backlog of SC/ST reservations. And accordingly the Constitution was amended by the Parliament.

Immediately after the announcement of amending the Constitution to clear backlog of reservation, there were deliberate and satirical reactions in the print media. The 'Times of India', Delhi edition dated April 3, 2000 observed in its editorial. "The main purpose of reservation today appears to be perpetuating the power of a Mai-bap Sarkar which would rather dole out reservation sops than encourage people to stand on their own feet and compete in a world of excellence".

Another prominent weekly 'India Today' remarked in its April 10th issue editorial that "if this is allowed there is no earthly reason why the Union Cabinet itself should not be subject to caste-based reservations. At a time when the Indian mind is prized commodity in the global market place, the Indian State is closing its doors to home-grown talent. The 50 per cent limit was an eminently sensible one that reconciled social justice with meritocracy. Now the balance is gone forever."

Earlier a five-judge constitution bench headed by Chief Justice A.S. Anand, ruled that "the employees recruited under the reservation policy cannot continue to claim seniority over their general category colleagues as a matter of right. Articles 16(4) and 16(4)(a) of the Constitution do not confer any fundamental rights nor do they impose any constitutional duties, but are only in the nature of enabling provisions vesting a discretion in the State to consider providing reservation if the circumstances so warranted". The apex court also held that " roster point" promotee (reserved category) could not count their seniority in the promoted category from the date of their continuous officiating in the promoted post vis-a-vis the general category candidates who were senior to them in the lower category candidate at the lower level, to the reserved candidate even if the reserved candidate was earlier promoted to that level".

Similarly the 13th August 1999 judgement of the Supreme Court in which the highest court of the country ruled that " keeping in view the national interest, in the criteria for admission to specialized branches of higher education i.e. engineering and medical (Postgraduate course) should be on merit and not reservation".

These two judgements of the highest court of the country within a span of two months indeed very short time have very wide-ranging and far-reaching adverse repercussions on the very-concept of social justice.

Reservation : Constitutional Provisions

The basic purpose behind reservation to the backward classes (SC/ST/OBC) in employments is not simply to give jobs to some persons of these communities but to increase their representation and participation in the services and uplift these people who were socially, educationally and economically neglected, deprived and deserted for a long in the social system of this land. In the absence of legitimate protection it would not be possible for these people to compete successfully with their more fortunate brothers and sisters in the matter of admissions in various courses of study and securing public employment. It was under this background that provisions for reservations for SC and ST have been made. With the same end in view, reservations were also made in Representation of People's Act, 1951.

According to Article 15(4) of the Constitution, "Nothing in this article or in clause (2) Article 29 shall prevent the State from making any special provisions for the advancement of any socially and educationally backward classes of citizens or for the Scheduled Castes and the Scheduled Tribes".

Article 16(4) reads as 'Nothing in this Article shall prevent the State from making provision for the reservations in appointments or posts in favour of any backward classes of citizens which in the opinion of the State, is not adquately represented in the services under the State".

In compliance with the Directive Principles of State Policy and the commitment made by, ' we the people of India' in the Preamble of the Constitution of the country, 'to secure Justice, Social, Economic and Political,' Article 46 states that "the State shall promote with special care the educational and economic interests of the weaker sections of the people, and in particular, of the Scheduled Castes and the Scheduled Tribes and shall protect them from social injustice and all forms of exploitation".

It is in this context that Govt. of India, Ministry of Home Affairs vide resolution No. 42/21/41 dated the 13th September, 1950 recognized reservations for Scheduled Castes and Scheduled Tribes.

And in addition to reservation in recruitment/appointments, the Constitution (7th Amendment) Act 1956 also provided for reservation in promotions and the facilities were available till the 1992 judgement on Mandal Commission was declared by which the said facility was restricted to 5 years from the date of judgement. The Scheduled Castes and Scheduled Tribes had been getting the facility of reservation in promotion since 1955. The Supreme Court in Indra Swahney Vs. Union of India (Mandal judgement) laid down that, the reservation under Article 16(4)...... is confined to initial appointment and cannot extend to reservation in the matter of promotion. However it allowed the present position to continue for five years, i.e., till 16.11.1997. What the peoples' power had given, the judiciary withdrawn said facility. The seeds of servere blow to the reservation were visible very much in the Mandal judgement. Nobody took note of the serious repercussions that had hitted the headmarch! Mandal judgement manipulated the whole system of reservation to the disadvantage of the beneficiaries - the weaker sections. Nobody cried, nobody shouted! The Constitution (77th Amendment) Act 1995 again restored the facility of reservation in promotion by inserting Clause (4A) to the Article 16 of the Constitution.

Reservations and Judiciary

Prior to the recent two judgements of the Supreme Court, in addition to Mandal Judgement of 1992 there were number of judgements delivered by the Supreme Court and various High Courts, which have affected the fate of the Scheduled Castes and Scheduled Tribes adversely as well as favourably. But most of the judgements were more against SCs/STs and less in their favour. And those, which seemed to be favourable, were also fraught with many a number of ifs' and buts' and difficult for implementation. Unexpectedly, the higher-ups entrusted with the job of executing the policy of reservation got the legal excuse to avoid implementation under such pretexts.

If we study various judgements we can observe that most of the judgements reflect the temperament, commitment and inherent urge of the bench constituting on the particular occasions and the socio-political scenario prevailing at that time in the country. This was in general as well as judgement pertaining to the SC/ST reservations.

In regard to Reservation for the Scheduled Castes and Scheduled Tribes, there has been conflict for many years as to which of the provisions of Part III or Part IV of the Constitution should prevail over the other. In Keshavanand Bharati Vs. State of Kerala it was the view of the Supreme Court that there is no disharmony between the Directive Principles and Fundamental

Rights because they supplement each other in aiming at the same goal of bringing about social revolution and the establishment of a welfare state, which is envisaged in the Preamble. In the recent past, the unenforceable Directive Principles have become the guiding principles to interpret the Fundamental Rights, as far as the concept of social justice and welfare state is concerned. But the very recent judgements of Supreme Court on reservation reflect the changing perspective of social justice, and dominant role of '*Hindutva factor*' which have considerably influenced the balance of justice.

Judicial Activism, Separation of Power and Sovereign will of the People

If one observes judiciously various verdicts on reservation policy, one can note that in the past few years, ever since the governments started changing every six months - instability of the State and Central governments, and ushering in of new era of coalition ruling, it seems the judiciary has assumed the role of both the executive as well as legislature. It is a change from committed judiciary to assertive and dominating judiciary. That is why the Chief Justice of India A.S. Anand could dare say in the controversy arose with presidential note about appointment of judges of the High Courts/Supreme Court in 1998, "I would like to assert that merit alone has been criterion far selection of judges and no discrimination has been done while making appointment." The 28th October 1998 judgement of the Supreme Court in regard to appointment of Supreme Court Justices, has empowered the Supreme Court and Chief Justice of India to bypass the executive. That is the reason Indian Judiciary has become very powerful, which it was never before!

No doubt, under Montesque's separation of powers theory, all the three wings of the State have their own areas of jurisdiction and operation. But, will of the sovereign people is supreme and that must prevail. In parliamentary form of government, sovereign will of the people is reflected through elected representatives who are committed to the welfare of the people. If that commitment was shattered every time, the faith of the people in them would be no more. That is dangerous signal for democratic process. Notwithstanding the independence of judiciary and separation of power, will of the people, i.e., sovereign will, must prevail.

It is in this context that the emphasis of Art. 46 of the Constitution that, "the State shall promote with special care the educational and economic interest of the weaker sections of the people, and in particular of the Scheduled Castes and the Scheduled Tribes and shall protect them from social injustice and all forms of exploitation." The indication is very clear in the Constitution. Even if the amendment to the relevant article is required to be made to facilitate the advancement of SCs/STs it must be done. That is the will of the people - 85 crores of people, sovereign will of the people!

Merit, Efficiency and Competency

Merit, efficiency and competency are the very word mostly used by antagonists of the reservation policy to bypass and dismiss the claim of the reservations. These terms are very cleverly used to confuse the provision of reservation.

Today, when every field of human activity is under pressure of corruptive practices, how can these terms/words be made judging criteria in regard to reservations only? Moreover, these words are relative terms. Despite stringent provisions, obligatory instructions, compulsory orders reservation policy is being diluted by those who are entrusted. Manipulation is most prevalent in the management. The latest judgement of 13th August, 1999 by the highest court of the country is a glaring example.

Despite Govt.'s best policy decisions for strict compliance of reservation policy, Scheduled Castes and Scheduled Tribes could never enjoy the required constitutional quota either in the services or in educational institutions. Though not many, some of the districts could be headed by Scheduled Caste Collector or Suptd. of Police, some could reach the level of Deputy Secretary, Joint Secretary and even Chief Secretary (Maharashtra and Uttar Pradesh). First time in 1975 IAS and IPS quota was fulfilled. This negligent upward mobility in the game of power politics had a severe shock to the high caste people. It was challenge for their monopoly of political and bureaucratic power. This they could not digest. After all how would they tolerate the encroachment in their sacred area of power politics? In this connection ill-intentioned remarks of then cabinet secretary T.N. Sheshan (an orthodox and communalist Brahmin): "There is no reservation in jobs.... They (Scheduled

Castes and Scheduled Tribes) are not competent and so they lose out." Therefore, the retired Welfare Secretary N.K. Krishan has very rightly observed that "the Centre is the bastion of discrimination." The move started to find out via media. It was much before submission of Mandal Commission Report to the Parliament that the concept of merit was introduced in debates, symposium and seminars. Akhil Bhartiya Vidyarthi Parishad took the initiative and then started the publicity. Creamy layer concept was also introduced in the same period by the same organisation.

Though the anti-reservationists were on their job to put an end to reservation or slow down the process for years, political parties could not open their mouths against reservation in public lest they should loose their vote banks. Double-standard policy was their game politics. Political parties would support reservations while the organisations affiliated to those very same political parties raise the issue of MERIT or ECONOMIC Criteria or Creamy Layer. Andhra Pradesh Chief Minister Chandrababu Naidu has gone much ahead and quotas has been fixed for each castes among the scheduled castes so that they keep on fighting for their own quotas and could never come together unitedly against their oppressors and exploiters.

There has been going on a long struggle for Supremacy and domination in India for power game. It is universal phenomenon. It is the nature. History, Politics, Religion, Economics or Sociology is directly or indirectly related with this struggle. Struggle is for supremacy. Alexander the Great, Napolean, Hitler, Mussolini and many others tasted their strength and luck. Earlier, struggles were led and fought in the name of individual leaders. In the recent past, focus has been shifted from individual to nations and now nation to 'ISM'. Before disintegration of Soviet Russia, USSR was united, strong and militarily well-built. And with the collapse of iron curtain the entire world has come under the shadows of USA. Globalisation of world economy has to be seen and studied from this perspective. The single solo domination of USA in the world affairs, economics and politics would also be dominated by this solo country. It is USA which directs and dictates both the Economic and political affairs of the world. In our own country also struggle for supremacy of power has been going on for centuries. Mythology is full of these stories *Dev and Danav* struggle is known to every body. Ramayana and Mahabharat are nothing but testimony of these struggles.

It is still going on and going on. Only the nature has changed. Supremacy of race to supremacy of religion and supremacy of caste is the change over. *Chaturvarnya System* and caste system is the outcome of this struggle. Some people may perhaps say that it is not relevant in the present context to raise this issue. They may also say that in today's context caste and religion are immaterial. This could be the view of the so-called Liberals. But reality is that caste and religion is as important in todays politics and power-game as it was in past. Despite all reforms and socio-political developments the caste and religion has not lost its identity, existence and relevance. The ills of present economic policy-under liberalisation and privatisation is to be viewed in this context also.

Monopoly of Few and Loss to Majority

The outcome of the struggle of thousands of years for supremacy has given birth to such a social and religious system wherein power is a monopoly of a few and the loss to majority. This social & religious system has been known as *"Chaturvarnya System"* which had divided the society in four varnas - *Brahmin, Kshatriya, Vaishya and Shudra*. This was again a graded system, at the top Brahmin and at the botton Shudra. Those vested with all powers - political power, bureaucratic power, economic power and feudal power do not want to be deprived of those powers. It was their monopoly for thousands of years. How can they part with these powers? It is this power which empower them to do any thing and to get any thing done in their favour. To keep on this power in their hands for further more thousands of years, they have played number of tricks, tactics and manipulations and as on date also they are busy in the same manipulations.

The New Economic Policy, under the name of Globalisation and Liberalisation, is on the one hand their new discovery to further deprive the Bahujans (SC/ST/OBC and Monorites) of their legitimate rights or their share in governance of the country and to put an end to the emerging aspirations of the majority of the oppressed and exploited people of this land. It is their heart-burning that the Bahujans (SC/ST/OBC and Minorities) through reservation policy have acquired a somewhat better, socio-economic position over the period of past 50 years. As on date many of them are Collectors, SPs, Under Secretaries and Deputy Secretaries,. This rise of the Bahujans was the direct result of reservation policy and that very policy is the cause for their heart-burning. In public sector undertakings also though not happy position, to some extent the Bahujans have acquired little bit good position. This all happened despite their dishonesty, manipulations, tactics and callous attitude toward reservations. Now they are afraid that if this move is not halted or stopped, some day in future these reservationists, the Bahujans, the oppressed and exploited, would overtake them and they would not be in a position to dictate and dominate. Keeping this in view, the new economic policy is being implemented vigorously by the govt. of anti-reservations.

Disinvestment and Privatisation

The basic and the foremost purpose of this economic policy, through disinvestment and privatisation, is to prevent the Bahujans (SC/ST/OBC and Minorities) from entering into services through reservations, to checkmate their promotions and put an end to their rise. As long as the reservation policy is in vogue and government departments and public sector Undertakings are there they cannot be prevented from entering into services. But soon after the disinvestment, the stake of government would automatically come down and after privatisation no reservation would apply. It is with this intention, strategy and tactics the process of disinvestment has been intiated by the BJP led NDA government

New Economic Policy and Bahujans

The new economic policy adopted and intiated by Narsimha Rao government and now being vigorously implemented by the BJP led NDA government, is totally and fully against the interest of the Scheduled Castes, Scheduled Tribes and Other Backward Classes. It is, therefore, in the interests of Bahujans to oppose it and reject it tooth and nail. As it is known, BJP is the party of pro-capitalist, pro-businessmen and pro-landlords, it would protect only their interest. The present govt. has withdrawn subsidies from those items which were essential to the poor and middle class people. On the other hand the same BJP led government have given number of concessions to big business houses, industrialists and capitalists. During the 2 1/2 years rule, the entire face of Indian Economy has been changed. And if allowed a second term, the whole country would be slave of the national and international capitalists, where the Bahujans, the oppressed and the exploited, would be again at the whim and will of the so-called meritorious superiors !!

References

1. The Costitution and the Constituent Assembly - A Lok Sabha Secretariat Publication - p. 19,123.
2. *Ibid.*
3. Fifty years of Indian Parliamentary Democracy - A Lok Sabha Secretariat Publication - p. 40.
4. Nakara Vs Union of India (AIR-1983 SC-130 Para 33-34).
5. Economic Thoughts of Dr. Ambedkar : M.K. Dongre p. 58,59.
6. The Managerial Revolution : James Burnhum p. 104.
7. Democratic Socialism : Ashok Mehta p. 54.
8. Thus Spoke Ambedkar - compiled by Bhagwan Das Vol.-I p. 38.
9. The Shorter Constitution of India - Durga Das Basu p. 2.
10. Ambedkar's Quest for Democratic Socialism : A Research Paper : Dr. Balchandra Mungekar, University of Bombay.
11. Economic Thoughts of Dr. B.R. Ambedkar : M.K. Dongre p. 64.
12. Fifty Years of India Parliamentary Democracy : A Lok Sabha Secretariat Publication p. 40.
13. The Indian Express (New Delhi Ed.) 17/9/2000 p. Business-9.
14. Outlook - News Magazine - June 25, 2001 p. 46, 47.
15. Frontline - October 13, 2000 p. 50,51-52.
16. *Ibid.*
17. *Ibid.*
18. Nav Bharat - (Hindi Daily from Nagpur) dated 20/6/2001.
19. Frontline - October 13, 2000 p. 106.
20. Fifty years of Indian Parliamentary Democracy : A Lok Sabha Secretariat Publication.

7
Minorities and Indian Constitution

Attacks on members of India's Christian minority are only isolated acts and there is no organised compaign against them....

Said Prime Minister Atal Behari Vajpayee in Rome on 25th June, 2000 during his 2 days visit to Italy, the temporal seat of Pope and international capital of the world Roman Catholics. He was speaking to the Italian newspaper **La Stampo**....[1] He further declared that there was no ethnic war being waged between Hindus and Christians.

This was what the Indian Prime Minister committed to the world Christians at Rome. And within less than 6 months time, RSS Chief K.S. Sudershan told the Centre *To throw out foreign missionaries....*[2]

What is reality? Who is telling lie ? The Prime Minister, who declared himself as the 'Proud RSS Swayamsewak for life' and who even declared that 'his status as a swayamsewak' (a right no one can ever take away from him) is dearer to him than even Prime ministership or RSS chief, whose dubious and double-standard statement about demolition of Babri Masjid made him laughing stock among the Indians?

Not only that, the RSS attacks on minority Christians are on the rise, the RSS chief has also started malicious and hate campaign against even Muslims. Speaking on the occasion of the release of a magazine of Vishwa Samwad Kendra (an RSS sponsored organisation) at Lucknow on 18th October, 2000, he said that *it was a matter of shame that Indian Muslims did not take pride in their culture. The blood flowing in the veins of Indian Muslims is the same as that of Lord Rama and Krishna. Their form of worship may be different but they cannot disown that they are part of the Indian culture, the same culture which has shades of Lord Rama. Despite being a Muslim country, Indonesia has not severed its link with Ramayana and Mahabharata. In Afganisthan, people do not take pride in Babar. But, in India, for a section of Muslims Babar is revered figure. This tendency was detrimental to the unity and integrity of the nation....*[3]

Dubious Attempt to 'Nationalise' Islam and Christianity ?

To Rashtriya Swayamsewak Sangh Chief K.S. Sudershan ' foreign churches are practising a divisive politics and hatching a conspiracy against India's interest. While on the one hand he has exhorted all Christians in the country to establish a national church' severing ties with those abroad,' simultaneously he said, 'it will be in the interest of the nation to expel foreign churches from India'. He even did not lag behind to charge "The Baptist church of having converted tribals in Tripura and persecuting non-tribal Hindus. They are not allowed to perform Durgapuja and other Hindu festivals or even offer prayers. Hindus in the Union territory are being terrorised and forced to move out. It is part of the larger conspiracy to secede the hilly region from India...[4]

It is really very surprising that the Proud Swayamsewak of Rashtriya Swayamsewak Sangh Atal Behari Vajpayee, the liberal face of BJP and RSS, has embarked upon 'denationalisation of Indian Economy and sell-out of 'patriotic national public sector undertakings' at throw-away prices, his Chief Swayamsewak has been advising Indian Muslims and Christians 'for nationalisation of their faiths'. According to a senior RSS leader, who was present at the Vijayadashmi function of Delhi Provincial unit at Raja Garden, Mr. Sudarshan said--

"It is advisable to have a totally Indian Church like the one in China and all foreign Churches and missionaries should be asked by the government to pack and go".

Why do RSS and its off-shoot organisations repeatedly speak always against the Christians and Muslims? Why do they want that these religious communities should follow the so-called Indian culture and feel proud of being the links with Rama or Krishna? What is the Indian culture and how far it has played its role in the national unity or national integration ? What China and Indonesia have done, not necessarily be emulated in this country. This country has its own unique culture- composite culture, unity in diversity, emerged during the past many centuries. Samrat Akbar did not impose his Islamic culture on the Hindus of this country. He allowed all the religions and communities flourish spontaneously without hindrances.

If missionaries need to be thrownout from this country then why should 'Overseas Friends of the BJP', VHP temples and RSS shakhas be allowed on the foreign land ? Then why should Indians and that too the *Hindutvwadis* preaching Hinduism be allowed abroad ? The RSS and its chief along with Vishwa Hindu Parishad are spreading hatred, ill-feeling about Indians in the minds of Muslims and Christians abroad culminating into vicious socio-religious atmosphere in the country. It is not the missionaries who are danger to the national unity and integrity, but it is RSS, VHP, Bajrang Dal and organisations like Shiv Sena are dangerous for the national unity and integrity, which are poisoning the hearts and minds of simple and innocent Hindus against the Christians and Muslims.

RSS chief wants missonaries to be thrownout. Bajrang Dal activists ready to take up AK-47s if the need arises. Because Muslims want to turn this country into an Islamic State but they shall not let it happen. By their own admission, the Bajrang Dal has become "Synonymous with terror for the opponents of Hindus". And this very attitude and posture adopted by the Saffron saviours of *Hindutvawadi* culture and Hinduism instigated people like Dara to burn alive Catholic missionary Graham Staines and his two small children Philip (10) and Timothy (6). It was an initiative to scare away foreign missionaries.

"Those who want to destroy the Hindus must fear us" was the reaction of Bajrang Dal All India Convener Dr. Surendra Jain. " We want them to fear us. After all, criminal elements do fear the police", continued he. And BJP President (then) Kushabhau Thakre gave him - the culprit Dara Singh- a clean chit : Bajrang Dal men are good nationalist. George Fernandes like Indira Gandhi, in her footsteps finds foreign hand every time. "The incident was part of a conspiracy from within and outside to crucify Vajpayee team" said he.

The gruesome burning alive of Australian Catholic missionary Graham Staines and his two kids on January 23, 1999 was not an isolated incident, as clarified by Prime Minister

Atal Behari Vajpayee at Rome. It was not really a stray incident. It was culmination of hate-campaign initiated, organised and propagated by VHP, Bajrang Dal and other RSS sponsored organasitions against the Christian missionaries.

Minorities under Continuous Attacks

"Ever since the Bhartiya Janata Party led NDA government assumed power at the Centre, there has been a low-intensity war against Christians in India, especially nuns and priests, by groups and organisations loyal to Sangh Pariwar. A wave of attacks against Christian evangelists and places of worship through 1998 culminated in the murder of the Australian missionary Graham Staines and his two sons.... A second wave of terror against Christian missionaries, that extends now to the states of Uttar Pradesh, Haryana, Punjab and Andhra Pradesh, has culminated this June in a series of bomb-blasts in churches in Karnataka, Goa and Andhra Pradesh...."[5]

And, again it was not isolated attack. According to the Director General of Police, Karnataka C. Dinakaran there was the same group of conspirators behind all the three blasts, that were managed in the churches of Andhra and Karnataka. "The fact of conspiracy is now clearly established. This points not only to careful and co-ordinated planning, but also to new levels and strategies of planned violence suggestive of a deadly seriousness of purpose. No longer need mobs be mobilised in the destruction of places of Christian worship as in the past....

The serial bomb blasts were in the nature of message of intimidation, not just to those who work for Christian organisations but to Church Congregations, from prayer meetings to Sunday school gatherings...."[6]

According to the United Christian Forum for Human Rights (UCFHR), there have been 35 recorded anti-Christian crimes between January and June this year (2000)[7]. Fr. Dr. H.R. Donald De Souza, deputy secretary general of the Catholic Bishops Conference of India told **Frontline** : "I read in all this a pattern of violence. These were similar explosive devices that were used. We suspect an organised movement by fundamentalist groups who have been emboldened by the in-action of the government...[8]

Attacks by fundamentalists on the Christians, their places of worships, schools and institutions run by them and the 'preachers of faith' are not isolated. There is a definite scheme, planning and systematic co-ordination, financed heavily by the godfathers sitting in different places. Whether it is Gujarat where tribals are being subjected to re-conversion to Hinduism, or Uttar Pradesh, Madhya Pradesh and Maharashtra, where nuns and fathers alongwith places of worships are the targets of attacks.

"The recent beating up of Fr Oscar Mendonca of St John the Baptist Church at Thane on 6th Aug. 2001 is the latest in a series of attacks by Hindu fundamentalists on Christian priests and organisations in Mumbai and the rest of Maharashtra.

Almost all the attacks have been prompted by allegations that the missionaries were converting adivasis and backward caste Hindus into Christianity.

The Bajrang Dal, which was involved in the Thane attack, figures in three other incidents. It disrupted the new year celebrations at St Francis D' Assisi church, Borivli, in 1998, objecting to the 'obscene' dresses of the revellers. Earlier, in November 1995, they attacked a peaceful dharna of the Bombay Catholic Sabha at Flora Fountain, injuring six of their members. The Sabha was demanding reservations for Scheduled Caste Christians.

In February 1998, a mob of 40 youngsters stormed the Catholic Hospitals Association of India camp at Latur, manhandled Fr Jeevandra Jadhav, the camp-in-charge, and molested and injured other residents including Sister Marlene Parakkadan. Three days prior to this, the Pune-based edition of *Tarun Bharat*, an RSS mouthpiece, *Saamna*, the Shiv Sena mouthpiece, had carried allegedly inflammatory reports credited to Jan Kalyan Samiti, an RSS affiliated, alleging that this Catholic group (involved in relief work after the 1993 quake and with health and education thereafter) was engaging in conversion.

In January 1999, around the time churches were being attacked in Dangs district of Gujrat, a church put up by adivasi converts in Kayre Sadarpada village, Peth taluka, Nashik, was demolished by locals under instigation from members of Vanvasi Kalyan Ashram, the social welfare wing of the Vishwa Hindu Parishad (VHP).

On May 9, 2000, VHP and Bajrang Dal activists barged into a Christian girl hostel at Abhona in the tribal taluka of Kalwan in Nasik and assaulted those watching a film of Jesus Christ.

In April 2000, a car and a shed at a Pota fathers' ashram at

Tabor in Kalyan were gutted under mysterious circumstances. The ashram had allegedly been receiving threats since it was visited a by a large number of Christians seeking spritual guidance.

Besides, there have been several instances where priests and nuns at missionary schools have been threatened. In one such incident in January 1997, a mob of Shiv Sainiks stormed into the Canossa High school at Andheri to protest against the 'conversion' of Hindu student. Their anger had been fueled by *Saamna,* which was carrying a series accusing this school as well as other missionary-run schools of forcible conversions.[8(a)] So what is the objective behind these attacks on Christians and Muslims? The nature of attacks has been very systematically planned.

For quite long time the Muslims were the targets of the attacks through communal riots. Malegaon in Maharashtra, Meerut and Aligarh in U.P., Hyderabad in A.P., Gulbarga in Karnataka, Jamshedpur in Bihar and such many other places all over India including Delhi were the places for their victimisation. During this period, the hate-campaign unleashed by the *Hindutvawadi* organisations helped their political organisations to consolidate their strength in the name of Hinduism and to save the Hindus from the attacks of 'Kafirs'. 'Hindus and Hinduism in danger' was the most uniting and cementing force to strengthen their political force and communal riots were one of the methods, designed for the purpose. This method helped them a lot to expand and strengthen the political base of the party. 1927 to 1947 by haunting the terror tactics of insecurity and survival in danger of Hindu samaj, was the earlier version of uniting method. In fact, the RSS was launched only with the sole objective of protection and organisation of Hindus alone.

Article 3 of the constitution of RSS says :

> "The aims and objects of the Sangh are to weld together the diverse groups within the Hindu Samaj and to revitalise and rejuvenate the same on the basis of its Dharma and sanskriti, that it may achieve an all-sided development of the Bharatvarsha."...[(9)]

Minorities Under Communal Scrutiny

And Shri Guruji - the second Sarsanghchalak of RSS in his *'Bunch of Thoughts'* (Bible of RSS) addressed the Muslims No.1

Internal Threat to the unity and integrity of the country. He observed :

> ".... It has been the tragic lesson of the history of many a country in the world that the hostile elements within the country pose a far greater menace to national security than aggressors from outside. Unfortunately, this first lesson of national security has been the one thing which has been consistently ignored in our country ever since the British left this land. Wishful thinking borne out of lack of courage to face realities, mouthing of high-sounding slogans by the persons at the helm of affairs to cover up the tragedies overtaking one after another, and opportunistic alliances of parties and groups with the hostile elements to further their narrow self-interests, have all combined to make the threat to internal subversion of our nationalfreedom and security very acute and real...."[10]

With this philosophical note about the national security, Shree Guruji wanted to build-up an atmoshphere of suspicion and doubt about a particular community and then he openly said:

"....First let us take the case of Muslims. Even to this day, there are so many who say, 'now there is no Muslim problem at all. All those ritous elements who supported Pakistan have gone away once and for all. The remaining Muslims are devoted to our country. After all they have no other place to go and they are bound to remain loyal...."[11]

How many times those *Hindutvawadis* would question and test their loyalty and integrity? How long and for how many generations do they need to prove their bonafides ? Captain Abdul Hamid's sacrifice in Indo-Pak war of 1965 was no testimony to all the time suspicious *Hindutvawadis*? Jaichand was no Muslim who betrayed Prithvi Raj Chauhan ! How do we recall the services of Abul Kalam Azad and Dr. Zakir Hussain ? But the Sanghi mentality is so poisoned with the minorities presence that Shree Guruji was not prepared to accept the existence of Muslims in national mainstream. While raising the issue of loyalty and credibility and their devotion to the cause of country he asked :

> "But what are the facts? Is it true that all pro-Pakistani elements have gone away to Pakistan? It was the Muslims in Hindu majority provinces led by Uttar Pradesh who provided the spearhead for the movement for Pakistan right from the beginning. And they have remained solidly here even after partition. In fact, the Muslims of Punjab, Bengal, Sind and NWFP which went over to Pakistan had totally rejected Muslim League in 1937 elections. It was only in later years, that because of the wrong policies of our leadership, the Muslims there were pushed into the arms of the Muslim League.... Have those who remained here changed at least after that ? Has their old hostility and murderous mood, which resulted in widespreadriots, looting, arson, raping and all sorts of orgies on an unprecedented scale in 1946-47 come to a halt at least now? It would be suicidal to delude ourselves into believing that they have turned patriots overnight after the creation of Pakistan. On the contrary, the Muslim menace has increased a hundred fold by the creation on Pakistan which has become a spring board for all their future aggressive designs of our country...."[12]

Shree Guruji did not term the 'Muslims' alone the internal threat to the country, but he branded even the Christians as 'Internal Threat' to the country. In the same 'Bunch of Thoughts', he observed :

> "The way they (Christians) are behaving towards other people forces us to conclude that the modern proselytising religions have very little of true religion in them. In the name of God, Prophet and religion, they are only trying to further their political ambitions. In true religion there need be no proselytisation, no change in the way of worship. Our religious missionaries who reached distant lands in ancient times did not force their religion on other people. (There was no such Hindutvawadi religion as today's in those days and, if any, Dr. Ambedkar has given

> detailed assessment of that religion in his 'Riddles of Hinduism' which is worth-reading for those who are interested to know in detail). And "So long as the Christians here indulge in such activities and consider themselves as agents of the international movement for the spread of Christianity, and refuse to offer their first loyalty to the land of their birth and behave as true children of the heritage and culture of their ancestors, they will remain here as hostiles and will have to be treated as such...."[13]

It is again the same very question of loyalty and integrity that is in doubt in the eyes of *Hindutvawadis*. Who are they to question the loyalty and integrity of the Muslims and Christians often and often ?

> ".... Within our Constitutional framework, Indians have no 'primary' indentity, least of all one defined religiously. Nor is Christianity or Islam 'alien' or new. Indian Christianity goes back to 52 A.D.—eight centuries before any thing resembling Hinduism as we know it today was consolidated here. Christianity is much odler in India than in Europe, today considered its 'Home'. Islam in India too goes back more than a thousand years. It evolved organically here, as part of this soil. Historians such as Romila Thapar argue that India has always been plural and multi-religious. Secondly, it is doubtful if most Christians or Muslims in India were 'forcibly' converted.... Had there been mass-scale forcible conversion—as distinct from a willful change of faith by, say, dalits, to escape caste oppression– India, would not have had a fairly well-dispersed population of Muslims or Christians in most of India........"[(14)]

As observed by Praful Bidwai in his article—Tapping a Rich Vein of Irrationality (Frontline - July 21, 2000) 'Indian Christianity goes back to 52 A.D. - eight centuries before anything resembling Hinduism as we know it today', it is abundantly evident that it was Hinduism which has been imposed on the natives of India by force, and not Christianity. The British, the Europeans came to India much later than the missionaries. And who co-operated with the Europeans to allow them consolidate their rule- those very Hindu Kings, Jamindars, Feudal lords and the so-called high caste people. It is they who betrayed the motherland to enjoy the favour of the Rulers !!

The right to religious conversion is a fundamental Constitutional right. Article 25 guarantes the right to freely profess, practice and propagate religion subject to certain restrictions. The freedom of religions is subject to the interest of public order so that it would not outrage the religious feelings of another class with a deliberate intent. What the *Hindutvawadis* are doing for the past many years amounts to outrage the religious feelings of the Christians and Muslims. And thus they are playing a fraud on the Constitution. It is none of the business of RSS chief to advise the Muslims and Christians to Indianise their religions and cut-off their relations with Mecca-Madina or Vatican. Also, the derogatary assessment of the humane service of Christian missionaries by Shree Guruji does not fit to his position and personality of the head of the so-called one socio-cultural organisation like RSS. What he has observed about the Christian Missionaries is most condemnable:

> "So far as the Christians are concerned, to a superficial observer they appear not only quite harmless but as the very embodiment of compassion and love for humanity ! Their speeches abound in words like 'service' and 'human salvation' as though they are specially deputed by the Almighty to uplift humanity ! They run schools and colleges, hospitals and orphanages. The people of our country, simple and innocent as they are, are taken in by all these things. But what is the real and ulterior motive of Christians in pouring crores of rupees in all these activities."....[15]

If this is the assessment of missionary activities by RSS, what to talk about the various Sewa Departments opened by RSS : Vanvasi Kalyan Ashrams, Sewa Bharti, Vidya Bharati under which 13,000 schools, 74,000 teachers and 17.5 lakh students are being prepared to outrage the religious feelings of other religions !

Politics of Communal Riots

Recently, one of the top functionaries of Bhartiya Janata Party boasted, counting the achievements of BJP rule. In the words that functionary BJP has been very successful to a most extent to put an end to the communal riots in the country. However the story is entirely different. It was observed that most of the time and also supported by the findings of the Commission of Enquiries that in most of the riots, either RSS, BJP, Bajrang Dal or Vishwa Hindu Parishad activists or their off-shoot organisational functionaries were involved. As mentioned in earlier paragraph by the All India Convener of Bajrang Dal, Dr. Surendra Jain— 'We want them to fear us. After all criminal elements do fear the police-', that is what the Sanghi loyalists use the methods of communal riots to terrorise and terrify the minorities so as not to allow them raise their heads and submerge in the *Hindutvawadi* majority will.

"Justice P. Jaganmohan Reddy of the Supreme Court headed the Commission of Enquiry into the communal disturbances at Ahmedabad and other places in Gujarat, on and after September 18, 1969. Its report noted that ' the agitation had received the blessings of the local Bhartiya Jan Sangh workers who did not want to involve themselves directly but suggested the formation of an organization known as Hindu Dharma Raksha Samiti with Harishchandra Panchal, an old RSS worker, as its convener'. The Commission found that the Hindu Dharma Raksha Samiti had issued pamphlets calling on the Hindus ' to prepare for "Dharma Yudha" without waiting for justice to be done by the Government to serve all economic and social relations with the community that has attacked their religion, viz. the Muslims.' The report noted the 'definite part played in various Districts which were affected by the workers of the Jan Sangh and Hindu Mahasabha organisations or by persons having leaning towards them. There is evidence definitely that they took a leading part in the Districts of Amreli, Banaskantha, Mehsana and Baroda...."[16]

The Report of the Justice Vithayathil Commission of Enquiry on the Tellicherry riots in December, 1971 said :

"I have no doubt that the RSS had taken an active part in rousing up anti-Muslim feeling among the Hindus

> of Tellicherry and in preparing the background of the disturbances. The same can be said about the Jan Sangh also. Athough there may not be any official connection between the Jan Sangh and the RSS, the RSS in generally regarded as the military wing of the Jan Sangh and the Jan Sangh, the political wing of the RSS. That the two organisations are regarded as one by the common people is admitted by P13W1 Chandrasekharan.... the Jan Sangh unit in Kerala has taken the same attitude towards the Muslims as the RSS....

"Chandrasekharan was the Secretary of the Hindus Samekshana Samiti-another united front and prominent RSS worker in Tellicherry."[17]

"The Report of the Justice Jitendra Narain Commission of Enquiry into the Jamshedpur riots in April 1979 has one chapter that deals with the RSS. Deoras addressed an RSS Conference on April 1,1979 just 10 days before the outbreak of the disturbances. The report observed that his speech amounted to communal propaganda and held the RSS responsible for creating a climate for the disturbances that took place. The Commission also concluded that a certain Dina Nath Pandey was,"a member of the RSS, his actions followed a line which was in fulfillment of the general scheme of the Hindu Communalists of Jamshedpur and that they were also aimed at achieving the plan announced in the leaflet circulated by them. His conduct had, thus, directly contributed to the outbreak of the riot at Jamshedpur, on the occasion of the Ram Navami Festival of 1979."[18]

Communal riots have also been used as the strategy to capture the political power by the communal groups. What happened in Surat on August 4 and 5, 2000 is a concrete example of politics of votes. 'Surat responded with alarming violence to the Vishwa Hindu Parishad's call for a bandh to protest against the killing of Amarnath pilgrims. During the two days, 18 incidents of stabbing, five of them fatal took place and property worth Rs.1 crore was damaged.... what followed, however, indicated that the violence was pre-planned. Shops were broken into and looted and it is no coincidence the looted shops were owned by Muslims. " It seemed as if it had all been worked out", said an official source. "It was designed to become violent.

Rumours were deliberately spread. We saw mobile phones in use every where. It was as if the violence was being directed". According to eye witness accounts Bajrang Dal activists looted shops in the Bhagal and Chowk Bazar areas...... There was two fold objective of that outburst, said a highly placed official. One was to polarise the votes. *The Vishwa Hindu Parishad thought it could generate more votes for the ruling party (BJP) through violence.* This view is substantiated by researchers at the Centre for Social Studies as well as by Desai, who says: "Whipping up religious sentiments always helps in getting more votes. Political parties preach one thing but practice something different. They incite communal felings and then step farward at election time and claim to be the protectors of voters". Desai believes that the VHP adopted this game plan. "The fear losing power prompted them to incite the riots" say an informed sources.... All that was manipulated because elections to the corporation were to be held in September 2000....[19]

The nature of communal riots in Mumbai immediately after the demolition of Babri Masjid has not a different story. 'To teach them lesson, was the main objective from both sides. The series of bomb blasts at different places on the day causing fatal injuries and destructions of properties was also planned to teach the lesson.' But who were victims? Innocent and poor people of Mumbai?

"The Shrikrishna Report is clear just where the blame lies for the 1992-93 riots. On the basis of the welter of evidence before him, the judge concluded that, "the communal passions of Hindus were aroused to fever pitch by the inciting writings in (the) print media, particularly *Saamna and Navakal"* (Marathi dailies from Mumbai) "From 8th January 1993. at leas"t, he concluded, "there is no doubt that the Shiv Sena and Shiv Sainiks took the lead in organising attacks on Muslims and their properties from the level of Shakha Pramukh to the Sena Pramukh Bal Thakeray who, like a veteran General, commanded his loyal Shiv Sainiks to retaliate by organised attacks against Muslims".

The Report also blamed the "effete political leadership, vacillation for political reasons and conflicting orders issued to the Commissioner of Police" for the State's failure to contain the attacks on Mumbai's Muslims'....Police officers and men, particularly at junior level," Justice Shrikrishna found, "appeared to have an in-built bias against the Muslims". This bias, he noted, "manifested (itself) in their reluctance to firmly put down incidents of violence, looting and arson which went on unchecked"....[20]

Among the minorities, even the Sikhs have not been spared by the *Hindutvawadi* organisations. 1984 communal riots, when hundreds and hundreds of Sikhs were made the target by *Hindutvawadis*, some of them were burn alive, while others were killed. 'Teach them the lesson was the slogan'. Buddhists or the Scheduled Castes and Scheduled Tribes have been routine victims of the *Hindutvawadi* atrocities. Jully 1997's police firing on the Dalits of Mumbai's Ramabai Nagar and inhuman atrocities committed on the Dalits in some of the villages nearby Nagpur are glaring instances of police-excesses in leage with *Hindutvawadis*. Though our Constitution has assured the minorities their life, liberty, cultures, language and institutions through articles 25 to 30, in reality, in most of the time, the same have proved dead-letters. The bureaucracy, the police and the politicians have failed the arrangements of the Constitution. This *Hindutvawadi* combination has been, continuously and consistenly, directly and indirectly, attacking the Constitution by way of flouting these very provisions of the Constitution.

Historical Monuments: Disputes to Demoralize Minorities

After communal riots, historical monuments are the second most important factors being used to terrorise and demoralise the minorities. Babri Masjid is not the isolated and the only example mis-used by the *Hindutvawadi* majority-community to teach the lesson to the minorities. There are so many monuments all over India being used and mis-used to rock the issues.

Our Constitution has guaranteed every religious denominations or any section thereof to establish and maintain institutions for religious and charitable purposes. Article 49 of the Constitution says :

> "It shall be obligation of the State to protect every monument or place or object of artistic or historic interest, declared by or under law made by Parliament to be of national importance from spoliation, disfigurement, destruction, removal, disposal or export as the case may be".

And as per Ancient Monuments and Archaeological Sites and Remains Act, 1958 and the Rules framed under the Act 1959, 'no construction can be under taken within a radius of 100 meters of the notified monument leave alone within the premises of a protected monument. Despite that, 'several structures temples dedicated to various gods of the Hindu pantheon have come up on the premises of the Sher Shah Suri mausoleum at Sasaram in Rohtas district (Bihar) and sought *post facto* legitimacy to those structures as places of worship.

"The matter was reported to the District Magistrate for his intervention and strict action. But the District Magistrate declined to take any action. Over the 25 years of unchecked encroachment temples dedicated to various gods of the Hindu pantheon have been built on this premises. The master mind behind all these activities is Jawahir Prasad, a former Bhartiya Janata Party legislator who has been threatening and intimidating local ASI personnal, in charge of the upkeep of the monument.

At New Delhi, The Vishwa Hindu Parishad, meanwhile, has served notice that it intends to take up the politics of Islamic monuments once again. On November 14, 2000 a group of 130 activists belonging to the VHP and Bajrang Dal attempted to perform a "Dev Mukti Yagna" at the spot where Ganesha idol is placed in the Quwat-ul-Islam mosque in Qutub Minar Complex"....[21]

One more example of communal attack on the historic monument is that of Fatehpur Sikri Palace in Uttar Pradesh which is under the rule of Bhartiya Janata Party for the past more than 3½ years. During this very period "The Archeological Survey of India (ASI) has irretrievably damaged a part of a Palace and a mound in Fatehpur Sikri, the historic fort-city built by Akbar in the 1560s.....

Members of the ASI team who undertook the excavation claimed that they were looking for a temple under the mound and a secret cell under the palace courtyard. While doing so, the archeologists dug up works of architecture nearly 500 years old. The team which carried out the excavations throughout the last two years, told vernacular dailies in Agra and Aligarh that certain historical documents they had found indicated that the Mughal emperor had built his fort capital after demolishing a temple....[22]

The Justice Vithayathil Commission of Enquiry Report has very rightly and very correctly declared as to who, most of the time, are the people for incitement and instigation of communal flare-up. BJP MLA Jawahir Prasad in Sararam of Rohtas District is the mastermind to disturb the communal harmony there, while BJP Rule in UP has taken the timely advantage of spreading rumour that Fatehpur Sikri Palace had been built after demolishing the temple.

The BJP has repeatedly reiterated that Kashi and Mathura are on their agenda. In addition to these two places, the place like Charminar of Hyderabad and Dhawalgiri's Buddhist Peace Stupa(Orissa near Bhubaneshwar) built by Japanese are most likely to be the next places of dispute. The temple constructed adjacent to the left side of Charminar is recent addition but it would not take much time to dispute the construction of Charminar and incite the communal flare-up.

The temple of Shankara constructed behind the Buddhist Peace Stupa at Dhawalgiri, 8 kms away from Bhubneswar (Orissa) has also been a recent addition to the place, and the same has been constructed with some definite ulterior motive by the communalists. One of the churches in Mumbai has also been claimed by Shiv Sena to have been constructed by the Britishers after the destruction of a temple. The famous Muslim Shrine-Mazar of Malang Shah Baba near Kalyan (Mumbai) had also been claimed by Shiv Sena as the original place of Hindu Devtas or Rishis'.

The world famous Buddha Gaya's Maha Boddhi Maha Vihar has also been brought under dispute by the *Hindutvawadis*. The statues of Buddha, shrewdly and cunningly, were declared as the statues of Shankara. Under the Act of 1949, the control, supervision and day-to-day maintenance was eutrusted to a committee dominated by Hindus. A move by Bhante Surai Sasai a Japanese Buddhist Monk in India, has already started to liberate the Mahaboddhi Maha Vihara of Buddha Gaya from the clutches of *Hindutvawadis*.

Goa is another place, likely to be in the hit-list of Hindutvawadi encroachment ".... If it has its way, Goa will be the Kashi of the west coast rather than the Rome of the East. A glossy booklet circulated by the Sangh Parivar seeks to establish that an important Hindu temple was destroyed by the Portuguese and a church was built in its place.

Also, the booklet claims that Goans have a 'north Indian'

heritage. It raises questions about the origins of Christianity in Goa. It asks : "How can anybody deny that siblings of certain families are both Hindus and Christians? There are many books that trace the history of its people to the north of India."

This is not the first time that the VHP has focused on Goa. It had wanted to take out an all-India march from the island of Diwar in October 1999. The plan never got off the ground, but Diwar has remained a fixation for VHP leaders.

The booklet quotes Jesuit historian Fr. Francisco da Souza, author of *Oriente Conquista*, as saying, "Diwar was as much venerated by the Hindus as the Holy Land is by us on account of a temple of many indulgences and pilgrimages, and even at present, on a certain day of the year, Hindus flock there to bathe."

The VHP booklet says, "The temple on the island is relocated at Narve in Bicholim taluka after the original was destroyed by the Portuguese. It was rebuilt by Shivaji in 1668. The temple is dedicated to Lord Shiva as Shri Sapta Koteeshvara. The holy *lingam*, made of an alloy of seven metals and consecrated by seven sages, was believed to grant freedom from sin by sight and the salvation by touch. Thus, the tradition of pilgrimage is traced to unknown antiquity."

Combining its argument "with the tradition of Vedic and Sanskrit learning recorded in various copper plates", the booklet concludes that Goa is equal to Kashi as a centre of pilgrimage as well as learning."[23]

After failure of the infamous Freedom of Religions Bill, introduced in Parliament by Bhartiya Jan Sangha's O.P. Tyagi in 1978, the year-back the Uttar Pradesh Regulation of Public Religious Buildings and Places Bill 2000 is another dubious initiative to destroy the minorities religious places which amounts to serious attack on the religious and cultural rights available to minorities under the Constitution of India. Not that, the RSS dominated and controlled BJP Govt. of Uttar Pradesh have got the said Bill passed by both Houses of the Uttar Pradesh Legislature in January 2000 and awaiting the President's nod, similar Acts viz. The Rajasthan Religious Buildings and Places Act, 1954 under Congress Rule of Mohan Lal Sukhadia in Rajasthan and the Madhya Pradesh Sarvanjanik Dharmik Bhawan Tatha Stan Viniyaman Adhiniyam, 1984 under the Congress stalwart Arjun Singh in Madhya Pradesh are not different. It is, therefore, "Samajwadi

Party leader Mulayam Singh Yadav has gone to town trumpeting the Rajasthan and MP legislation to tell the minorities in UP that what the RSS is doing in their state while in power had been done by the Congress in the neighbouring states years ago....[24]

The re-construction of Somnatha temple with the active and direct support of Sardar Patel and the same having been inagurated by the then President Dr. Rajendra Prasad has embolded the communalists to repeat Somanatha in Ayodhya and else where. The BJP has always tried to give this incident the official colour. But Pandit Nehru made it very clear 'on July 12, 1950 by writing to Dr. K.M. Munshi' : I have been feeling a little uncomfortable at your reference to the re-building of the Somnatha temple. As a Government we cannot undertake the building of any religions edificies."....[25]

Explaining the Government's stand on the issue of Somnath temple, Pandit Nehru in a letter to the Chief Ministers, wrote :

"You must have read about the coming ceremonies to Somanath temple. Many people have been attracted to this and some of my colleagues are even associated with it in their individual capacities. But it should be clearly understood that this function is not governmental *and the Government of India as such has nothing to do with it* : While it is easy to understand a certain measure of public support to this venture, we have to remember that we must not do anything which come in the way of our State being secular. That is the basis of our Constitution and governments, therefore, refrain from associating themselves with anything which tends to affect the secular character of our State. There are, unfortunately, many communal tendencies at work in India today and we have to be on our guard against them. It is important that governments should keep the secular and non-communal ideal always before them"....[26]

The Bhartiya Janata Party has cunningly and cleverly misused the Somanath issue to misguide the masses that Nehru Government was associated with the re-construction of Somnath temple. And as such, Government must handover the Ayodhya - Babri Masjid dispute land to the Ramjanmabhoomi Nyas. After Ayodhya, their next agenda is Kashi and Mathura and such as in the lines many more places of religious importance. The main objective behind this strategy is to synchronise the reach of minorities to expand their area of influence and make them submit to *Hindutvawadi* majority community.

References

1. The Times of India, (Mumbai) June 26, 2000.
2. *Ibid,* October 3, 2000.
3. *Ibid,* October 19, 2000.
4. *Ibid,* October 16, 2000.
5. Frontline–July 9, 2000, p. 22.
6. *Ibid.*
7. *Ibid.*
8(a) The Times of India, (Mumbai)–August 11, 2001.
9. The RSS : Myth and Reality : Dinanath Mishra–p. 208.
10. Bunch of Thoughts : M.S. Golwalkar–p. 177, 178, 189, 194.
11. *Ibid.*
12. *Ibid.*
13. *Ibid.*
14. Frontline - July 21, 2000, p. 103.
15. Bunch of Thoughts : M.S. Golwalkar–p. 188.
16. The RSS and the BJP : A Division of Labour : A.G. Noorani–p. 38, 39.
17. *Ibid.*
18. *Ibid.*
19. Frontline–November 10, 2000, p. 41-42.
20. Frontline–August 12, 2000, p. 12.
21. Frontline–December 22, 2000, p. 45.
22. The Times of India (Mumbai)–January 4, 2001.
23. The Times of India (Mumbai)–October 21, 2000.
24. The Asian Age (New Delhi) April 11, 2000.
25. Frontline–February 2, 2001, p. 96, 97.
26. *Ibid.*

8
Nation, Nationalism and Constitution

What is Nation ?

"A nation," E. Barker says "is a body of persons inhabiting a definite territory and thus united together by primary fact of living together on a common land. They are drawn from number of races and they come from different breeds.... While living together for a sufficiently long time they developed two forms of sympathy. The first is a common capital of thoughts and feelings acquired and transmitted in the course of common history; a common capital, or tradition, which include as a rule common language, a common religion (which may, however, assume a number of different forms), and architecture, in literature, in social habits and otherwise. The second is the common will to live together for the future freely and independently, thus, having common thoughts and aspirations, and thereby exercising their right of political self-determination"[1]

Living together for a long time and sharing a common legacy with a determination 'to live together and die together' feelings bind the people to make a nation. A nation is, thus, the expression of the peoples' conciousness of unity. 'We-ness' and the common bond of cementing the people emotionally, culturally and socially, irrespective of a demarcated territory, make a nation. Palestianians and Jews had no demarcated territory for a long, still they could constitute a nation.

We have a common legacy of thousands of years. We have survived number of invasions and aggessions. Alexander the Great and Chengiz-Khan's invasions also could not destroy this great nation, inhabitated by the natives - aboriginals- mulnivasis! Renam, however, in his famous essay on Nationality, had observed that it was not race, language and land that make a nation. "A nation", according to him is, "is a living soul, a spiritual principle. Two things, which in truth are but one, constitute this soul, this spiritual principle. One is in the past, the other in the present. One is the common possession of a rich heritage of memories, the other is the actual consent, the desire to live together, the will to preserve worthily the undivided inheritance which has been handed down .... The nation like the individual, is the outcome of a long past of efforts, and sacrifices, and devotion.... A heroic past, greatmen, glory—I mean the glory of the genuine kind,—these form the social capital, upon which a national idea may be founded. To have a common glories in the past, a common will in the present; to have done great things done together, to will to do the like again,—such are the essential conditions for the making of a people.... Forgetfulness, and I shall even say historical error, form essential factor in the creation of nation; and thus it is that progress of historical studies may often be dangerous to the nationality.... But the essence of the nation is, that all its individual members should have things in common; and also, that all of them should hold many things in oblivion....[2]

The oppressed and exploited people of this land—The Dalit-Shoshit Samaj, despite their terrible and unbearable oppression and exploitation, torture, humiliation and even having been subjected to in– human treatment for centuries , decided to forget and forgive and devote their all to this very land—as their motherland, the great nation. There was nothing common, their sufferings, their agony. But firm resolve to live together and develop this land—the nation, to such a great height of development and progress that today it stands as a nation—a great and powerful nation !

Among the minorities, even after a traumatic results of Partition in 1947, the remaining Muslims and Christians decided to live together and contribute to the development and progress to this country. However, it is irony of fate that to Shri Guruji—M.S. Golwalkar, the second Sarsanghachalak of RSS (Chief), minorities are still a great threat to this country!

Nationalists and Nationalism

Ever since India became free, the credentials of the minorities—the constitutional minorities—Muslims and

Christians, have come under continuous fire by the so-called nationalists—the Hindu nationalists. They (minorities) have always been branded as anti-nationals by the same very so-called Hindu nationalists. It has, therefore, become essential to know as to what is 'nationalism' and who are the 'nationalists'!

According to Dr. D.R. Jatav, "Nationalism in general is an ideology based on devotion to or love of one's country either by birth or by choice. In particular, there are as many nationalisms as there are nations. The real basis of nationalism is cultural, something spiritual. Nationalism is closely related with man's life, pride and activity. Nationalism is a force in the history of mankind. It cannot be overlooked now and at any time, by the emerging forces—social and political—in the different parts of the world"[3]

To Dr. Ambedkar, "Nationalism means the desire for a separate national existence for those who are bound by this tie of kinship. Secondly, it is true that there cannot be nationalism without the feeling of nationality being in existence.... nationality does not in all cases produce nationalisms. For nationality to flame into nationalism two conditions must exist. First, there must arise 'will to live as a nation'. Nationalism is the dynamic expression of that desire. Secondly, there must be a territory which nationalism could occupy and make it a State, as well as cultural home of the nation"[4]

K.S. Sudershan, the present RSS Chief, has also the same views about nation and nationalism. According to him, "....a society having mental and emotional bonds with a particular well-defined territory and imbued with a sense of 'we-ness' acquires the nomenclature of 'Nation' in that particular piece of land. The great men who contribute to its protection, progress and prosperity evoke deep feelings of reverence and gratitude in that society. And the attachment to the values of life and traditions borne out of a long existence in that land also become a major link for binding the people of that nation to one another. Apart from that there are many factors like language, history, festivals, feeling of having a common enemies and friends, common economic and political interests, common aspirations etc. which strengthen this feeling; but none of them is indispensable for the formation of every state'[5]

It could well be observed from the above that the basis of

nationalism is cultural and spiritual. It is that very feeling of attachment to a particular piece of land—a territory, the residence for years—and for centuries. It is also a will to live together. Common interest and common aspirations help to build-up and strengthen the feeling of nationalism. It is a very strong feeling of 'one-ness'. 'The attitude of glorifying the pride and protecting the interest of one's own country is the basic tenet of nationalism and the attitude of loving one's own country is patriotism'[6]

Judged on the basis of the basic tenets of the concept of nationalism, nobody can challenge the loyalty, dedication and patriotism of any other persons, born and brought-up and dedicated for the betterment of this country irrespective of religion, caste, class or creed.

There is no barometer with a particular community or religious sect to measure the nationalistic feelings or dedication of some other community or religious sect. All those, who are born and brought up on this land and whose ancestors have lived here for generations could never be singled out and need to prove their bonafide, loyalty or their dedication towards this country. As such it is totally wrong and mallicious when Shri Guruji - Golwalkarji doubts the integrity and loyalty of Muslims in India after Partition. He questions :

".... Have those who remained here changed at least after that ? Has their old hostility and murderous mood, which resulted in wide spread riots, looting, arson, raping and all sorts of orgies on an unprecedented scale in 1946-47, come to a halt at least now ? It would be suicidal to delude ourselves into believing that they have turned patriots overnight after the creation of Pakistan. On the contrary, the Muslim menace has increased a hundred-fold by the creation of Pakistan which has become a springboard for all their future aggressive designs on our country"[7]

It is also very clear from the above that those who do not have the sense of 'one-ness' or 'we-ness' and desire to live together, they cannot be called nationalists or patriots. Who are those, who do not subscribe to this concept ? Can we call those Hindus nationalist and patriots, who are selling the secrets of the country and spying for other countries?

Hinduism and Nationalism

In the RSS dictionary Hinduism and nationalism are one

and the same thing. Hinduism has become synonymous of nationalism. That means only Hindu is national and all others, if not anti-national, are not national. And if the attitude of glorifying the pride and protecting the interest of one's own country is the basic tenet of nationalism, what to call the sacrifices of all those, who laid down their lives for protection of the country. Those include Sikhs, Muslims, Christians and Buddhists, in addition to Hindus. The sacrifice of captain Hamid in the Indo-Pak war of 1965 is not a rare example. There are hundreds and hundreds of Muslims and Christians who sacrificed their lives for protecting the interests of the country. Do they not belong to the nationalist race ?

According to Dr. Ambedkar, " ....Hindu society is a myth. The name Hindu is itself a foreign name. It was given by the Mohammedans to the natives for the purpose of distinguishing themselves...., There is no Hindu consciousness of kind. In every Hindu the consciousness that exists is the consciousness of his caste. That is reason why the Hindus cannot be said to form a society or a nation".[8]

'Nationalism is closely related with man's life, pride and activity. The sprit of nationalism has been disruptive. It has destroyed many nations, though at the same time, it has also created other ones. It, thus, both destroys and preserves'.[9] According to Dr. Ambedkar, the Turks were bound to the Arabs with the ties of religion. The religious tie of Islam is the strongest known to humanity. No social confederacy can claim to rival the Islamic brotherhood at the point of solidarity. But Arab nationalism broke the bonds of Islam and fought against his fellow Muslim, the Turk, for its independence. It won, but Turkey was completly dismantled.[10]

'Another example is that of Czechoslovakia. The Slovaks nationalism compelled the Czekhs to recognise the fact that they were a distinct people.... A deeper study to the disruption of Turkey and Czechoslovakia shows that neither local autonomy nor the bond of religion is sufficient to withstand the force of nationalism, once it is set in motion. In fact nationalism sometimes is so blind that it causes enemity and anger even among those who have lived together for centuries past."[11]

Our immediate neighbour Pakistan, which separated from this land on the basis of religion i.e. Islam, could not retain her entire territory and people in the name of religion. 1971 witnessed a brutal Partition of Pakistan and creation of Bangla Desh in the name of language and against the terror and tyranny of Punjabi militarist domination. That was the force of nationalism. As such Hindu society in which caste consciouness is much stronger, must not unusually boast of Hinduism - which is a most loose and thin thread of unity. Indian nationalism is based not on any caste feeling, or religious feeling but its most powerful base is 'the feeling of living together as a secular nation'.

Nationalism and Secularism

The secular spirit of Indian nationalism dates back to many centuries. Ashoka the Great and in the recent past Emperor Akbar are two distinct examples of secular nationalism. Christian missionaries and Christianity contributed a lot to create awareness and awakening among the neglected and the deprived. That helped to strengthen the nationalist feeling, and not disruptive activities as blamed by RSS Chief K.S. Sudershan.

"Religion is the foundation whereupon depends the social solidarity. It is the social solidarity which can lead the people to human happiness, national unity, military strength and political stability. According to Dr. Ambedkar, men cannot live by bread alone; they have a mind which needs proper food for thought; religion instils hope in men and puts them into action.... Religion should not be a symbol of inhuman treatment, ignorance and ignominy. They should essentially be a binding force behind the national spirit"[12]

We are known as a secular nation. Our Constitution has very clearly and in unambigous terms defined the concept of secularism. Article 25 guarantees that every person in India shall have the freedom of conscience, and shall have the right to profess, practise and propagate religion, subject to restrictions imposed by the State. It is nobody's business as to what is the teaching of a particular religion. But it should not be against the national interest. National well-being and national interest should be the top most objective of every religion. Tolerance and not hatred should be the base of religion.

"Dr. S. Radhakrishnan, the philosopher, former President of India, in his Discovery of Faith stated that the religious impartility of the Indian State is not to be confused with the secularism or ethism. Secularism as defined here is in accordance with enormous religious tradition of India. It is for living in harmony with each other. The fellowship is based on the principle of diversity in unity which alone has all quality of creativeness"[13]

Hinduism, Fascism and Nazism

Excess of anything is always dangerous. It destroys the very basis of the thing or concept. That is why Buddha's middle path is always preferable. '.... Buddhism is neither materiatistic, nor purely spiritualistic. It is a doctrine of dynamic realism which means that matter and mind are real and they constitute the one whole existence. The Buddhistic realistic world outlook is quite in consonance with the middle path of Buddha. The doctrine of the Middle Path means the first instance the middle way between the two extremes of optimism and pessimism such a middle position is a synthetic whole, tending neither one way nor the other'[14]

".... Hindu religion", as observed by Dr. Ambedkar, "was once a missionary religion must be admitted. It could not have spread over the face of India, if it was not missionary religion. That, today it is not a missionary religion is also a fact which must be accepted.... Hindu society as such does not exist. It is only a collection of caste. There is no Hindu conciousness of kind. In every Hindu the consciousness that exists is the consciouness of his caste. This is the reason why the Hindus cannot be said to form a society or a nation"[15]. It was, therefore, RSS which took over the responsibility of organising Hindus only in the name of religion. And for that, to creat the myths of 'Rama' and 'Krishna' and whatever the other instincts and emotions of various castes could be exploited to merge them all in one single and unified concept and they did it for the last 75 years. The very birth of the organisation was for that purpose. And there was no place for the Shudras and Ati-Shudras in their scheme of things, what to talk of minorities ? It was very much evident from the concept of graded social-order.... Who should be on the top and who should be on the bottom. That is why Dr. Ambedkar questioned : " Does Hinduism recognise Equality?... Does Hinduism recognise liberty ?... Does Hinduism recognise fraternity?".... And then he himself replied that, "....Hinduism is a denial of equality, both social as well as religious". As regards liberty doctor Saheb observed, ".... Hinduism denies freedom of vocation. In the scheme of Manu each man has a vocation preordained for him before his choice. Hinduism allows no choice.... Hinduism compels people to serve ends choosen by others. Manu tells the shudra that he is born to serve the higher class.... In Hinduism inequality is a religious dictrine adopted and conscinetiously preached as a sacred dogma.... Indeed inequality is the soul of Hinduism". And therefore Dr. Ambedkar said, "....The philosophy of Hinduism from the point of view of justice reveals in a glaring manner how Hinduism is inimical to equality, antagonistic to liberty and opposed to fraternity"[16]. If this is Hinduism and we seeit, it cannot be equated with nationalism! And both Savarkar and Dr. Moonje were very proud of it.

Fascism and Nazism or (National Socialism as it was originally known in Germany) are the direct consequence of the failure of the discriminatory treaty of varsailles imposed upon Germany and fragments of Europe after the First World War in which the self-development instincts of those natives were badly crushed by the super powers to expand their colonisation and eliminate the probable contenders.

The Slogan of Fascism 'all within the State, none outside the State; none against the State', further deprived the people of their liberty, equality and all other rights, exactly on the same lines the Hinduism in this country had been practising in the name of religion. Fascism demanded extreme loyalty and patriotism at the cost of others. Italians should alone be patriots and none others. In India the *Hindutvawadis* also claim that only they are loyal to the land—motherland, and none else ! Fascism also presents 'a complete repudiation of the assumptions, ideals and methods of democracy, 'liberalism and socialism'. Individual has no place in the society; it is the State which matters. There is no individual will, it is the will of the State, that counts. Violence was the only method and instrument known to Fascists. Adjustment, compromise and peaceful settlement was nowhere in their scheme of things. Supremacy of the State was the final watchword.

Nazism or the National Socialism conceived, developed and expanded by Hitler in Germany and used as an instrument of state policy is not very different from Fascism. The purity of race, the purity of language and the purity of literature/culture were one of the most important ingrediants of the Nazism. Their's was the slogan 'Germany for Germans only'. 'The superiority of the German and Nordic race and blood over the rest of humanity. According to Nazi theorists the race of 'blood' of a special group determines its outlook and made of thought. But as the Nordic race is indowed with the finest human qualities and is responsible for the greatest achievements of mankind (?) its purity to be maintained, and all the elements alien to the Nordic Stock, especially the Jews or Jewry, must be exterminated'.[17]

Fascism never believed in popular sovereignty which is creation of democracy. It also denounced democracy because it gives power to the masses to decide their own fate. As mentioned earlier, the demand for presidential form of government by BJP leaders and the likes reinforce the thinking of RSS/BJP of 'one superior leader like Mussolini or Hitler' who were once the ideal for Hedgewar. The question of Women's Reservation Bill, which has been vigorously pushed by the BJP and similar elements in other political parties are well-aware of the probable dangers to their political hegemony because of fast emerging mass awakening among the Dalit-Shoshit Samaj and their will to assert their democratic rights to choose their political rulers. The recent outburst of Pravin Togadiya, International General Secratary of Vishwa Hindu Parishad, who in reply to one question said, " It (Government) should hand over the Ramjanmabhoomi to the Nyas. Though the matter is sub-judice, if Parliament wants, *the court can be bypassed*"[18]

Seema Mustafa, an eminent journalist and Resident Editor of Indian Express (Delhi Edn.) in an article—Communal Politics : Towards Fascist State, published in The Economic Times (New Delhi—September 23, 1991) had very rightly and timely observed that, :

> "....The Babri Masjid—Ramjanmabhoomi issue has created an environment which is conducive to the creation of a fascist state. The BJP, which is basically a fascist force, has grown in strength over the years, from a lone member in the Lok Sabha Shyama Prasad Mukherjee in 1952, it has grown in to a political force

> ....In the absence of an organised secular offensive it came out the winner in U.P. ... The party succeeded in infusing a feeling of 'minorityism' in the majority community, playing an imagined grievances by portraying the Muslims as the pampered usurpers. And in spreading its communal doctrine the BJP spared no effort or expense. It was a loud, aggressive compaign with little children having been inducted to shout *Jai Shri Ram*.

Her prediction, formed in 1991 that, :

> ".... And it will not be an exaggeration to say that given the present situation it has better chances of forming government in Delhi with a decisive majority, than the National Front, or the Congress (1), in the not so distant future", has come to be proved hundred percent correct. 1996 Lok Sabha elections catapulated BJP led coalition under Atal Behari Vajpayee at the Centre, though for 13 days and in 1998 for 13 months ! Today BJP led NDA is comfortably sitting in the Centre with her allies fully tightlipped!

There has been lot of similarity and affinity between the ideology and policy conceived by Hitler and Mussolini in the name of Nazism and Fascism in Germany and Italy and that of the *Hindutvawadi* revivalists in the name of RSS, BJP, VHP, Bajrang Dal and many other off-shoot organisations. The idea of recruiting 30 lakh *Bajrangis* and one lakh *'Ram Bhaktas*, for construction of Ram Temple at Ayodhya, even against the judgement of the Supreme Court indicates and reflects their liking for violence and scant regard for judiciary !

The purity of race, the purity of language and the purity of literature/culture, three important ingrediants of fascism are most visible in designs, policies, programmes and actions of RSS, BJP, VHP and Bajrang Dal. Not this alone, what happned 75 years back before formation of RSS and after that and as to how RSS activities had been greately influenced by the fascist ideology, has been elaborately analysed and confirmed by Maria Casolari in his research essay—Hindutva's Foreign Tie-up in the 1930s, published in Economic and Political Weekly (January 22, 2000). He observed :

> " Hindu Nationalism had much more than an abstract interest in the ideology and practice of fascism.... The interest Indian Hindu nationalism in fascism and Mussolini must not be considered as dictated by an occasional curiosity, confined to a few individuals rather, it should be considered as the culminating result of the attention that Hindu nationalists, especially in Maharashtra focussed on Italian dictatorship and its leader. To them, Fascism appeared to be an example of conservative revolution".

According to the same author and the contents of the Report quoted by him in his research essay :

> " ....(4) Through the RSS the Maharashtrian Brahmins have been dreaming of establishing in India a 'Peshwa Raj' after the withdrawal of Britishers. The RSS flag is the Bhagwa Flag of Peshwas—Maharashtrian rulers (who) were the last to be conquered by the British—and after the termination of British rule in India, the Maharashtrians should be vested with political powers."

Hinduism Threat to Indian Constitution

In the backdrop of Ram Mandir and raising of the disputes of many other religious places and creating controversy in the name of religion, the RSS and its off-shoot organisations viz VHP, Bajrang Dal and many other local out fits patronised by Sangh are working vigorously on the same legacy of Mussolini and Hitler, who were the most favourable and adorable ideals for RSS founders, Hedgewar and Dr. B.S. Moonje.

The recent initiative announced to the Press number of times by VHP Functionaries that they were recruiting 30 lakh *Bajrangis* for construction of Ram Temple of Ayodhya and rowdism exhibited by their activists at Varanasi during the shooting of Deepa Mehta's *Water* and *Chaddi-Banian* protest (under wear-banians) in- front-of veteran film superstar Dilip

Kumar's residence at Mumbai, as well as destruction of Cenema Hall in Varanasi during the screening of *Mohabbatein,* are some of the instances of violent assertation and exhibition of fascist tendencies, in the name of protection of *psedo- Hindutvawadi* culture. Opening of military schools in every district of Maharashtra and, that too, by the RSS affiliated/supported public trusts and societies alone, during the short span of 4 year's BJP-Shiv Sena rule in Maharashtra, is a part of their larger strategy of creating a fear psychosis for minority communities, as done by Hitler to Jews in Germany which amounts to militarisation on the same fascist line. "..... Hedgewar himself was among the promoters of a compaign in favour of militarisation of society, according to fascist pattern. On January 31, 1934 Hedgewar presided over a conference about Fascism and Mussolini.... A few months later, on March 31, 1934 Moonje, Hedgewar and Laloo Gokhale had a meeting, the subject of which was again the military organisation of Hindus, along the Italian and German lines". During this meeting, what Dr. Hedgewar spoke and hinted at is very important in today's context, when RSS Chief is advising the Centre 'to throw away Christian Missionaries' and 'Muslims to cut off their loyalty to Mecca and Madina to 'Indianise them', and his retentless pursuit for scrapping of the present Secular Indian Constitution is on the top of their 'Saffron Agenda'. What Dr. Hedgewar then spoke in the meeting is very important for the secularists of the country to keep in view He said, :

> ".... I have thought out a scheme based on Hindu Dharma Shashtra which provides for standardisation of Hinduism throughout India.... But the point is that this ideal cannot be brought to effect unless we have our own Swaraj with a Hindu as a dictator like Shivaji of old or Mussolini or Hitler of the present day Italy and Germany.... But that does not mean that we have to sit with folded hands untill some such dictator arises in India. We should formulate a scientific scheme and carry on propaganda for it."[19]

Really, they did not sit with folded hands. During the last 75 years, they moved steadily, tactically, slowly as well as speedily and after 75 years of strenous efforts, and through various conspiracies, social as well as political, with the help of communal riots and opportunistic political alliances, they proved that what did they decide long back, they are in a position to achieve it or in a different language—to capture it with the help of fake socialists, half-hearted Mandalists and Ambedkarites alongwith Periyar's unfaithful Dravidians. Saffronisation of education and imposition of Sankrit by back-door, a symbol of Brahminical imperialism, distortion of history, review of the working of the Indian Constitution and changing the complete face of Indian economy during the short span of 2½ years coatition rule, are clear indications for Indians—Bhartiya Janata, and the so-called democratic socialists, socio-political leaders to wake-up from their deep slumber and save once and for all this great country—the country of Buddha, Mahavir, Kabir, Nanak and Jyotiba Fule, which was once proud of great worriors like Ashoka the Great, Samrat Akbar and Shivaji Maharaj; from slipping into the hands of future Mussolinis or Hitlers, who are not very far off from the Constitutional reach !

References

1. Principles of Social and Political Theory : E. Barker p. 53.
2. Dr. Babasaheb Ambedkar : W and S. Vol. 8 P/35 to 37.
3. Political Philosophy of Dr. Ambedkar : Dr. D.R. Jatav p. 47.
4. Dr. Babasaheb Ambedkar : W and S. Vol. 8 - Pakistan or The Partition of India p. 39.
5. Why Hindu Rashtra - A Suruchi Prakashan, New Delhi p. 9.
6. Gods, False Gods, and the Untouchables : S.K. Biswas p. 160.
7. Bunch of Thoughts : M.S. Golwalkar p. 178.
8. Dr. Babasaheb Ambedkar : W and S. Vol. 1 p. 50.
9. The Political Philosophy of Dr. Ambedkar : Dr. D.R. Jatav p. 48.
10. *Ibid.*
11. *Ibid.*
12. Dr. Ambedkar : Life and Mission : Dhananjay Keer p. 499.
13. S.R. Bommai Vs. Union of India - AIR - 1994 SC - 2015, 2016.
14. The Buddha and Karl Marx : Dr. D.R. Jatav p. 216.
15. Dr. Babasaheb Ambedkar : W and S. Vol. 1 p. 55, 56.
16. Dr. Babasaheb Ambedkar : W and S. Vol. 3 -Philosophy of Hinduism.
17. Fundamentals of Sociology : P.S. Gisbert p. 103.
18. The Times of India (Mumbai Edn.) August 26, 2001.
19. Economic and Political Weekly - January 22 - 28, 2000 p. 220, 221.

9

Constitution, People and Politics

Addressing the Constituent Assembly on 26th November 1949, the last day of concluding session, Dr. Rajendra Prasad, Chairman of the Constituent Assembly and First President of Indian Republic observed :

> "We have prepared a democratic Constitution. But successful working of democratic institutions requires in those who have to work them, willingness to respect the view points of others, capacity for compromise and accommodation. Many things which cannot be written in the Constitution are done by conventions.... Whatever the Constitution may or may not provide, the welfare of the country will depend upon the way in which the country is administered. That will depend upon the men who administer it. It is trite saying that a country can have only the Government it deserves.... If the people who are elected are capable and men of character and integrity, they would be able to make the best even of a defective Constitution. If they are lacking in these, the Constitution cannot help the country. After all, a Constitution, like a machine is a lifeless thing. It acquires life because of the men who control it and operate it, and India needs nothing more than a set of honest men who will have the interest of the country before them".[1]

Is there any hope in the hope of our former President Dr. Rajendra Prasad, who hoped that a set of honest men who will have the interest of the country before them, would emerge some time to come? While expecting a positive outcome, he further observed :

> ".... We have communal differences, caste differences, language differences, provincial differences and so forth. It requires men of strong character, men of vision, men who will not sacrifice the interest of the country at large for the sake of smaller groups and areas and who will rise over the prejudices which are born of these differences. We can only hope that the country will throw up such men in abundance".[2]

No doubt, Constitution is only a lifeless document and it requires men of very strong character and will-- power, could we spot out such men of high moral character and vision during the last 54 years? The answer cannot be affirmative and would not also be final. There is still some hope that the country will throw up such men, if not in abundance, to some extent, to fulfil the desired and destined goals, set-up by our Constitution-makers.

Thus, the Constitution is only an instrument, a means to achieve the ends or goals destined before the country. It all depends upon the men who manage the affairs of the State and control the reigns of administration. Constitution is like a machine which does not operate spontaneously or automatically. It acquires life because of the men who control it and operate it. And, therefore, former President of India said that 'India needs nothing more than a set of honest men', to operate successfully and honestly Constitutional machinery without their own selfish interest.

Sir Alladi Krishnaswami Aiyar, one of the members of the Drafting Committee, elaborating the important characteristics of the Constitution in the Constituent Assembly, observed on November 23, 1949 :

> "....Altogether it may be claimed that the Constitution gives sufficient scope for the achievement by the Indian Republic of all those great objects which are contained in the Preamble to the Constitution. The Constitution contains within itself the necessary elements of growth, flexibility and expansion. To a large extent, any Constitution depends upon the people who work it. It is the human element that after all is the most important in the working of any institution ....[3]

Dr. Ambedkar, Chairman of the Drafting Committee and architect of the Indian Constitution, replying to the debate, observed on November 25, 1948 :

> ".... Because I feel, however good a Constitution may be, it is sure to turn out bad because those who are called to work it, happen to be bad lot. However bad a Constitution may be, it may turn out to be good if those who are called to work it, happen to be a good lot. The working of a Constitution does not depend wholly upon the nature of the Constitution...."[4]

Our Constitution came into effect from 26th January, 1950. We have already completed half a century of successful working of the Constitution. During the same very period, our neighbours—Pakistan, Sri Lanka, and even other countries, which were liberated from the slavery of Europeans, and which adopted their own constitutions, have not only changed those but replaced those constitutions number of times according to convenience of the respective ruler or political party. On the other hand our Constitution withstood the test of time, notwithstanding the crucial period of emergency imposed upon the country by Smt. Indira Gandhi. There might be some lacunae in certain provisions but that did not come in the way of rulers or proved insurmountable hurdle in the revolutionary socio-economic development of the country. The first amendment to the Constitution took place in June 1951 which was a comprehensive change covering various difficulties experienced immediately after enactment of the Constitution. Since then almost more than 90 amendments have been made in the Constitution including the most controversial 42nd amendment. There is no bar to the amendment of the Constitution. More than 90 amendments during the last 50 years are ample indications as to how much flexible the Constitution is. Despite that why did there arise a need to review the Constitution?

The recent move of the BJP led NDA Government for the appointment of Constitution Review Commission, under the chairmanship of Justice M.N. Venkatachaliah, does not appear without biased motive. And what Prime Minister Atal Behari Vajpayee said in the Central Hall of the Parliament on the occasion of Golden Jubilee of the Indian Republic and Indian Constitution that, "the people are impatient for faster socio-economic development. The country is also faced with a pressing challenge to quickly remove regional and social imbalances by reorienting the development process to benefit, the poorest and the weakest", do not support the bonafide of his move. A.G. Noorani, therefore, very correctly observed that 'no Constitution can accomplish that goal, it can be realised only through policies pursued by men who work the Constitution'[5].

The Indian Constitution has never become an hurdle or obstacle in the socio-economic development of the country. Right from first Constitutional amendment in 1951 to 1971's Abolition of Privy Purses and Nationalisation of Banks, nowhere in between the Constitution came in the way and of late, even the Supreme Court has come to help and support the measures of peoples' welfare in terms of Directive Principles of State Policy. 'A Constitution may indicate the direction in which we are to move, but the social structure will decide how far we are able to move and what pace.... On the basis of this criteria, two thoughts are offered. First, the Constitution and its seamless web have met India's needs. The inadequacies in fulfilling its promise should be assigned to those working it and to conditions and circumstances that have defied greater economic and social reform during the short fifty years since Indians began governing themselves. The country has achieved greatly against greater odds. Second, the society and its hierarchical structure have shown themselves to be far more flexible and adaptable than might have been expected - due directly to incentives in the Constitution, and coincidentally from forces coming from within and outside society'.[6]

The ends or for that matter the goals of the Constitution are very much clear-the Welfare Society, based on the liberty, equality and fraternity wherein justice will prevail. To achieve these goals, the past 50 years passed through various stages. The first 17 years were fully dedicated to protect the existing Constitutional philosophy through political coalition within the same ruling block. Consultations, discussion and implementation was the most important aspect of this period. Pandit Nehru never tried or misused his unchallengeable political stature to impose his views upon his colleagues. On the contrary, he allowed full scale debate and deliberations before being finally decided, though party interests were taken care of, national interest were never allowed to slip out uncared . The exact goals and targets were fixed through Five Years Planning and state machinery, as well as political party net-working were also fully associated. It was a beginning for revolutionary socio-economic reforms, though methods and means sometime, seemed to be not in conformity with the democratic spirit. Notwithstanding this lacunae, Nehruvian period was one of the best periods in which secularism, democracy and socio-economic reforms were guarded with Constitutional commitment.

Smt. Indira Gandhi's period from 1966 to 1976 witnessed turbulent years. Most of the time, means and methods were twisted and distorted for her own survival. It can also be cited as an example as to how the Constitution was terribly misused to her own advantage and for the benefit of her family. However, the apparent Constitutional goals remained the same or rather those were projected very high-sounding ventures—like *Garibi Hatao!* It was during this very period committed bureaucracy and judiciary took the shape. Supersession of Supreme Court Judges and appointment of Justice A.N. Ray as Chief Justice was the highest culmination of distortion and misuse of the Constitution. Here, the ends were not the Constitutional goals but supremacy of an individual and perpetuation of dynastic rule. Imposition of emergency was the final story of subversion of the Constitution.

It was exactly after twenty years that the process of subversion and distortion has been initiated. No doubt, the people are impatient for faster economic development', but the means and methods adopted by BJP led NDA Government have not shown those results. On the contrary, the methods have proved reversing the original achievements of the past 50 years.

The present BJP led NDA Government, though, has an *Agenda for Governance* of the country, as announced through NDA Manifesto, it is now the main agenda of BJP, RSS and VHP, which is under implementation. In Germany, Hitler captured, political power through the same very constitution but soon after consolidation of the position, destroyed that very constitution. He had, then, his own constitution replaced with the old. Smt. Indira Gandhi once experimented with the Nazi

Style of constitutional working for 18 months. However, the experiment could not last long. Torture, tyranny and loss of liberty led to her fall from grace. Dubious ends did not hold for a long the dubious methods !

BJP has its own agenda apart from NDA Agenda—the larger Agenda :

Establishment of Hindu Rashtra for Hindus. And then, their slogan would be *'all within the state, none outside the state; none against the state'*. Already the majority of bureaucracy, from top to bottom, has their commitment with Hindu Rashtra. Displaying the photographs of gods and goddesses in the office premises and worshipping the said deities regularly even during office hours amounts to disregard to and violation of secular Constitution of the country. BJP never lost opportunities to project itself a nationalist and patriotic party. It took maximum advantage of all the alternatives and opportunities. It did not miss to use even the T.V. Serial *Ramayana* of Ramanand Sagar and B.R. Chopra's *Mahabharat* to push ahead its agenda of *Hindu Rashtra* and to consolidate Hindu Vote Bank. Arvind Rajgopal, Asstt. Professor of Sociology in the University of California at Berkely USA, in an interview with Darryl D' monte (Frontline : August 18, 2000 P/78) has very correctly observed to the point that ".... The Hindu nationalist party never lost sight of the fact that its audience was highly divided and had to be addressed in different languages and intonations. Advani addressing villages, would say : 'Ramjanmbhoomi is not a political matter, it is religious; we want to restore the temple of Ram to its former glory'. In the capital, he would say ' I am not a religious man, this is entirely a political issue; I am a secular person in fact".

The double-speak of RSS and BJP leaders is not new thing. Religion was extensively misused in the name of secularism, with their own version of secularism both by Indira Congress and Bhartiya Janata Party. What Indira Gandhi did during eighties, BJP is doing today. A.G. Noorani's observation (Frontline : Jully 21, 2000 p. 31) that :

> "In the June 1983 elections to the Jammu and Kashmir Assembly, Indira Gandhi tried out her strategy of competitive communalism for the first time.

> In valley, she projected herself as the champion of rapproachment with Pakistan, while in Jammu she portrayed herself as the saviour of Hindus. Although the strategy failed to yield dividends in Kashmir, she had the satisfaction of swamping the BJP in Jammu".

Later, Rajiv Gandhi allowed *'Shilanyas'* at the Ramjanmabhoomi place to grab the communal opportunity to consolidate the party vote-bank. The present experiment of Atal Behari Vajpayee with the Kashmir problem and his projection of initiative to settle the same with Pakistani rulers is not different from what Indira Gandhi did in 1983 and Rajiv Gandhi in 1985. All the time Constitutional authority was misused to the advantage of the party and for political gain. Atalji's recent statement in Lucknow that *Solution to Ayodhya issue by March* is a part of that larger strategy adopted by BJP and VHP, hand-in-hand, keeping in view the forthcoming Assembly elections in Uttar Pradesh.

There could never emerge a clear-cut majority verdict either in favour of Congress or Bhartiya Janata Party, (BJP) or NDA, except earlier few years in favour of Congress. People have never voted for majority communalism authorising BJP for construction of Ram Temple at Ayodhya or for that matter establishment of *Hindu Rashtra* based on Hindu nationalism. However, it has been very unfortunate that the secular nationalist forces are divided and not in position to counter the move of cultural nationalism of Hinduism, though this group of majority community is in minority and unaware of the consequences. As long as the nationalist secularists remain divided, the BJP shall gain more and more strength in the distant future and the Constitution of the country itself would be in danger of being replaced when committed bureaucracy and judiciary fall in line with Hindu Nationalism. The trend has already been set. It is only the question of time and then the prophecy of Dr. Ambedkar would not be ruled out:

> "....The Constitution can provide only the organs of the State such as the Legislature, the Executive and the Judiciary. The factors on which the working of those organs of the State depend are the people and,

the political parties they will set up as their instruments to carry out their wishes and their politics. Who can say how the people of India and their parties will behave? Will they uphold Constitutional methods of achieving their purposes or will they prefer revolutionary methods of achieving them? If they adopt the revolutionary methods, however good the Constitution may be, it requires no prophet to say that it will fail. It is, therefore, futile to pass any judgement upon the Constitution without reference to the part which the people and their parties are likely to play...."[7]

References

1. The Constitution and the Constituent Assembly : p. 193, 169, 174.
2. *Ibid.*
3. *Ibid.*
4. *Ibid.*
5 Frontline–March 3, 2000 : p. 30.
6. Working a Democratic Constitution–Indian Experience : Granville Austin : p. 166
7. Dr. Babasaheb Ambedkar : Writing and Speeches : Vol. 13.

Index